SURVIVORS

OF AFRICA'S OCEANS

Other titles by the author

For Valour, the history of Southern
    Africa's Victoria Cross Heroes (1973)

Die Uys Geskiedenis (1974)

Heidelbergers of the Boer War (1981)

Delville Wood (1983)

Longueval (1986)

The Comrades (1987)

Rollcall, the Delville Wood Story (1991)

Cross of Honour (1992)

South African Military Who's Who
    1452–1992 (1992)

Bushman Soldiers, their Alpha and
    Omega (1993)

SURVIVORS

OF AFRICA'S OCEANS

IAN UYS

FORTRESS
PUBLISHERS

Published by Fortress Publishers (Pty) Ltd
P O Box 679
Germiston 1400
Republic of South Africa

ISBN 0-9583173-5-6

Book design: Insight Graphics, Pretoria,
 with the author
Set in 11 on 12 New Baskerville
Printed by Galvin & Sales, Cape Town

Contents

Acknowledgements

I am indebted to many who have assisted me in this work. Principal among them is Bob Kennaugh, who materially assisted with the chapters on the *Nova Scotia*, the *Llandaff Castle* and the *Birkenhead*. Many of the photographs used are due to his research. I am grateful also to the authors and publishers whose works I have referred to, especially Random House UK Ltd re Tony Large, as well as the individuals who have freely told me of their experiences, which have been recorded in their own words as far as possible. I am grateful to Derek Walker for the loan of his scrapbook on the *Oceanos*. The librarians at the Johannesburg Africana Library, The South African National Museum of Military History, the Germiston public library and the Don Africana Library, Durban, have been extremely helpful.

The *Grosvenor,* a painting by Peter Bilas.

Prologue

The survivors of sea disasters off Africa have had to contend with terrifying circumstances; high seas and storms, being torpedoed or boarded by pirates, fire at sea, leaking ships, collisions with other vessels or striking rocks and the prospect of abandoning ship, swimming in the ocean and contending with shark attacks, drifting in open boats or on rafts and suffering from the tortures of thirst and hunger, to the dangers of exposure to the elements or being cast up on an inhospitable shore.

Southern Africa's worst sea disaster was the sinking of the *Nova Scotia*. It had the greatest loss of life as a result of being torpedoed, fire at sea and rapid sinking, followed by fighting among survivors on rafts and attacks by man-eating sharks.

Until the advent of mass air transport, travellers had to contend with long and often dangerous sea voyages. The author is a descendant of Captain Benjamin Boyes of the *Ligonier*, whereas his wife is related to Captain Edward Smith of the *Titanic*. Whether as captains, crew or passengers, the sea no doubt instilled in them all at some stage an element of fear. Yet, most survived . . .

The necessary qualities to survive harrowing ordeals must largely depend on the circumstances themselves. The physical strength necessary to launch a heavy raft may not be as important as the mental strength to persevere on the raft when it is adrift for weeks on end. Tony Large of the *Laconia* showed this, as did Alda Ignisti of the *Nova Scotia*. The two strong stokers who shared her raft kept wanting to give up, but she held onto them both throughout their 36 hours in shark-infested waters.

Flexibility, fortitude and mental strength are vital. Courage alone cannot suffice, for risk-taking must serve a worthwhile purpose. In the 1500's survivors of Portuguese shipwrecks on the south-east African coast embarked on a veritable 'death-march' northwards to Mozambique, losing hundreds of men, women and children *en route*. Under the same conditions Nuno Velho Pereira led 125 Portuguese and lost only eight.

The unwavering determination to survive is necessary when the ordeal may be protracted. This was exemplified by Anthony Steward's solo voyage in *NCS Challenger* around the world, then his shipwreck, fighting off sharks and having to survive on a desert island.

How one reacts in moments of extreme stress also dictates to a large extent who survives. When the captain and officers of the *Oceanos* deserted, it was the disciplined actions of the tourist company staff and the calmness of the passengers, coupled with the skill of military personnel, that resulted in no lives being lost.

At times the stoicism of doing your duty and sacrificing your life is necessary for the survival of others. This was demonstrated by the young, untried troops during the *Birkenhead* sinking, who stood fast on the sinking decks rather than endanger the women and children in the boats.

When all is lost and death stares you in the face it is essential that you remain calm. Panic-stricken people cannot reason. Acceptance of the inevitable was demonstrated by the blacks who danced on the deck of the sinking *Mendi*.

Why was the *Waratah* included when there were no survivors? Because a passenger chose not to be a casualty. Claude Sawyer dreamt repeatedly that the ship would founder, so remained ashore at her last port of call. Anyone who ignores his gut-feel or sixth-sense does so at his peril.

Your attitude is everything. If you are squeamish about what you eat you can end up starving. A *São João* lady's prudishness near the end of the march northwards doomed herself and her family.

It is undoubtedly the subconscious mind which determines one's attitude, which in turn plays a crucial role in times of extreme danger. It could influence whether you live or die. If your mind is the key to survival, your upbringing should engender a positive mental attitude, which gives you the leading edge – the will to survive.

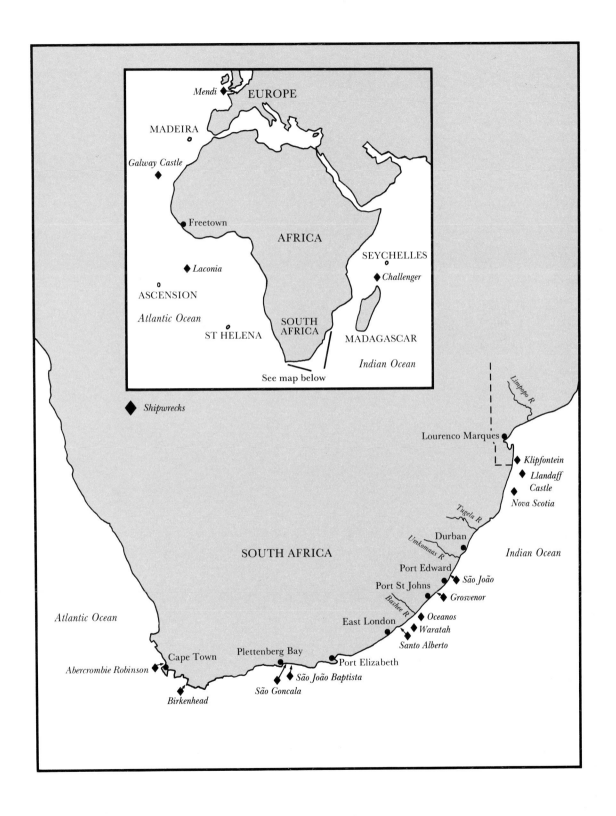

Mendi

EUROPE

MADEIRA

Galway Castle

Freetown

AFRICA

Laconia

SEYCHELLES

Challenger

ASCENSION

Atlantic Ocean

ST HELENA

SOUTH
AFRICA

MADAGASCAR

Indian Ocean

See map below

Shipwrecks

Limpopo R

Lourenco Marques

Klipfontein

Llandaff
Castle

Nova Scotia

Tugela R

SOUTH AFRICA

Umkomaas R

Durban

Indian Ocean

Port Edward

São João

Port St Johns

Grosvenor

Bashee R

Oceanos

East London

Waratah

Atlantic Ocean

Santo Alberto

Cape Town

Plettenberg Bay

Port Elizabeth

Abercrombie Robinson

São João Baptista

Birkenhead

São Goncala

The missing padrao – a painting by Peter Bilas (commissioned by Grahame Wilson) to represent a possible landing by Bartholomew Diaz on Robben Island on 6 June 1488, to erect a cross (padrao). This marked the beginning of known voyages between Africa's oceans.

CHAPTER 1

Castaways

South Africa's rugged coast has seen more than its share of ship-wrecks since the days of the Portuguese caravels in the 15th century. Some authorities contend that before that the Phoenicians had sailed around South Africa. Herodotus gives an account of a Phoenician fleet sent by the Egyptian Pharaoh Necos from the Red Sea southwards, which returned through the Strait of Gibraltar.

The prevailing winds made it possible for the square-rigged ships of the time to circumnavigate Africa clockwise from the Red Sea, but not anti-clockwise. The voyage lasted over two years, allowing the explorers time to plant and reap crops *en route*. In 1827 George Thompson of Cape Town reported the finding of ship's timbers which resembled the cedar from the Lebanon.

Subsequent investigation showed this to be brown coal with streaks of iron pyrites. In 1992 excavations were done at the site of another possible Phoenician galley, but nothing has been proved to date. Although any such voyages may be lost to antiquity, there are sufficient sea disasters to form a compendium of sea dramas and survivors comparable to any in the world.

Since the Portuguese caravels had explored the African coast under Bartholomeu Diaz in 1488 and Vasco da Gama in 1497, the authorities had become greedy and sent large, heavy carracks and galleons to transport spices from the East. Overloaded and badly caulked they were prone to wallow dangerously in storms.

In about 1504 a Portuguese ship went aground near the present Mossel Bay with a probable loss of all hands. Other ships such as the *São João de Biscainho* and *São Jeronimo* disappeared and may also have been wrecked on the east coast. The inhospitable wild coast was to claim a victim almost exactly a century before the first white settlement was established in South Africa.

São João:
11 June 1552

The *São João* left the Malabar Coast of India on 3 February, 1552, under Captain Manuel de Sousa Sepulvedo. He had with him his wife, Dona Leonora, their children and over 500 others. His galleon was laden with pepper, cloth, Chinese porcelain and slaves. After a long, slow voyage they sighted the South African coast on 13 April.

The ship was then subject to one storm after the other. They were blown to within 120 kilometres of the Cape of Good Hope, then lashed by westerly gales they ran before the wind in an easterly direction. About 630 kilometres east of the Cape the wind changed to easterlies. They resumed their westward voyage until the wind dropped three days later.

The ship began to leak and the rudder broke. The ship's carpenter found that three of the pintles holding the rudder were missing. Then another violent westerly storm burst upon them. The rudder became loose and the mainsail was carried away by the wind. While taking in the foresail the ship veered and was struck abeam by three huge waves, which broke all the stays and shrouds on the starboard side.

The mainmast then snapped and fell to the starboard. The crew cut away the shrouds and rigging, which all disappeared overboard. A mast was then jury-rigged. However, the rudder snapped in half and the ship wallowed dangerously in the swells. The foremast then snapped and carried the bowsprit with it.

Without mast, rudder or sails the galleon was at the mercy of the elements. Captain De Sousa then had a makeshift rudder constructed and used the cloth from the cargo for sails. It took the crew ten days to complete these rudimentary repairs, then set sail for the African coast. On 8 June De Sousa anchored his ship in 12 metres of water off the coast, just north of the present Port Edward and Wild Coast Sun. He went ashore with his wife and children and 20 men, together with provisions, powder, weapons and some cloth for bartering. De Sousa transported passengers ashore in the ship's boat, but on the third trip it sank in the waves, taking some people with it.

They intended to construct a caravel from the timbers of the galleon, but on the morning of the third day the anchor chain parted and the *São João* was driven onto the rocks. It broke in two and within an hour each of the halves broke in two. The cargo of the richest laden ship that had ever sailed from India then spilled out and littered the beach.

About 40 Portuguese and 70 slaves were drowned, but the rest managed to reach the beach. A temporary fort was then constructed near a source of fresh water. Built from crates and barrels, it served as a shelter for the injured to recuperate.

Two days later eight of the local blacks came to trade milk for iron and nails. Other tribesmen then shouted to them not to barter with the whites. Despite De Sousa's entreaties that the milk was necessary for the children, the cow was driven away.

After 12 days most of the injured had recovered and the captain gave a speech in which he said that their only hope of survival was to head northwards along the coast to Delagoa Bay, where Portuguese ships occasionally stopped to trade. On 7 July, 1552, the priest led the procession of the captain, his wife in a litter carried by slaves, 180 Portuguese and over 300 slaves.

The expedition had to cross numerous rivers, sometimes deviating inland to do so. Many fell by the wayside, succumbing to exhaustion, thirst, starvation, illness and exposure. Dona Leonora was later forced to walk, which she did bravely. In the first month they covered 480 kilometres. Leonora's 11-year-old son, who was carried on a slave's shoulders, was lost when they fell behind.

After three months the survivors reached the southern banks of the Lourenço Marques River. Only 200 of the original 500 remained. They were met by a friendly chief, who warned them of a warlike tribe to the north. He ferried them across the river until De Sousa, who was slightly deranged, attacked them with his sword, shouting, 'Dogs! Where are you taking me?'

Dona Leonora bravely intervened and the canoe trip continued. Thereafter they reached the Lourenço Marques Bay, where the local king offered them food and shelter if they laid down their weapons. Leonora protested that they would be lost, but De Sousa complied with the despot's request. He and his family were then robbed of all their jewellery and money. Other Portuguese survivors were also molested and robbed.

During the chaotic days which followed, 90 people banded together and set off northwards. They were followed by De Sousa, Dona Leonora, their two children and a few others. They were then attacked by blacks who tore their clothes off. The aristocratic Leonora flung herself to the ground and covered herself with her long hair. She then made a hole in the sand and buried herself up to her waist and refused to leave, despite De Sousa's entreaties.

He then asked Leonora's old nurse for her torn shawl, with which he covered his wife. Leonora told Andrè Vas, the helmsman, 'Now you see how we have been humiliated and cannot go further but must die here for our sins. Carry on, try and save yourselves and remember us to God. Should you someday reach India or Portugal say how you left my husband and I with our children.'

The party then left them with five slaves. De Sousa tried to care for his wife and children by fetching them fruit. He returned to find that one of his children had died, so buried the child. The following day when he returned with food he found his wife and other child dead. After sitting and staring at them for half an hour he allowed the slaves to assist him in burying them.

De Sousa then lost his reason and stumbled into the jungle, never to be seen again. A Portuguese poet wrote, 'O salty sea, how much of your salt, Are tears of Portugal?'

One of Leonora's relatives, Pantaleao de Sa, struggled onwards. Although naked and hungry he conquered his exhaustion and reached a native village. He was told that the chief had an ulcer on his leg which wouldn't heal. De Sa said that he was a great doctor, then privately made a mud poultice using his urine and placed it on the ulcer.

When the ulcer healed within a few days the superstitious blacks elevated him to the status of a God and he was offered half the chief's land and goods. He turned it all down and instead requested a guide to Mozambique.

On 25 May, 1553, eight Portuguese, 14 slaves and three slave girls reached Mozambique. They were the sole survivors of the more than 500 who had sailed on the *São João*. The tragic experiences which they overcame in seeking safety, ranks them second to none among the world's history of survivors.

São Benedictus:

24 April 1554

The fact that there were survivors who returned to Portugal meant that the story of the *São João* became known to other seafarers. It didn't seem to have taught them anything, for the following year the same events occurred.

On 24 April, 1554, the *São Benedictus* (also known as the *São Bento*), the largest ship of the Portuguese fleet, was wrecked at the Bashee River mouth, north-east of the present East London. Although 151 people drowned, 98 Portuguese and 224 slaves reached the shore.

The captain was Alvares Cabral. He insisted that they take as much iron as possible to trade with the locals for food. They tramped northwards, passing the site of the *São João* shipwreck and during the course of their journey met some of its survivors.

Hunger, thirst, exhaustion and clashes with black tribes thinned their ranks. Many of them dropped out to avoid the privations and to live off the land. On 2 June a very weak Captain Cabral was drowned when trying to cross the St Lucia River. Those who remained reached the Maputo River on 3 July, a mere 62 (56 Portuguese and six slaves) survived of the original 322.

They were then attacked by lions and one night five Portuguese were taken by lions. The others sought shelter in Bantu villages and heard the man-eaters scratching on the hut doors. Manuel de Mesquita Perestrelo, 44, was one of the few to survive their further ordeals. Five months later, when rescued by a passing ship, only 20 Portuguese and three slaves remained.

Perestrelo was to have a distinguished career. In 1562 he commanded a squadron on the Gold Coast. The following year he was imprisoned in Lisbon's castle on an unspecified charge. He escaped to Spain, from where he petitioned Portugal's king and was pardoned.

In 1564 Perestrelo wrote a book about his experiences, which became the oldest book dealing exclusively with events on South African soil. From 1575–6 Perestrelo mapped the south-east coast of South Africa. His 'Roteiro' became much used by subsequent navigators. He died at Alenquer, Portugal, in about 1580.

Santo Alberto:

21 March 1593

Almost 40 years after the *São João* disaster, a further stranding of a Portuguese ship was to show that the qualities of good leadership make all the difference to the fate of shipwrecked people.

While sailing back from India the *Santo Alberto* sprung a leak on 21 March, 1593. Among the aristocratic passengers was Nuno

Velho Pereira, 53, recently captain of *Sofala*. He was an intelligent man and directed that as the leak was mainly in the stern all heavy items should be thrown overboard or brought forward to the bow.

Three days later the ship stranded near the mouth of the Umtata River and broke in two. The stern drifted near the rocky beach and Pereira had a seaman swim ashore with a line. The bow, which held the captain and some passengers, was then attached to the stern. By using this 'bridge' 125 Portuguese and 160 slaves reached the shore.

On 27 March Pereira was chosen as commander of the expedition which would walk northwards to Mozambique. Pereira had the wreck stripped of copper and iron, which he used to barter cattle from the local tribes. A mother and daughter were carried in a litter by slaves, proving a considerable handicap to progress. They reached the Umtata River on 4 April.

Pereira didn't follow the shore, due to the lack of food and water and difficulties experienced by the previous shipwrecked parties. He struck inland, where crossing the rivers was easier, and navigated with the ship's instruments.

At one stage they passed near the present Bulwer and Richmond. They followed the Umkomaas river valley and then walked along the ridges to the Umgeni. Within a month of being shipwrecked they were west of the present day Durban. By then Pereira had accumulated a herd of 26 cattle.

At the end of May they had reached the Tugela River. They were generally well received by the black chiefs and the sick and infirm were left in their care. During June they followed the Pongola River and for the first time saw elephants. After reaching Kosi Bay they followed the route which the previous survivors of other wrecked ships had followed.

They learnt that a Portuguese ship was trading at Delagoa Bay, so Pereira sent some men ahead to ensure that it remained there. A messenger then arrived from King Inhaca, who assured them of his hospitality. The messenger was a former slave, who had been with the *São João* many years before.

On 30 June they reached the ship and were welcomed, especially as they still had 19 cattle with them. Only eight Portuguese had been lost in the three month trek, some of whom had been old or infirm. Although 95 slaves had dropped out, in many cases it was voluntary, as they sought their freedom by escaping.

On the return journey the ship was sunk by an English squadron. Pereira was taken to England and held for ransom, which was paid a year later. He died in about 1610.

São João Baptista:

29 September 1622

This Portuguese carrack was involved in a sea battle with Dutch ships for 19 days, in which she lost 20 killed and was forced to run for land. The crew and passengers disembarked somewhere between Algoa Bay and Plettenberg Bay. The march from there to Mozambique was the longest of any Portuguese castaways.

Captain Pedro de Marais was a cruel, obstinate despot, who tortured and killed his followers under any pretext. Those killed were then eaten, as were any dogs encountered *en route*. The weak, irrespective of age or sex, were abandoned. Only 27 of the original 279 who gained the shore eventually survived to reach Mozambique.

A detailed account of this march was left by a soldier, Francisco Vaz d'Almada, who had seen service in India. He told of the inhabitants they met, at first Hottentot and later Bantu, and of how civilised people eventually behaved in order to survive. When they were desperate and starving it became a matter of every man for himself.

São Goncalo:

1630

While sailing from India this great ship began taking in water, so ran for land and reached Bahia Formosa (Beautiful Bay), which was later renamed Plettenberg Bay. A hundred people were landed, while repairs were effected. The pumps were found to be clogged with pepper and before they could be cleared a storm blew up and wrecked the ship near Robberg, drowning the 130 aboard.

The survivors had heard horrifying tales of the overland trek, so decided to try and escape by sea. It took eight months to build two small ships. During that time they camped close to Robberg and had friendly relations with the local Hottentots. They left behind a stone inscribed, 'Here was lost the ship *São Goncalo* in the year 1630. They made two boats.'

One of the ships sailed successfully to Mozambique, while the other set off for Table Bay. The latter were picked up by a passing Portuguese ship, to be wrecked in turn at the mouth of the Tagus River near Lisbon.

The location of their settlement near Robberg was discovered recently when the foundations for a house were excavated. Of all Portuguese castaways in south-east Africa, those from the *São Goncalo* were the most successful.

Grosvenor:

4 August 1782

There were at least 16 ships wrecked on South Africa's eastern coast between 1593 and 1782, when an English East Indiaman, the *Grosvenor* of 729 tons ran ashore about 48 kilometres north of the present Port St Johns. It differed from the Portuguese sagas in that the shipwrecked party travelled southwards along the coast.

The ship left Ceylon on 13 June, 1782, with a crew of 132 and 18 passengers, of whom six were children. The greatest hardship for them would be to be cooped up for months on the small ship, which was no more then 160 feet by 34 feet. As Britain was at war with

Wreck of the *Grosvenor*, from a contemporary drawing (*Willcox*).

Holland, Dutch man-o'-wars would have to be avoided and there would be no re-provisioning at the Cape.

The cargo was valued at £75,000 and it is unlikely that she ever carried the fabulous bullion later ascribed to her. The passage across the Indian Ocean was beset with one gale after another.

On approaching the South African coast at Pondoland, north of the Umzimvubu River mouth, the captain miscalculated his position in misty weather. Captain John Coxon's charts showed them to be 640 kilometres out to sea! When told by Second Officer Shaw that he had seen lights ahead before a curtain of rain descended, Coxon refused to believe him. Shortly afterwards breakers were seen ahead, but it was too late to turn and the *Grosvenor* ran aground.

The waves pounded the wreck where it lay on an outer reef, 400 metres from the beach. Some survivors either swam through the breakers or clung to timbers until thrown ashore. Local natives stood one side watching them dispassionately.

Two Italians tried to swim ashore with a rope. One was drowned when dashed against the rocks. The other reached the shore with the rope, which enabled a thick hawser to be attached to some rocks. The other end was tied to the *Grosvenor's* mizzen mast and some men pulled themselves ashore along it, although nine died in the attempt.

The ship then broke in two and part of the bow section, with 100 people on, was carried by the waves into shallow water. Ultimately 123 people reached safety. The blacks were aggressive and Coxon decided that in their own interest they should leave the site of the wreck and make for the Dutch settlements along the coast to the south-west.

Captain Coxon agreed to splitting the group. Two men would remain at the site of the wreck while 52 seamen would lead them under Second Mate Shaw. The central group included the first officer, Logie, being carried on a stretcher, three white women, four Indian maids and six children, while Coxon would lead the rearguard. Their intention was to walk to Cape Town, which they believed was not far away.

Although the *Grosvenor* was not a treasure ship, she did carry some Indian alluvial diamonds. A rich merchant, William Hosea, carried some while Captain Coxon himself carried 12 small parcels. Of more importance was the evidence that a lawyer, Charles Newman, carried off a massive fraud perpetrated by officials of the East India Company.

The local blacks were extremely antagonistic and harassed and plundered the party at every opportunity. The British had a few cutlasses and firearms, but no gunpowder, so were virtually defenceless. Coxon threw away his hat and wore a turban, advising the others to make turbans from the bales of silk and muslin which had washed ashore.

They carried a Dutch flag, instead of English colours, as they hoped that the emblem might ensure them greater respect. It didn't, as the First Frontier War of 1779 still rankled with many of the Xhosa, who hated the Dutch. Coxon consulted with Colonel James, deferring to his knowledge of military matters and relations ashore.

The shipwrecked party had scarcely left when they were surrounded by hundreds of local inhabitants who threatened them with assegais and threw stones at them. After a number of his people were wounded, Coxon tried to show the blacks that they meant no harm. He was beaten to the ground with sticks and had to be rescued by his men. The whites managed to fight them off.

The following afternoon they were accosted by 60 locals. The paymaster, Mr Hap, used sign language to explain how they happened to be there. The blacks then gave edible roots and maize to the women and children. Shortly afterwards they met a Cape Malay man who had deserted from the Dutch. He told them that the journey ahead would be terrible, and refused to act as their guide.

During the next day the castaways were again attacked. The blacks lined the sides of a valley they were passing through and threw stones, injuring many of them. Coxon was stabbed in his hand, but he managed to wrestle the assegai out of his attacker's hand. He led his party out of the valley, while the men in his party threw stones back at their persecutors. These were easily deflected by the blacks' shields.

The battle continued for three hours. Afraid that they would lose the iron tips of their assegais, the blacks removed them and threw the sharpened hafts at the party. A lawyer, possibly Newman, was hit behind the ear and fell unconscious. The blacks then withdrew.

The next day they reached the village in which the Cape Malay lived. They were refused any food, but the headman instructed two men to act as their guides. Shortly afterwards they were again attacked by locals, including women and children. They were stoned, then attacked and all their food stolen or spoilt. The white women, who had their clothes torn and jewellery ripped off, were threatened with death if they resisted.

The following day, Sunday 11 August, they reached the Ntafufu River. They dug nearby and found fresh water, but had very little food. Coxon agreed that Shaw proceed with the seamen in the hope that they would find help. He would follow with the slower group of 47 souls.

It was brutal, but practical. Rather let the stronger push ahead and perhaps send back relief than have them all move at the pace of the slowest and probably die. Two of the wealthier men, William Hosea and Colonel James, promised high rewards to those who would remain to act as bearers.

Coxon then left Hosea, Logie, their families and others who were slowing them down. He and his group reached the Umtata River, where they searched for a crossing. Neither they nor Hosea's group were ever seen again.

Shaw's castaways

Shaw's party of 52 seamen had scarcely left Coxon when they were attacked by blacks and robbed. They struggled on and came across more locals, who gave the milk they had to their dogs, rather than let the hungry whites have it.

They reached the Umzimvubu River on 13 August, where a number of men gave up. Among them were sailors, two aristocrats and a servant. The stronger swimmers, including Seaman William Habberley, then assisted the rest of the party across the river. Their route then traversed bushy country and hills. The elderly Captain Talbot was exhausted and insisted on being left behind. His servant, Blair, wanted to remain with him, but he wouldn't have it.

On Monday, 19 August, they reached the Small Umgasi River mouth. They were met there by friendly blacks under Sango, whose white wife had been a castaway 40 years earlier. A gold watch-chain was bartered for a young ox, which was slaughtered and eaten. The skin was used to make rough shoes. The party felt strengthened and continued their trek until they reached unscaleable cliffs, which they had to bypass.

Shortly afterwards, on the 21st, the group divided into those who wished to continue along the coast with Thomas Page, the carpenter, and those who chose the inland route with Shaw. The latter group were driven by hunger to eat the leather oxhide they had used for shoes, then ate what they thought was cabbage. It turned out to be poisonous wild tobacco and they were to suffer from violent stomach cramps. Eventually, after traversing a densely wooded area, they decided to return to the coast

On Sunday, 25 August, they came across a hut belonging to a black beachcomber. There they found a collection of seafoods, which they thankfully devoured. The following day they reached the mouth of the Umtata River, which was running strongly. Six sailors swam across, whereas Shaw and the others decided to find a crossing higher up.

Early the following morning four men tried to swim the river, but must have drowned, as their clothes were seen floating on the stream. Shaw's group, consisting of nine men, continued walking and at midday found a three foot snake, which they killed and ate. Shaw had lost his flint, so they had to carry smouldering wood.

They crossed the river at the end of August and three days later reached the Bashee River. They were joined by one of the sailors who had been with Coxon's party. His news was sobering and upset them all. Habberley was the only person fit enough to swim the river, so he made nine trips backwards and forwards, assisting his comrades across the river.

On 8 September they came across a beachcomber, who assisted them to find shellfish and oysters. By the 11th it was apparent that Shaw was exhausted and extremely ill, possibly as a result of the oysters he had eaten. They set up camp to try and nurse him, but he died on the 18th. Habberley had served him for five years and was devastated. They buried Shaw on the banks of the Shixin River.

Two days later Habberley led his companions across the Kora River. They were then attacked by 20 blacks who cut the metal buttons off their jackets. Thereafter a Malayan fisherman and blacks offered them food in exchange for a watch chain and other articles, but in both cases took the items and gave them nothing.

On 1 October they reached the Kei River. There they met George

MacDonald, a carpenter's mate, who had been in Page's advance party. He complained that when he had begged milk from the local blacks, they had given it to their dogs. They left him there the following morning.

Habberley later wrote, 'Wednesday the 2nd of October – In the morning, having provided ourselves with shellfish, we continued along the river in search of food, leaving here McDonald, the carpenter's mate, who said he was not able to go up the country with us, but would endeavour to swim over, which we thought was impossible for him to do, for when we left him, he was so weak that he could barely stand, and what became of him afterwards we never knew . . .'

His party was followed by locals and again attacked, but they had nothing left to be stolen. A Portuguese-speaking black then showed them where to cross the river. After crossing the Kei and reaching the coast, James Stockdale was so weak that he had to be left behind.

The remaining men stumbled southwards until they reached the Buffalo River mouth. Owing to the strong current and the presence of elephants they turned inland, where on 15 October they were assaulted by 20 Xhosas. They were hit with sticks and their meagre food supply stolen. Habberley was knocked unconscious and badly injured.

A few days later they reached the Keiskamma River and found the water to be salty. Rain brought them some relief, then they caught a stray dog, which they killed and ate. On Monday, 21 October, John Sussman died and the following day Laurence Jones.

A raft was built and Habberley pushed Taylor, a merchant, and Williams across to the opposite bank. They left Trotter behind, who had not wanted to risk the crossing. He changed his mind after they had crossed, but by then the raft had drifted away in the strong current.

The Great Fish River was reached on 31 October. By then the three men were suffering from scurvy. They were attacked by local warriors, who threw Williams into the river and stoned him until he sank. Habberley and Taylor fled, but were pursued. Taylor was caught and beaten to a pulp, while Habberley managed to conceal himself. At sundown he crept to his friend's side, to find that he was still alive.

The next day, Friday, 1 November, they struggled onwards. Taylor became steadily weaker and died on the Sunday at the mouth of the Kleinmond River. Habberley was too exhausted to bury him, so removed his clothes and let the current carry his body away. Habberley stumbled on alone for another week, his fourteenth since the stranding. His legs were swollen, whereas his body was skeletal.

He reached a black settlement, east of the Cowie River, and was given roast meat and milk. As his strength returned he offered to assist the black women with their chores, which amused them immensely. At the next village he was also well received and slept in a hut.

To his delight he then met Thomas Lewis, one of Shaw's party who had swum the Umtata River and later joined Thomas Page's party. He explained that Page had died before 19 of them reached the Fish River. Their group then split up into smaller parties and struggled onwards, eating whatever dead whales, seals or birds they came across.

Lewis had remained behind at the Bushman's River as he was too exhausted to continue. Two Italians, Feancon and Paro, were in neighbouring villages. They had cured the local headman of a painful ulcer and were honoured throughout the area. The four men remained with the friendly villagers until a messenger arrived some time later to advise them of horsemen nearby.

Despite the headman's protests they left and after a few days met the Boers. To Habberley's surprise he saw that two of his former shipmates were their guides. It was on Tuesday, 14 January, 1783, that they met the search party led by Captain Heligert Muller of the Swellendam Burgher Forces. They were welcomed, fed and clothed – and knew then that they had survived!

Carpenter Page's party

As Shaw's party had the only flint, Page's group had to carry burning wood with them. They had the young boy, Law, with them so had to find relatively easy river fords and routes. By the time they reached the Umtata River two members had died. After fording the river higher up its course they again reached the coast on 28 August.

They were overtaken by six men who had left Shaw when they swam the Umtata River. The combined party crossed the Bashee River on improvised rafts, but Page and Auld, the vat maker, died before they reached the Fish River. The group then split up into two parties of seven each.

The first party reached the Buffalo River within six days, then entered a nightmare world of giant sand dunes. Instead of going inland and bypassing the dunes, they struggled on over 100 foot high dunes. Four of them died in the barren area, leaving Di Lasso, Leary and Price who reached the Sundays River.

The second party of seven reached the Buffalo River, where they met Thomas Lewis. He was too weak to accompany them so was left behind. On reaching Algoa Bay they also had to struggle through the dunes. The youngster, Law, became sick and they stopped for him to rest, but he died. By 5 November only four of them remained and they were reduced to drinking their urine to keep going. Lillburne then collapsed and died.

The remaining three men then reached their limits. One of them, Warmington, suggested that they draw lots to decide who should die, so that the others could drink his blood and live. This was rejected by Evans and Hynes. Warmington then collapsed, saying that he could walk no further.

At 10 am Evans and Hynes saw what they thought were three large birds on the beach. They staggered forwards, hoping to catch one, only to find that it was Price, Di Lasso and Leary. Two of the latter were then sent back for Warmington. The six continued their journey until they reached the Swartkops River, where they found a beached whale carcass and Hottentot figs.

While making a fire and cutting up the whale they were found by two armed horsemen. One of them, John Battores, was Portuguese and understood Di Lasso's Italian. They were taken to the farm of Christiaan Ferreira, near the later Port Elizabeth. Then they left for Daniel Kuene's farm, where Price remained because of swollen legs.

The other five castaways were taken from one farm to another until, on 4 December, they reached Swellendam. The Muller-Holthausen rescue commando was sent by Governor Van Plettenberg to find and rescue as many of the *Grosvenor* survivors as they could. Eventually 18 of the original 123 castaways were saved, among them seven Lascars and two Indian maids.

The maids were servants to Mrs Hosea and Mrs Logie. They said that Mr Logie was almost dead when they left. Colonel and Mrs James had already left, but they passed them as the colonel could hardly move and had to be assisted by four seamen. They had then stayed with the Malay and supported themselves on shellfish, as the natives wouldn't let them reside with them.

The white women either died or were absorbed into local tribes, as no trace of them was found. In 1828 Lieut Francis George Farewell passed through the area and wrote, 'I found the wreck of the *Grosvenor* . . . a carpenter [Joshua Glover?] and armourer [John Bryan] had lived near this place until lately, the son of the latter being at this time in my employ.

'There were also two women, who had lived on the spot some time, but upon an irruption of the natives from the westward, all the tribes that inhabited that part of the coast were killed, when these women fled, hid themselves in the bush, and were then starved to death.'

The rest of the party either died of privation, were murdered by the blacks or forced to live among the Xhosa tribes. Many years later a group of half-castes were found in the area of the wreck, which indicates that the wives of men murdered by the blacks then lived with them.

The Diamond sequel

Legends of a treasure trove began in 1880, almost 100 years after the shipwreck. A number of unsuccessful attempts were made to recover the expected bullion and chests of precious stones, but nothing has ever materialised.

Rumours of treasure on the *Grosvenor* abounded. A trench was dug in the rock to try and undermine the wreck site, but nothing of value was found. An estimated R1 million has been spent in fruitless searches for her alleged treasure.

In December, 1925, Johann Bock and his son, Frank, were strolling down a cattle path southwards towards the Kei River mouth. The youngster stooped and picked up a strange pebble. It glinted in the sun and they were intrigued. Bock senior thought that it might be a diamond, so applied to the magistrate at King William's Town for a prospecting licence. He then split this with a son, John, and his lawyer.

A grandson, Derek Bock, of Hennopsmeer, Transvaal, later wrote, 'My grandfather made a thorough search of this portion of the ground. Oh yes, there were diamonds there all right . . . The area he staked out was only about four paces in diameter, but in one day alone he unearthed 63 stones and in a fortnight had found more than 300. The diamonds were easy to recover. They were either on the surface or buried in a few centimetres of sand.'

Government officials had come to the conclusion that there couldn't be diamonds there and that Bock senior had 'salted' the area. He was arrested under Act 11 of 1888, but released on R1,000 bail. They also did some digging and found diamonds.

Counsel for the defence put forward a theory that the diamonds had come from a survivor of the *Grosvenor* or some other shipwreck. It was rejected as pure surmising by the court. Bock, 73, was found guilty and jailed for three years. He broke down and wept. After serving his sentence he died.

Professor Percival Kirby, the acknowledged expert on the *Grosvenor* wrote in 1960 that although she was not a treasure ship, diamonds had been carried by Coxon and Hosea. Although they succumbed near the Umtata River, McDonald had reached the Kei River mouth in a weak state and probably died there. Did he have the diamonds with him, to be found 143 years later?

The bottle of diamonds was removed by the authorities after the trial and taken to Kimberley, but no one knows what happened to them then. The library at Kei Mouth established a small museum, a corner of which was devoted to the Bock saga.

CHAPTER 2

Pirates and Traditions

In the days of sailing ships, families that travelled together were often subjected to extreme hardships. The Boyes family were no exception. One can but imagine the trauma and helplesness felt by the parents, as their children were exposed to extreme danger.

Ligonier:

April 1829

Benjamin Boyes was born in Hull in 1785. His father deserted his mother and disappeared, so his uncle, a shipbuilder, was his father-figure. One can assume that he went to sea as a young man and possibly fought at Trafalgar in 1805, for later he served under Captain D'Acres in South America. When his captain was imprisoned in a stockade Benjamin crept up to the pallisades and threw a hatchet over, thereby enabling D'Acres to hack his way to freedom.

On another occasion he was shipwrecked off the coast of South Africa. He swam ashore and then searched for something to eat. He found a barrel which had been washed up and thought that it contained salt meat. He stuck his hand in and began pulling at the contents, then to his horror found that it contained the dead cabin boy, who had been jammed into the barrel by the violence of the sea.

Some of his fellow sailors made it ashore. They constructed a raft and in order to test its seaworthiness put Boyes on it and sent it out to sea. It disintegrated and he would have drowned in the waves but for the presence of mind of a Boer on horseback. The man had a long whip and when he saw the boy struggling for his life he rode into the waves and held the whip out to him. Boyes managed to grasp it's end and was pulled to safety.

Boyes married a wealthy Jewess, Sarah Brand (b 1794) in about 1814. Her father was a London jeweller who had been given the freedom of the city, the qualification apparently being that he owned over £500. He owned a small estate outside London, to which he would drive his family two or three times a week.

After his death his widow married a Mr Bealby, whose children succeeded in getting the properties which had belonged to Brand. Boyes was urged by Sarah to dispute the matter, but he allowed himself to be persuaded by Bealby to sign papers not to proceed with claims and to accept £400 instead of £4,000.

Captain Boyes then purchased a small sailing ship and he, his wife and children saw a great deal of the world. By then their children were Benjamin, William (b 1816), Walter, Alfred, Ettie and Ellis. He apprenticed his eldest son to his friend, Captain Ellis. During a heavy storm the mate sent young Benjamin aloft, contrary to Ellis's orders, and he was blown into the sea and lost.

During a voyage, when 14 days out from England, the baby girl,

Ellis, died. Sarah would not have her buried at sea. She dressed the little body carefully and placed it in a camphor chest, leaving the lid slightly open. The child was then buried in England.

On 31 August, 1924, Boyes left Gravesend i the cutter *Nereide.* This single masted vessel of 69 tons had a narrow beam and a deep draught. Its cargo was ballast and its destination New South Wales, Australia. There was a crew of six men aboard, besides Sarah and two children, presumably William and Walter. They crossed the equator on 27 October and stopped at Mogadore Island, then arrived at Cape Town on 2 December. They loaded up a cargo of Cape wines and left on 14 December.

They had with them all Sarah's furniture, which was done up in matting. During the voyage she gave birth to a son, Alfred. At the time she grieved so much over her mother's failing health, that for three months after his birth the baby sighed and grieved noticeably.

When they reached Sydney, Boyes applied for a grant of land and was given 10,000 acres. In order to validate the claim he had to erect a building on it. When he heard rumours of a penal settlement being established nearby, Boyes was scared off. He ignored Sarah's appeals and warnings and sold the ship and her furniture. He refused to erect even a small shanty and instead purchased passage back to Europe for his family.

He thereby lost all claim to what was to be a valuable estate. On his return to England, Boyes left his family there while he spent what money remained in touring the Alps. Another son, George, was born in England.

In January, 1829, Boyes bought a small condemned government Cutter, the *Ligonier.* He loaded cargo for St Helena and had with him a complement of 10; Sarah and the four boys, a maid, a crew of three and an apprentice boy. He bought Sarah a gold watch before the voyage, which she was very proud of.

They sailed in a convoy with a French man-of-war for protection. In the West Indies one very misty day they were separated from the convoy, then became aware of a silent black hulk which approached swiftly. They knew it to be a pirate ship, although they couldn't see anyone aboard. As it came alongside the deck of the pirate ship suddenly became alive with dark, fierce-looking Lascars from the East Indies.

The pirate captain then boarded their ship. Sarah hurried down to the children in the cabin. She saw her gold watch, took it and hid it under some bunker coal, saying to herself, 'It will take you some time to find that!' Boyes spoke to the pirate captain and called on Sarah to bring them wine. While she carried wine to the cabin he took the telescope and looked through the porthole. The mist was lifting and the convoy could be seen nearby.

The pirate seized a pen and paper and hurriedly wrote, 'Met Capt Boyes, Lat –, Long –, at – O'clock, date –, no harm done him.' He then made Boyes sign it before returning to his own ship. It rapidly disappeared before the French vessel could train its guns on it.

In *Cutlass and Yardarm* Eric Rosenthal described the encounter as follows: 'The next pirate victim whom Henry Solomon encountered was Captain William (sic) Boyes, who was bringing the cutter *Ligonier* from London to St Helena. Aboard was a crew of three and an apprentice boy, besides Mrs Boyes, her family and a maid. How such a party could undertake the voyage is hard to credit, for the *Ligonier* was little larger than a lifeboat; yet she had safely reached equatorial waters when she was boarded by pirates. At the critical moment, a man-of-war appeared, the Russian corvette "Krotski" [*sic*], and the evildoers made off.'

They then appear to have lost the convoy again, as they sailed about for months. An average three months voyage had stretched to almost six. They exhausted their provisions and the crew had broached the cargo, but Boyes wouldn't touch it. In addition they had virtually run out of water. They had to cook their food in salt water and had to depend on rain showers to replenish their water barrels. Somehow they always seemed to miss the main part of the cloud and only got the edge of it. They all became weak, especially the children.

When they reached St Helena the wind was against them and they had to tack three times to get into the bay. They then saw a man in a ferryboat with a keg of water. Sarah called to him with a trumpet. 'For God's sake, give us some water.'

No persons were allowed aboard, nor allowed to have any dealings with them, until the port captain had boarded the ship. A sentry stood nearby, but the man managed to get the ship between them and managed to get the water aboard. The children were each given a sip or two in turn. When they had each had some Sarah began with the first one again, and so on . . .

After a short rest at St Helena they left for Table Bay on 1 July with a cargo of empty casks. After an uneventful trip they arrived on 14 August. The vessel had to have barnacles removed, the reason for their slow voyages. At Cape Town they found canals running down the sides of the streets. In the summer vast swarms of mosquitos would breed and the people would come out in the mornings, all red and swollen from the way they had been bitten during the night.

People who went out at night carried lanterns, as there were no street lamps and the roads were either very muddy, dusty or dirty. Nevertheless, Sarah refused to go on board another ship and insisted that Benjamin sell his. Accordingly a notice appeared in the

Government Gazette of 28 August, 1829 advertising it for sale:

'Sloop *Ligonier*. On Monday the 31st instant will be sold without re-
serve, at the Commercial Exchange, at 12 o'clock precisely, the
above vessel, with stores, etc, complete, as she lies in Table Bay. An
inventory may be seen, and further particulars learned, on applica-
tion to the undersigned.

S B Venning

24th August, 1829'

In 1830 Benjamin Boyes, mariner, lived at 21 Plein Street in Cape
Town. Sarah was anxious to obtain regular employment for her
sons ashore. She had to make some provision for her family at
Cape Town as there was no prospect of Benjamin being able to support them. William and Alfred were apprenticed to a shoemaker
and Walter to a cabinetmaker.

William's master's surname was Williams and his shop was on the
site of a later 'picture shop'. One day he said to William, 'Here you
are, Boyes,' handing him a newspaper. 'Here is an advertisement
asking for a governess. I advise your mother to go to Wynberg and
see Lady D'Urban.' Lady D'Urban was born Anna Wilcocks in 1780.
Her husband, Sir Benjamin, was governor of the Cape from 1834–8
and they had stayed on in the Cape afterwards.

Sarah was very reluctant to do so, as the bus fare to Wynberg was
two shillings each way, but as she was anxious to get employment
she went to see her. Lady D'Urban was pleased with her and gave
Sarah a book, for her to study the current method of teaching. She
then had to appear before a committee and was at length appointed
as teacher in the Industrial School. This was about 1836 as the
school was opened then.

The building was near to Waterloo Green in Kenilworth and 40
girls attended the school. They used to do beautiful needlework
and all the gentry, who used to have their country residences out
there, used to have their work done by these girls. Many of them
would remember Sarah when their luscious fruit ripened and
would send her a basket of fruit, with a small silver or gilt-edged
card inscribed something like, 'With Col and Mrs —— compliments
to Mrs Boyes.'

Sarah also kept a post office, and they would get their letters
from her and post them there, which was a great convenience.
From 1841 to 1861 Sarah was postmistress at Plumstead, at six
pounds per annum, which probably included quarters. The post
office was situated on Plumstead Road. The Boyes family thus managed to live simply and respectably.

Her sons William and Walter, who were apprenticed to the shoemaker in Cape Town, later recalled walking to the town at six in

the morning and out again at six at night. Another little girl, Ellis, was born and named after her baby who had died at sea.

During 1842 Sarah became the principal of the Industrial School for Girls. A note in the calendar for 1843 read, 'A school of industry, established by Lady D'Urban, affords instruction to about thirty girls, in sewing, reading, writing and other elementary branches. This institution depends largely on voluntary subscriptions for its support.'

Lady D'Urban was a small, dainty lady and used to enjoy Sarah's company very much, as Sarah could tell of so many experiences and adventurous stories. Lady D'Urban used to be brought to the school in a type of chair and Sir Benjamin would accompany her on horseback. When they reached the school he would lift her out and carry her into the schoolroom, place her in a chair and leave her for the afternoon.

After some time it was decided to change to a new system of teaching – the Lancaster system. Sarah did not understand this and, although Lady D'Urban did her best to keep her in the school, the other members of the committee were in favour of a new teacher who understood the new method, so Sarah left.

She still retained her position as postmistress, however, but moved to Plumstead. During Governor Maitland's time there was talk of moving the post office back to Wynberg, but Sarah went to see Maitland himself. He added his influence behind her and she was enabled to keep it.

Lady D'Urban, whom Sir Benjamin loved dearly, died at Wynberg on 23 August 1843. Before Sir Benjamin left to fill a new appointment in Canada in 1846 he went to Sarah and said to her, 'Mrs Boyes, will you please make me half a dozen neckerchiefs, for there is no one else that I know who can make them so well for me.' He used to wear a peculiar kind of neckerchief, with a large button-hole on one side. Through this the other end would be drawn, then the two ends would be buttoned in some way and tied in a small bow.

Queen Victoria granted a tract of land to Benjamin Boyes for having assisted Captain D'Acres to escape during the South American wars. Admiral D'Acres later came to South Africa as admiral of the squadron stationed there. Rear-Admiral Sir J R D'Acres was Commander-in-Chief at Simonstown from 1844–5.

As the postcart for Simonstown passed through Wynberg, Benjamin used to receive the mailbags there. Admiral D'Acres recognised Benjamin at Wynberg when the postcart drew up to deliver the mail. He invited him to be his guest at Admiralty House in Simon's Town. For three weeks Benjamin lived at the expense of the Imperial Government, 'not wisely but rather well'.

Benjamin and Sarah both died in 1869, aged 84 and 75 respectively. Sarah was said to have been very stern and strict, very reli-

Rear-Admiral Sir James D'Acres (*SA Navy*).

gious but not very likeable! It is understandable that she appeared to be shrewd and difficult, for she had been the main breadwinner for her last 40 years. Throughout that period she would never forget the moment of terror when the pirates had boarded her husband's ship, the *Ligonier* or the wasting away of her children afterwards when the food and water ran out.

Birkenhead:

26 February 1852

A spectacle of soldiers standing in rows on the deck of a sinking ship, while women and children are taken to safety, usually conjures up pictures of the *Birkenhead*. Yet, this is exactly what happened in Table Bay a decade earlier. On 28 August, 1842, the *Abercrombie Robinson* was anchored in the bay with 600 troops and 80 women and children aboard. Nearby lay the convict ship *Waterloo*, with 219 male convicts bound for Tasmania, 30 guards and 19 women and children aboard.

At 5 am a gale parted the anchor chains of the *Abercrombie Robinson* and she was blown ashore at the mouth of the Salt River. A line was taken ashore from the ship, while surfboats set out from the beach to rescue the passengers. The soldiers of the 27th and 91st Regiments stood firm until all the women and children had been evacuated, before they began disembarking.

At 10 am the *Waterloo* ran aground about 500 metres from the *Abercrombie Robinson*. It was an older vessel and rapidly broke up. More than 200 of the people aboard the *Waterloo* were drowned, among them the guards of the 99th Regiment.

The 1,400 ton iron paddle-steamer *Birkenhead* was launched among considerable controversy in December, 1845. Its designer and builder, John Laird, had not convinced the admiralty of the future of iron ships, as they were concerned at the effect the iron would have on compasses.

Originally intended to be a warship for the Royal Navy, the frigate was converted to a troopship by the addition of a poop. It had eight water-tight compartments and two engines, built by George Forrester & Company.

One of the first important tasks of the *Birkenhead* was in August 1847, when it towed the SS *Great Britain*, which had run aground 11 months earlier. The *Birkenhead* left Portsmouth for the last time on 3 January, 1852, two years before the outbreak of the Crimean War. It proceeded to Cork to pick up troops, then set out on the long passage to South Africa.

The *Birkenhead* carried a complement of 23 officers and 469 men as reinforcements for Lieutenant-General Sir Harry Smith in the Eighth Frontier War at the Cape's eastern frontier. The voyage was interrupted by stops at Madeira, Sierra Leone and St Helena for coaling and provisions. She arrived at Simon's Town on 23

February, after 50 days at sea, during which four women had died – three in childbirth and one of consumption.

During the next two days 350 tons of coal and provisions were loaded and the government despatches for Sir Harry were received. The Royal Naval paddle-steamer sailed from Simon's Bay at 6 pm on 25 February, 1852, bound for Algoa Bay. The iron troopship was under the command of Captain Robert Salmond and had 638 people on board. They were mainly drafts of men from 10 regiments. 20 women and children were among those on board.

The cargo included 350 double-barrelled carbines of a new design for the 12th Lancers and some wine. The officers' horses and their bales of fodder were kept on deck as there was insufficient room below decks.

Captain Salmond came from a long line of seamen, dating back to the 1500s. His father and four brothers all died at sea, as well as one of his two sons while still in his teens. He held no commission in the Royal Navy, which at first caused some strain between himself and the commanding officer of the troops, Major Seton. A very good working relationship then followed.

Among the regiments represented were the 2nd Foot (Queen's Royal West Surreys), the 6th Foot (Royal Warwickshires), 12th Foot (Suffolk Regiment), 43rd Light Infantry (1st Bn Oxford & Buckinghamshire), 45th Foot (1st Bn Nottinghamshire and Derbyshire Regiment), 73rd Foot (2nd Bn Royal Highland Regiment), 74th Foot (2nd Bn Highland Light Infantry) and the 91st Foot (1st Bn Argyll & Sutherland Highlanders).

Major Alexander Seton, 38, of the 74th Highlanders commanded all troops on the ship. His family seat was at Mounie Castle, Aberdeen, and had connections with Mary, Queen of Scots. A thoroughly professional soldier, he had passed out at Sandhurst in 1847 and spoke 15 languages. He had, in fact, succeeded to a death vacancy and been promoted lieutenant-colonel, but neither he nor anyone else on board knew it.

His second-in-command, Captain Edward Wright, 38, of the 91st Highlanders was a tall, heavily-built man. An experienced commander, he had served in South Africa five years before. All other officers were much younger than them.

An early portrait of Major Seton (*from his family records*).

That evening it was clear and calm with only a gentle breeze. At 2 am the following morning the ship struck rocks at Danger Point and stuck fast. Tons of water poured through the ripped hull and drowned soldiers in their hammocks. Men shouted and ran along the narrow corridors, seeking the safety of the deck.

The young recruits, many of whom had been signed on in Ireland, did not have time to dress. They snatched up their tunics, stumbled through the dark passages and struggled to reach the hatches and deck beyond. In the confusion white-faced women grabbed their children and tried to reach the boat stations.

Captain Salmond rushed to the bridge half-clothed and gave orders to stop engines and to lower the bow anchor. Officers were to assess the damage and report back, while the men were to form ranks on the deck. The women and children were to be collected together.

Mr Archbold, the gunner, set off flares but when they died darkness resturned. The magazine was flooded, so he couldn't fire the guns or set off more flares. The pumps were hurriedly manned. Both lifeboats were impossible to launch. A small gig's ropes snapped as it was lowered, drowning most of its occupants. Another small boat was then launched for the women and children.

Salmond thought that only one compartment had been holed and that there would be sufficient buoyancy in the others to keep the ship afloat. He ordered the engines astern and as the *Birkenhead* tore free, it hit other rocks and water rushed in and killed the engines. The bilge buckled and the watertight bulkheads were broken.

In the engine-room Mr Whyham, his engineers and stokers stared in horror as the hull plates tore apart and cold sea water poured in. The boiler fires were doused by the water and steam billowed upwards. Whyham reported to the captain then shouted for his engine-room crew to evacuate. They thankfully climbed up the ladder to the upper deck.

Salmond then asked Seton to send 60 men below to work the chain pumps. Others tried to release the eight lifeboats, but rusty bolts and rotten tackle made it virtually impossible. Only three, which would hold 60 people each, were freed. The seven women and thirteen children were then led to them.

Second-Class Boy William Mathews was a proven survivor. While serving on HMS *Illustrious* he and another boy played in the rigging and he fell 60 feet into the sea. An officer dived overboard and brought the unconscious boy to safety. While standing about on the *Birkenhead* he was sent below to fetch an overcoat.

Meanwhile Seton had ordered the hatches to be battened down to contain air in the hull. Mathews found himself entombed in the sinking ship and banged desperately on the hatch cover until the seaman who had been screwing it down opened the bolts and allowed him out.

Seton ordered his troops to muster on the poop-deck, to take weight off the bow. Showing perfect discipline, they did so, supporting injured comrades and standing up smartly as though on parade. Hundreds of soldiers stood barefoot, most in nightclothes, but some with whatever bits of uniform they had donned in the panic to escape the flooding troop quarters.

As the ship rolled in the swell, the 30 horses on board panicked and orders were given for them to be pushed overboard. Cornet

The Wreck of the Birkenhead – a contemporary painting (*McPherson Collection, Africana Museum*).

Ralph Sheldon-Bond, 23, of the 12th Lancers organised the party which did so. The regiment's chargers kicked and whinnied as Bond and half a dozen men struggled to get blindfolds on them, before pushing them overboard. Some of the horses were attacked by sharks as they swam and screeched in terror as the water reddened about them.

The young officer then rushed below to check the few cabins that had not yet flooded. He came across two children who were screaming, so grabbed them and rushed them to their hysterical mother at a lifeboat. He was offered a place in the lifeboat, but refused it and returned to take his place with his men.

Lieutenant John Francis Girardot of the 43rd Regiment was a tall and able officer, the son of a parson and clearly a professional soldier. As third in command of troops, he took charge of the men at the pumps.

Unlike him, Ensign Gould Lucas of the 73rd was wealthy and aristocratic. To him the army was merely a step in the direction of his ambitions. Lucas asked the ship's carpenter what the trouble was and the reply was, 'We have struck a rock and we are going down fast.' Lucas then asked the carpenter not to tell the men as he feared that they would panic.

Salmond had ordered the women and children to be gathered under the poop-deck. Lucas and several soldiers tried to reassure the women, but some tried to break past them, screaming their husbands' names. Lucas superintended the loading of the women and children, a task which he described as 'difficult', as he had to tear women from their husbands' arms and force them into the boats. Their men dutifully stepped back into the lines.

HMS Birkenhead – a painting by Peter Bilas (*by permission of Dr Allan Kayle*).

The first cutter away was commanded by the coxswain, John Lewis. The second, which was filled with the women and children, was under the Master's Assistant, Mr Richards. A gig under Dr Culhane was the only other boat launched.

An authority states that Richard Nesbitt, 14, fell into the sea when being passed from the *Birkenhead* into the boat. 'He grasped the gunwale, his fingers being crushed as the ship rolled over, and he was caught between ship and boat. He was dragged aboard, to find his mother and brother already there.'

According to the Nesbitt family Ensign Henry Nesbitt and his younger brother, Richard Athol, 14, had come with their mother, Annie, and family to join their father, Lieut-Col Alexander Nesbitt, the quartermaster at Algoa Bay. Mrs Nesbitt and the younger children were in one of the lifeboats while the two boys swam for the shore.

Born at sea *en route* to Mauritius in 1838, Richard did his best to keep up with his older brother. When Richard became exhausted he clung to one of the overloaded boats. A sailor tried to beat him off with a boathook, but one of the ladies then fell across him to protect him. He was to bear the scars from the boathook wounds for the rest of his life.

Women and children on the poop by Thomas Hemy, showing Seton clutching his sword (*Africana Museum*)

On the poop someone shouted, 'God bless you all.' Then, some 15 minutes after the first collision, the bow tore off at the foremast. The stern rose and men were pitched into the sea. The funnel then crashed to the deck, smashing the paddlebox and crushing the men who had been working on releasing the boats.

The vessel broke in two with a screech of tearing metal and splintering woodwork, and the poop began to sink. The soldiers who were manning the chain pumps in the darkness of the lower deck were drowned at their posts. Lieutenant Booth of the 73rd had just relieved Lieut Girardot and died with the men.

Captain Salmond knew that the stern would sink soon, so he climbed a few steps up the mizzen rigging and shouted, 'All those that can swim, jump overboard, and make for the boats! This is your only hope of salvation.'

Two officers, Captain Wright and Lieutenant Girardot, then begged the men, who were standing in rows on the deck, not to do so, as the boats would be swamped and the women and children drowned. Colonel Seton reinforced this by yelling, 'You will swamp the cutter containing the women and children. I implore you not to do this thing and I ask you to stand fast.'

A few of the men went overboard, but the majority stood firm.

Captain Wright later said, 'It struck me as one of the most perfect instances of what discipline can effect, and almost led me to believe that not a man on board knew the vessel was likely to go down.'

As the passengers pulled away they saw the lines of red-coated soldiers standing to attention, and the crew standing with them. Shortly aferwards the deck suddenly dropped and threw Captain Salmond into the water. The officers and untrained young soldiers stood firm.

Ensign Lucas shook hands with Seton and said that he hoped they would meet on shore. Seton shook his head, 'I do not think we shall, Lucas, as I cannot swim a stroke.'

Lucas later wrote, 'I dared not jump into the water as it was literally alive with men. A dreadful sight it was. Some in their last dying efforts, others striking out manfully and suddenly going down with a yell of agony – their shrieks seem still to ring in my ears; some pulling others down in their efforts to keep above water.' He went overboard just before the stern sank. It took virtually all those who had stood on the poop to a watery grave.

The ship was gone within 20 minutes of striking the rocks. The top of the mainmast and and the main topsail yard remained protruding from the water, so some of the soldiers and crew swam towards them and climbed up the shrouds to find a place to hang onto.

Drowning was to be preferred to the horror which faced those in the water. Sharks attacked the horses and circled the wretches who struggled through the cold water and kelp towards the shore. Many acts of heroism took place as men tried to save others.

Captain Salmond swam from the sternpost of the ship, which had just sunk, to a portion of the forecastle decks which was floating about 20 yards from the main part of the wreck. Something struck him on the back of the head and he was seen to sink.

Private Page of the Queen's Regiment and 27 men hung onto a mess table in the water. Page was the only one to survive as the others released their holds because of exhaustion or when taken by sharks. Private Boyden, also of the Queen's, climbed on top of a bale of floating hay. A cabin boy who paddled past on a door shouted, 'Come on, Jack Straw!' The nickname stuck to Boyden for the rest of his service life, even when he later served as a colour-sergeant.

Major Seton hung onto a plank until he saw two cabin boys in difficulties nearby. He pushed the plank to them and, when he realised that it couldn't support all three of them, he let go.

Captain Wright and five others managed to board the floating fore sponson, from where they managed to pull another ten men to safety. The boats were soon full and no more men could be rescued. The first cutter held 36 men, the second 35 people, including the women and children, and the gig nine men. In total 80 people out of the complement of 638.

Lucas had swum to one of the paddlebox boats which floated upside down with five soldiers and the ship's quartermaster, Henry Maxwell, hanging onto the keel. The boat drifted out to sea, past the mast to which many men desperately clung. Another current then swung it in towards land.

At 3.30 am Ensign Alexander Russell, 16, of the 74th Highlanders offered his place in a boat to a man who was struggling in the water. As he swam behind the cutter he was attacked by a shark and dragged under.

William Mathews, the youngster who had escaped from being locked into the sinking ship, grew weak as he swam towards a cutter. He cried out for help and the women begged the sailors to allow him aboard. Richards approved and he was dragged aboard in the nick of time.

The young lancer, Cornet Bond, had put on one of Mackintosh's life preservers and inflated it in the water. He saw that the sea was covered in struggling forms and the air full of their cries and shouts. He swam astern of one of the boats, hoping to be picked up, and hailed it when 60 yards away but couldn't reach it. He saw two men swimming near him disappear with shrieks.

Realising that there would be no rescue from the overloaded boats, he swam for the shore, a couple of miles distant. When nearing land he became entangled in a dense jungle of kelp. Although exhausted, he managed to drag himself through and at last reached the rocky beach. While walking up a track he saw his own horse standing knee-deep in the water. Five of the 30 horses eventually reached land.

As it was then daytime Bond led his horse to shore, then went to assist nine of his comrades who were trying to land on a raft. He clambered along the beach until he could point out to them the best place to come ashore. After some difficulty they scrambled ashore at 7 am.

Three other men were then noticed clinging to a spar and being tossed about by the waves. They were naked, like many others who had scrambled from their berths without time to dress. According to Bond, 'Those just saved stood at the water's edge, praying for an opportunity of lending them a helping hand.

'The three men were helpless to direct the spar; it required all their energies to maintain a grasp on it. The waves would bring them close to the land, but receding, would carry them bloody and bruised back again into the boiling surf. At length they were shot violently up, were seized by ready hands, and dragged, breathless and spent, high and dry upon the shore.'

As day broke Lucas found that his group on the upturned boat were still a mile from shore. He saw an oar floating nearby so swam to fetch it. The oar then enabled the men to work their boat close inshore. During the early afternoon Lucas saw two men swimming past. One kept returning to assist the other and eventually they both disappeared under the water. Eventually Lucas and his party reached the rocky beach.

Of the men who had climbed the mast's rigging only 45 remained. They had clung to the ship's mainmast and hung on throughout the night, to be rescued the following day at 2 pm by the schooner, the *Lioness*. By that time they were parched and weak. It also took on the survivors from the boats. All the women and children were saved. The gig rowed 50 miles along the coast before landing.

Where the gig landed at Hawston, near Hermanus (*Murray*).

John Archbold, the gunner, had fallen overboard when the ship broke up. He spent the night spreadeagled on a bale of hay, then at daylight joined the group with Captain Wright's raft.

Captain Wright and the men on the sponson drifted to Walker Bay and in the early afternoon fought their way through the thick kelp. They then marched inland to seek help. To keep their spirits up Wright led them in singing. At 3pm they met a wagon driver, who directed them to a fisherman's hut. That night Wright walked a further 12 kilometres to a farm belonging to Captain Smales, formerly of the 7th Dragoon Guards. From there he sent provisions back to his men.

The next day, Friday, 27 February, Captain Wright, Lieutenant Girardot and Cornet Bond met on the beach opposite the wreck and searched for more survivors. Some rafts had washed ashore with dead bodies lashed to them. Other bodies that washed up had been savaged by sharks.

For three days Wright and Jeffreys, the ship's purser, scoured the coast for 32 kilometres and found two survivors. The crew of a whaling-boat found two other survivors who had been in the sea for 38 hours. The civil commissioner of Caledon, Mr Mackay, and a party of men under the local field-cornet, Jan de Villiers, assisted Wright in burying the bodies on the beach and collecting personal items which had washed ashore.

Her Majesty's paddle-sloop *Radamanthus* then arrived and sent boats to pick up 68 men who had made it to the beach on makeshift rafts and bits of wreckage. Of the 290 troops who had stood on the poop-deck when the *Birkenhead* went down, there was no sign.

Of all on board, 193 were saved, but 455 lost, two-thirds of the original complement. Captain Salmond and Major Seton were among the dead. Among the survivors was Colour Sergeant O'Neill of the 91st Foot, who had also survived the wrecking of the *Abercrombie Robinson* ten years before. He claimed that immediately after the wrecking they were paid in Spanish dollars, which gave rise to the rumour that the usual gold with which they were paid was lost with the *Birkenhead*.

The survivors were taken for a court-martial aboard HMS *Victory* at Portsmouth and all were acquitted. Captain Salmond was found to have navigated too close to shore, possibly through his compass's magnetic needle being deflected by the nearby mountains or underestimating the inshore current. Many of the survivors felt that the captain had acted with great courage and presence of mind.

Captain Wright stated, 'The resolution of all hands far exceeded anything that I thought could be effected by the best discipline. Everyone did as directed; there was not a murmur among them. Orders were carried out as if the men were embarking instead of going to the bottom.'

One of the Duke of Wellington's last public acts was to commend the men of the *Birkenhead*, 'They have shown under the most difficult circumstances the utmost subordination, order and discipline.'

The King of Prussia instructed that the official account of the *Birkenhead* disaster was to be read out to all his regiments as an example to them of discipline and bravery.

The discipline which prevailed was to be an inspiration for future sea disasters. The axiom of 'Women and children first' was to become accepted procedure thereafter. Fifty years after the tragedy it was immortalised by Rudyard Kipling in verse, 'Soldier an' Sailor Too':

> To take your chance in the thick of a rush, with firing all
> about,

Is nothing so bad when you've cover to 'and, an' leave an'
linkin' to shout;
But to stand an' be still to the Birken'ead drill, is a damn
tough bullet to chew;
An' they done it, the Jollies – 'Er Majesty's Jollies – soldier an'
sailor too!
Their work was done when it 'adn't begun; they was younger
nor me an' you;
Their choice it was plain between drownin' in 'eaps an' being
mashed by the screw,
So they stood an' was still to the Birken'ead drill, soldier an'
sailor too!

Kipling eulogised the Royal Marines in his poem, although there
were only a handful aboard. The principal glory must go to the
officers and young soldiers, who were untrained for such an envi-
ronment, yet set a tradition which is accepted throughout the
Anglo-Saxon world.

Captain Edward Wright was to become a full colonel and in 1870
was initiated into the Order of the Bath. He died at Chelsea in
1871.

Ensign Lucas returned to South Africa a few years later to take
up a position as a magistrate in Natal, eventually becoming the
Chief Magistrate of Durban. He later returned to England where
he retired.

Richard Nesbitt served in the Frontier Armed and Mounted
Police and Cape Mounted Riflemen from 1861. In 1880 he founded
and commanded Nesbitt's Irregular Horse and Nesbitt's Light
Horse. After distinguished service in the South African War he retired to Redhouse, near Port Elizabeth, where he died in 1905. Henry
Nesbitt's son, Randolph, was to win a Victoria Cross in Mashona-
land in 1896.

In 1902, on the 50th Anniversary of the sinking, among those
who signed the Roll Call were Lieut-Col John Girardot, Captain
Sheldon-Bond and Captain Lucas. Girardot died on 11 September,
1902, aged 73 years.

Salvage

The Admiralty did not appear to be overly concerned at the loss of
the *Birkenhead's* cargo, as the wreck was sold by their agents at the
Cape shortly afterwards. In 1854 A H Adams and a team of divers
explored the wreck and found engraved silverware which had belonged to Lieut-Col Seton, as well as papers and other artefacts,
which unfortunately weren't recorded. The silverware was returned to Seton's family.

In the 1890s a Mr Bandmann obtained permission to dive for

the reputed £240,000 sterling gold thought to be aboard. Of any treasure found, a third was to be given to the government and any relics, which had belonged to the officers or men, were to be handed to their relatives. The salvage failed.

One of the most notable salvages was made by the South African strongman, Tromp van Diggelen. In June 1958 his team announced that the bow was overgrown with marine life, that the paddles stood erect on the sea floor, but that the stern was missing. They recovered some anchors and copper and brass fittings, but no gold or the ship's bell.

In 1983 Dr Allan Kayle of Johannesburg began organising a scientific salvage. By 1986, when the new War Graves and National Monuments Act was promulgated, over 300 artefacts had been collected.

Bond's nameplate. Those of Seton and Lucas were also found (*Dr A Kayle*).

Among the items found were nameplates of Major Alexander Seton of the 74th Highlanders and of Cornet Ralph Sheldon-Bond of the 12th Lancers. None of the reputed gold specie and bullion was found, which may have been buried with munitions against bedrock under tons of sand. On the 134th anniversary of the sinking a salvage crew managed to bring up some valuable sovereigns from the wreck.

In October 1988 the official division of the artefacts took place at the Cultural History Museum at Cape Town. The portion of the artefacts claimed by the National Monuments Council was shared between South Africa and Britain.

A plaque was fitted to the lighthouse at Danger Point to commemorate those who perished in the *Birkenhead* disaster. The rock lies approximately one-and-a-third nautical miles south-west of the lighthouse and can be clearly seen. This isolated part of Africa's coastline is rarely visited.

During building operations in 1991 a bulldozer uncovered the remains of three men in an unmarked grave near the wreck site. The War Graves Committee had the grave excavated by the National Monuments' Council archaeologist, Dr Janette Deacon. They were ceremoniously reinterred in a Simon's Town garden of remembrance in August 1993.

Although hundreds of men perished there in 1852, their stoic discipline set a tradition which has become embodied in unwritten maritime law – 'the stronger shall not claim the right to survive over the weaker' and 'women and children must first be saved'.

CHAPTER 3

Foundered, Collided and Torpedoed

By far the most sea disasters off the South African coast took place in the nineteenth century, due to storms and shipwrecks. In the early twentieth century one of the great mysteries of the seas was to occur off the Transkei coast when an ocean liner disappeared. The riddle which has perplexed the world for so long may soon be solved by a team of intrepid skindivers.

Waratah:

27 July 1909

The stormy seas off South Africa's coast has also claimed numerous ships, among the better known was the Australian liner the *Waratah*, which disappeared between Durban and East London. It was an unlucky name, for ships named *Waratah* were lost in 1848, two in 1887 and another in 1894.

She was a twin-screw passenger and cargo steamship of 9,339 tons, built on the Clyde in 1908, was 465 feet long with a beam of over 59 feet. Lund's Blue Anchor Line then used her on the Australia run. The *Waratah*, named after an Australian proteaceous tree bearing crimson flowers, had a speed of 13 knots and was one of the largest ships on the route. She was criticised for being 'top heavy' by some crew and passengers, but no official notice was ever taken of this.

Captain Josiah S Ilbery was proud of his ship with a crew of 119 and luxurious accommodation for 100 passengers. He was commodore of the Blue Anchor Line, which he had served for over 40 years, and expected the *Waratah* to be his last command. An experienced mariner, he had sailed in clipper ships and had a great deal of experience of storms at sea.

The *Waratah* left on her maiden voyage to Australia on 5 November, 1908. No trouble was reported during the voyage, although it was noted that it was difficult to load her evenly. This was aggravated by the fact that a cargo-passenger liner used a great deal of water and fuel, which changed the ship's stability during the voyage.

She left London on her second voyage on 27 April, 1909, then returned from Adelaide, Australia, on 7 July. On board were 93 passengers and a cargo of 10 000 tons of flour and frozen meat. One passenger, Claude G Sawyer, and English Engineer and businessman, refused to continue the voyage from Durban. During the trip from Australian he had recurrent nightmares.

He dreamt that he stood at the rail and that a medieval knight, in bloodstained armour, rose from the ocean with a bloodsoaked cloth in one hand and a sword in the other. The apparition's mouth

Captain Ilbery (*RK*).

The *Waratah* (*Livermore, Murray*).

seemed to say "The *Waratah!* The *Waratah!*" Sawyer believed that he was being warned, especially as he felt that the ship was top-heavy.

The *Waratah* left Durban on 26 July and the following morning at 6 am overtook and exchanged signals with the *Clan MacIntyre* near Port St Johns. Neither ship was equipped with radio, which came into general use only after the sinking of the *Titanic* three years later.

The *Clan MacIntyre* asked her name by lamp and she replied, '*Waratah*, for London.'

The high superstructure of the *Waratah* (*Murray*).

'*Clan MacIntyre*, for London. What weather did you have from Australia?'

'Strong southwesterly to southerly winds across'.

'Thanks, goodbye. Pleasant passage.'

'Thanks. Same to you. Goodbye.'

The *Waratah* remained within sight until 9.30 am before her hull slipped below the horizon. There was a north-easterly wind blowing, the pressure dropped and the wind died abruptly. Then the pressure shot up and a full gale blew out of the southwest. The *Waratah* was about 12 miles offshore when she ran into a head sea. Brutal short, quick waves were followed by 40-foot waves, while the sky was purple-black and full of flying clouds.

The Capsizing

Shortly afterwards Colonel Joe Conquer, one of a signalling party of the Cape Mounted Riflemen who were carrying out live shell practice near the mouth of the Xora River, saw a ship 'proceeding very slowly in a south-westerly direction and making very heavy weather'.

Joe Conquer later reported, 'I watched this vessel through a telescope and I can still see her in my mind's eye. She was a ship of considerable tonnage with a single funnel, two masts, a black hull, the upper works painted yellow.

'I watched this ship crawling along and saw her roll to starboard and then, before she could right herself, a following wave rolled over her and I saw her no more.'

According to Emlyn Brown, 38, who researched the ship's disappearance, Conquer's report was not taken seriously. 'And yet he was a decorated, highly respected officer who had been trained as an observer and made careful notes of the position of the ship he had seen.

'Why was his report not taken seriously? I believe it was because the Cape Mounted Rifles did not want to be involved in any way in the sensationalism surrounding the ship's disappearance and the subsequent inquiry, which was a complete whitewash.'

While doing his national service in the navy a few years earlier Brown had heard of a CSIR report about a shipwreck located off the Xora River mouth. Further checking revealed that it was the position given by Conquer.

Brown added, 'I have evidence that Conquer made an official written report in which he located the site, and I have material written by Conquer himself in which he describes vividly what he saw. He was not the kind of man to fabricate it all. Anyway I do not believe the riddle of the *Waratah* will be solved by historians or by armchair logic but by action. This is the stuff that dreams are made of, and you have to fight to make the sea let go of it.'

The *Waratah's* crew (*RK*).

The 1st-Class Music Saloon (*Murray*).

What was agreed was that the *Waratah* had vanished between Durban and East London. No survivors or trace of any wreckage was ever found. The *Clan McIntyre* was following the same course and must have passed the scene of the disaster some hours later. When she failed to arrive at Cape Town three naval vessels were sent to search for her, but no trace was ever found.

A fund of £5 000 was then raised by public subscription to charter a ship for a comprehensive search. The *Wakefield* left Durban in February 1910 and followed a 30 000 kilometre zig-zag course across the Indian Ocean as far as the Antarctic, but no trace of the *Waratah* could be found.

The Inquiry

The Board of Trade inquiry was opened at Caxton Hall, London, on 16 December, 1910. With no survivors, collecting evidence had been extremely difficult. There was no plan of how cargo had been stowed or evidence of its stability at the time.

The expert witnesses called claimed that the ship was properly designed and constructed and that she had sailed in a seaworthy condition; she was adequately manned and her rigging and lifesaving equipment in good condition.

Among the 'amateur' witnesses was a physics professor, William Bragg, who had sailed on the first homeward voyage from Australia. He said that one morning a starboard list was so bad that water would not run out of the baths. The list had continued for a few days. When a water ballast tank was filled to correct this, she merely listed to port.

Able Seaman Edward Dischler, an experienced sailor, said that when the *Waratah* rolled she went right over and didn't recover for some time, so that portholes had to be kept closed to prevent the seawater from coming in. He added, 'She was the unsteadiest ship I ever voyaged in.'

A steward, Frederick Little, who had left the ship in Durban to find work there, said that there had been talk among the officers and stewards and that he had heard some stewards say that she was top-heavy.

Another passenger who had sailed on the maiden voyage, Worthington Church, said, 'I thought she was very top-heavy. I had a conversation with Captain Ilbery, who said he was not altogether satisfied with the ship.' Other passengers seemed satisfied with the behaviour of the vessel.

Then Claude Sawyer was called. Despite his allusion to the warning dream he appeared to be a stable person. he said that when the ship rolled she recovered very slowly and that the 3rd officer had said that it was top-heavy. One morning he had noticed from his bath water that the ship was lying at 45 degrees. The pitching was of greater concern, for when she was in a trough between waves, instead of rising to the next wave, she would plough through it. The *Waratah* would take on a lot of water and recover slowly.

On 28 July, the night the *Waratah* disappeared he had dreamt of it. 'I saw the *Waratah* in big waves. One . . . went over her bows and pressed her down. She rolled over on her starboard side and disappeared.' He never varied his story, which he had dreamt before news of the missing ship was received.

In February 1911 the Board reported their conclusions: that the *Waratah* had capsized in a gale of exceptional violence, the first great storm she had encountered.

Aerial sighting!

In 1924 a South African Air Force pilot, Lieutenant D J Roos, sighted a wreck lying on a submarine ledge near the mouth of the Bashee River, north of East London, while flying a mail route. A few years later he drew a map to assist an air search sponsored by *The Star*. The air search failed due to bad weather. Lieutenant Roos died in a motorcycle accident.

His son, Brigadier Tom Roos, was a former military attaché to Portugal and later lived in Cape Town. Speaking of his father he said, 'He was always convinced that he had seen the *Waratah*. For many years the map that he drew was lost. Then one day I was going through the family album and I found an authentic copy of it.'

Hole in the ocean

The absence of any wreckage pointed to a capsizing. The fact that no bodies were found could largely be ascribed to this and to the numerous sharks in the area.

In 1960 Captain Byles of the 28,000 ton *Edinburgh Castle* experienced heavy seas in the area in which the *Waratah* had disappeared. The distance between the waves was 150 feet, when suddenly one appeared 300 feet away, so that the ship pitched and charged head-on into it at an angle of over 30 degrees, almost as if she had dropped into a 'hole in the ocean'.

In 1962 a retired seaman, W Recknell, wrote to a Durban newspaper that he was at sea at the time the *Waratah* disappeared. He had heard officers talking of their ships dropping into an 'air pocket' in the area, which was caused by a rift in the ocean.

The *Sunday Telegraph* stated, 'This phenomenon is unique to the southern ocean, when a combination of gale, current and ocean bed contours tugs the sea apart to form an enormously deep vacuum, into which a ship can plunge and be buried by the waves.' In 1971 Geoffrey Jenkins wrote of such an occurrence in his novel *Scend of the Sea*.

In 1979 George Young, shipping editor of the *Cape Times*, wrote to John Harris that if the *Waratah*, with her wooden hatches, had hit such seas the load of water on the forward well deck would have filled the holds and she would have gone down like a stone. His theory is well supported by what happened to other ships in the area, such as the *Edinburgh Castle* and the *Bencruachan*. In the latter case the weight of water pressing on the foredeck had almost broken it off and she had to return to Durban.

Mr Owen, chief officer of the *Waratah* (*RK*).

In July 1989 the *Sunday Star* reported on Emlyn Brown's expedition to find the *Waratah*. The wreck had been located in 1977 by the Durban-based CSIR vessel *Meiring Naude*. Cape Town historian and author, Peter Humphries, who said that he had been investigating the riddle for 50 years, dubbed the search 'a fiasco'.

He said that when last seen from the *Clan MacIntyre* on 27 July, 1909, at 10.30 am the *Waratah* was about 17 miles due east of the Bashee River mouth, the present search area. Her speed of 13,5 knots, plus the Mozambique Current, running up to four knots, meant that when the *Waratah* hit heavy weather between 4 pm and 6 pm she would have been much further south-west.

'From several plottings that I have done in a number of vessels, she could have been as far to the south-west as to be off the Fish River mouth when she encountered the storm.' He said that the present search was being carried out largely on the supposed evidence of Joe Conquer.

'I was told by the late Lieutenant-Colonel Bertram Woodhead DSO, of the Dukes, that Joe Conquer was quite widely known as a bull . . . I checked with the late Lawrence Green, who had quoted Conquer in one of his books. Lawrence told me he had not checked the accuracy of Conquer's statement but never allowed the facts to spoil a good story.'

Mr Humphries believed the *Waratah* was making for shelter in

Port Elizabeth when she got further inshore than the skipper intended, wallowed and hit a submerged rock, tore her bottom out and 'went down like a stone'.

Professor J K Mallory, retired professor of oceanography at the University of Cape Town, disagreed with him and believed the *Waratah* was the victim of a freak wave – the 'hole in the sea' phenomenon about which he has written a treatise.

In June 1989 a Johannesburg newspaper ran a competition, in which readers could guess where on a map grid the *Waratah* would be found. The prize offered was a cruise on the *MTS Oceanos*.

Whatever the fate of the *Waratah* was, it was the premonition of disaster which had ensured that there would be a survivor. Had Claude Sawyer not dreamt of its end, he would surely have been among those who disappeared.

Mendi:
21 February 1917

'If I should die, think only this of me
'That there is some corner of a foreign field
'That is forever England . . .'

This excerpt from Wilfred Brookes's sonnet 'For the Fallen' could well be applied to the sea, for there is a corner of the English Channel which will forever be Africa's!

The 4,230 ton troopship SS *Mendi* left Cape Town on 16 January, 1917, with the last batch of the South African Native Labour Corps, some 800 blacks from all parts of South Africa. The ship was commanded by Captain Henry Arthur Yardley, who had been master of a number of ships since 1901. On board he had a crew of 89, which included some West African 'Kroo' men.

The medical officer was Captain Lewis Eccles Hertslet, 38, who had served as a medical missionary in Natal. He was deeply religious, married and had four children. Hertslet joined up in 1916 and was working at the Wynberg Military Hospital when asked if he would volunteer to go to France with the Native Labour Contingent, as he could speak black languages. Although one of his brothers had been killed at Gallipoli, he didn't hesitate to sign on.

The ship was 370 feet in length and 46 feet in the beam. She had been in the Liverpool-West Africa service and had possibly been named after the Mendi tribe in Sierra Leone. She was chartered by the British government in the autumn of 1916 and fitted out as a troopship with four holds.

Nigerian troops were then loaded in Lagos and transported to Mombasa for service in the East African Campaign. On her return trip the *Mendi* loaded the SANLC troops and five million pounds in gold bullion at Cape Town, then sailed in convoy with the *Kenil-*

The Transport *Mendi*
(*Murray*).

worth Castle and other liners. They called at Freetown and Lagos, where coal and provisions, including coconuts, were loaded.

At these ports the whole ship's complement took part in lifeboat drills. The boats were lowered and found to be in good condition. The rafts were also tested and found to float satisfactorily. The gold bullion was transferred to HMS *Cornwall* and the convoy then continued unescorted.

The Native Labour Corps included educated men such as the Reverend Isaac Wauchope Dyobha and Joseph Tshite, a schoolmaster from near Pretoria. Dyobha was a Xhosa, educated at the Lovedale Mission, who had been one of the five evangelists who went to Nyasaland (Malawi) in 1876. They returned the next year because of fever.

He subsequently taught at Uitenhage, then became an interpreter at the Port Elizabeth Magistrate's Court. After entering the ministry of the Congregational Church he served at Beaufort West. Dyobha is believed to be the first black to have written a poem in English. He joined the SANLC as a clerk/interpreter.

Jacob Koos Matli worked in Johannesburg and was at his tribal land on sick leave when he was recruited. 'At the end of November (1916) our Chief called us and told us that the British Government had asked for some soldiers from the Union Government to go overseas in order to partake in the First Great War . . . I was chosen as a leader of our tribe (the Bahaduba) and amongst these men there was one George Mathibe who had just returned from German West.

'He asked the chief that he should be our first leader as he already had a bit of experience and would show me the way to lead

William Bonafacious
Mathumetse (*Clothier*).

men as I was still a young man . . . We left for Cape Town the following day.' Matli's group were used as stokers and later also as lookouts.

William Bonafacious Mathumetse, 16, had been forbidden by his father, a pastor of the Lutheran Church, from joining up. When William persisted, he was told to go and ask his grandfather, who lived 30 miles away. The old man, Thomas Mokone, had been a fearless warrior in his time. He grabbed his battle-axe and danced about, then led his grandson back to his home, where he harangued the parents until they gave the necessary permission.

Thirty-four days after leaving Cape Town the *Mendi* at last steamed into Portsmouth. Despite the danger from U-boats the troops then had to be transported across the English Channel to Le Havre, Captain Yardley had heard of threatening mist, although the weather then was only overcast. They left Plymouth at 4 pm on 20 February, 1917, escorted by the destroyer HMS *Brisk*.

By 5.30 pm it was almost dark and lookouts were posted in the crow's nest and two on the forecastle head. At 7.30 pm oil lamps were lit. Among the half dozen white officers of the Native Labour Corps was Lieut Samuel Henry Richardson, 34, from Durban. He was married to a sister of Captain Garnet Green, the last man to leave Delville Wood when the South African Brigade had been relieved there seven months before.

At about 11.30 pm it became foggy and the whistle was sounded at one minute intervals. After midnight Captain Hertslet was relieved by Lieutenant Richardson. They sat up talking until 1.30 am on aspects of the new testament. The blacks slept fully dressed, most wrapped in their blankets, in the troop decks.

At 4 am Second Officer Rayne and Fourth Officer Trapnell came on watch. The weather was still very thick and misty and the *Mendi* continued at slow speed. Other steamers' whistles were heard in the area. At 4.30 am Captain Yardley saw that the weather was becoming thicker, so he went down to the chartroom.

The escort HMS *Brisk* drew up alongside and asked whether they couldn't increase speed, but Yardley chose to continue at slow speed. They were then about 11 miles south-south-west of the Isle of Wight and he feared colliding with other traffic.

At 4.57 am Trapnell shouted, 'Raine! I think there is a vessel near us.' He sounded the *Mendi's* whistle and almost immediately the SS *Darro*, a twin screw steamship, burst out of the fog and at full speed smashed into the starboard side of the *Mendi*. The bow of the *Darro* struck near a watertight bulkhead, opening up No 1 and No 2 holds to the ocean.

The two ships then drifted apart, leaving a gaping hole in the side of the *Mendi*. Men struggled out of their blankets in the dark,

Capt L Hertslet, Lt S Emslie, Major F Guest, Lt S Richardson, Lt L Van Vuren; Inset: L Deary (*Clothier*).

trying to escape the freezing water, and struggled toward the exits. At least one of the exits was jammed closed and approximately 140 men were trapped.

Matli was in the hold when he heard, 'a very big sound like a cannon's and the ship blowing its whistles all the time. Everybody was putting his lifebelt on and in full kit. We started to run to the upper deck and the steps were crowded. I was pressing myself into the middle of the crowd, in order to have a chance of getting to the steps, when I realised that I was being pulled back by someone.

'I had no chance because the man who was pulling me back was a very big man and hefty, so, as soon as he passed me I held on to his jacket and he did not seem to mind, because he kept on shoving and pushing other men until he got on deck. I relaxed my grip on his jacket and jumped over the rails of the steps on to the deck.'

Captain Yardley had been thrown to the deck by the force of the collision. He then rose, ordered the engines to be stopped and sent Trapnell to have the boats lowered and signal with four blasts that all hands go to their boat stations.

Captain Hertslet was woken by the collision. 'My first thought was, "We've run into a fishing boat"' . . . my second, "Better go and see what's doing". I put on my tunic, boots and coat quickly. While doing this I noted a change in the ship's siren, which had been sounding all through the night. It changed to a rapid series of hootings, which we had been warned would mean "Every man on deck at once!"

'As I was getting my coat on Richardson came down running and said to myself and Emslie "Come on you chaps" and dashed off. I

41

ran along the passage to the saloon, and up the stairs to the passenger-deck. All was dark but I looked over the rail and saw a lot of broken planks floating alongside, which seemed to confirm my idea of the fishing boat.

'I walked along the deck and saw our native troops all running or walking quietly to their allocated places on the deck. These places had been given to us, during the passage, ready for such an emergency. I now noticed that some of the men were fastening their belts to themselves as they ran to their places. And then . . . the ship gave a strange sort of lurch on to one side . . . and then I discovered like a fool I'd left my lifebelt in my cabin and . . . I . . . couldn't swim!

'I scouted around the smoking-room and the nearest part of the deck, but no spares (lifebelts) were visible . . . so I had to make up my mind very quickly whether to risk going back to my cabin to get the belt, or chance going overboard without it.

'I decided to get the belt, and hustled below . . . said a hasty farewell to all my kit, grabbed my leather attache case, previously filled for such an emergency, slung my belt round me and tied the tapes and dashed out again. By the time I got to the staircase leading to the deck, the ship had heeled over so that the edges of the stairs were almost horizontal and I had to walk on them to get up at all and when I reached the doorway I could only slide down to the rail!'

Matli searched for his friends. 'I turned round on deck, and saw that some men were already in the sea and a group of our company was standing at attentiton as if someone had ordered them to fall in line. I went to them, there I found George Mathibe in the front row. I asked him if there was anyone who could tell us what to do, and as I was talking to him I saw a white man leaning against the rails of the ship and looking into the sea.

'I left my Company and went to him. I did not know what he was or who he was, as it was very dark and misty. As I came to him I realised that he was a Captain and I told him about the men who were at attention and asked what we were supposed to do, but he did not speak to me or turn to see who I was.

'I left him and went back to my Company who were now busy trying to untie one of the lifeboats hanging on the sides of the *Mendi*. I told George Mathibe what I said to the Captain and that he did not answer me. Then George said I must take off my overcoat. I did so and he said to me, "Koos, we are about to die, but one of us will live to tell at home how members of the tribe had died with the ship *Mendi*, but I hope it will be you so that you will be able to relate the story.

'I told him I was going back to the Captain again. I left them and tried to speak to the Captain again, but this time he turned back, went down some flight of steps, opened a door and shut it behind him. I was just about to turn away when I heard the sound of a gun being fired from the room the Captain had just entered.'

The Death Dance   Richardson and some others helped men out of the forward holds. Some of the boats were smashed while being launched. Men then tried to release the 46 rafts which were lashed to the deck. Most of the blacks couldn't swim and dreaded leaving the sinking ship.

It was then that the Rev Wauchope Dyobha cried out to the men on the steeply slanted deck: 'Be quiet and calm, my countrymen, for what is taking place is exactly what you came to do. You are going to die . . . but that is what you came to do. Brothers, we are drilling the death drill. I, a Xhosa, say you are my brothers. Swazis, Pondos, Basutos, we die like brothers. We are the sons of Africa. Raise your war cries, brothers, for though they made us leave our assegais in the kraal, our voices are left with our bodies.'

They took off their boots and stamped the death dance on the slanted deck of the sinking ship. Oral tradition would keep alive the story of the brave black men who danced as the ship sank.

Hertslet then heard the shout, 'All overboard! . . . boats! . . . she's sinking!' For a moment he stood almost paralysed, gripping the deck rail. 'What should I do? There, about 15 or 20 yards from the ship's side, lay one of her boats, fastened to us by a rope. Men were sitting in her, others were swimming towards her, and several were trying to climb in.

'Again I had to decide quickly . . . to jump or not to jump . . . I couldn't swim, and I had a heavy overcoat on, over which was fastened my lifebelt and I carried a despatch case with chocolate and restoratives in it. There really wasn't much choice, the boat seemed the only hope of safety so I scrambled onto the rail and jumped feet first.'

As he jumped he saw Lieut Richardson carrying something. 'Pheuf! The water was cold! Eight degrees above freezing they told us afterwards. I remember going under, wondering if I'd ever come up again, but the belt held me up, and then I took two or three spasmodic, floundering and despairing strokes and got to the side of the boat . . . but I couldn't get in!

'Of course I couldn't, I had my long overcoat on which in a minute had got soaked and heavy with water, to say nothing of all my other clothes and military boots. Of course, the lifebelt held me up a bit and I was able to hold on to the edge of the boat.

'I was hanging on near an oar which one of the men was trying to row without a rowlock. I remembered that I had noted the rowlock hanging by a small chain near its socket so I put my hand inside, pulled it out and jammed it into place and the man was able to row.

'Then came a cry, "Cut the rope quickly or we shall be dragged down" . . . This someone did with an axe, and four men started to row away from the sinking ship, dragging me and some others along in the water.'

After the officer had left him, Matli returned to his Company. 'When I reached the spot there was no one in sight. I looked for the boat they were trying to untie, and noticed that the front of it was still tied on the *Mendi* and the back was hanging into the water. By this time the ship was sinking. The nose was deep in the sea and the back of it was slanting downwards towards the nose.

'I was standing very badly, holding myself onto the rails of the ship and I thought to myself, if I left my grip I would plunge downwards where the ship was fast sinking. I climbed over the rails, held onto the hanging boat and got into it. I put one foot into the sea and then followed with the other one, and as soon as I left holding the boat with my hands I went down into the sea.

'I swallowed some water and then came up to the surface. As I came up for air, a searchlight shone into the sea and I saw a group of men holding onto something. I started to swim towards them, but the light went off. The light shone again and I was not far from the group of men. I swam until I reached them. Then I found they were holding onto a life-saving tube [lifebuoy?]

'I asked the man in front of me to shift aside, so that I could also have a place to hold onto, and he said there was no space. This man was a Swazi. Well, there was only one thing to do and I did it. I jumped onto his back and held him by the shoulders, with my knees dug into his ribs.

Sixteen-year-old Mathumetse initially held back from leaving the ship. 'There was great panic and confusion, and on the deck we were told to get onto lifeboats and leave the ship, as it was sinking. Below there was a sea of darkness, but the men plunged into the rough, cold water, singing, praying and crying.'

He was among the last to jump, then splashed around, repeating the Lord's Prayer over and over. Others sang tribal songs and prayed. Eventually Mathumetse found the bodies of two blacks who had died in the icy water and were floating in their lifebelts. He pulled them together, placed his feet on one and the rest of his body on the other, and rested.

The ship went down by the head, canted to the starboard until the final moment when it swung to port, then was gone. Lieutenant Samuel Emslie, 61, had retired as Chief Licensing Officer for the

Transkei before joining up. It was later said that he had refused to take a place in one of the boats, as there was no room for the blacks. He couldn't swim and drowned when the ship sank.

Lieutenant Richardson was last seen trying to cajole blacks into abandoning ship. Captain Yardley was sucked underwater initially, then rose to the surface of the icy waters. About 120 men were in the boats, while hundreds floated in the freezing water, shouting, singing, praying, crying and dying.

Matli saw the ship go down. 'The sinking ship then blew three times and as it did so I looked back. The light was shining right where the ship was and I saw two men in sailors'uniforms plunge into the sea. The ship now sank and we were circling around where the ship had been.

'I am sure it was when the ship sank, that many men lost their lives, because as it sank it made a great hollow and many men were not far from it. So by the time the water covered that empty space many had gone down into it.

'As for those who were sick and were in the hospital cabin of the ship, I don't think there was one that got saved, because when the ship started sinking there was something like a small nut that shifted and blocked the hospital door.

No steps were taken by the *Darro* to lower boats or rescue the survivors. She stood off and floated nearby while the *Brisk's* lifeboats rowed among the survivors, trying to rescue them. The cries of the men dying of hypothermia echoed in the misty dawn.

'Ho, so and so, child of my mother, are you dead that you do not hear my voice?' and 'Ho, to me, men of so and so, that we may all die together,' was increasingly heard. Tshite, the schoolmaster, encouraged those around him with hymns and prayers until he died. A white sergeant was supported by two blacks who swam with him and found place for him on a raft.

Hertslet thought that he was dying, 'It was intensely cold . . . and very soon I couldn't feel my legs at all . . . and after a bit my arms began to get paralysed and numb. I besought them to pull me in . . . but no one was in authority, and everyone seemed to be obsessed with the idea of getting away somewhere from something . . . I think some feared a German submarine.

'After what seemed to be hours, but was probably less than half an hour, I couldn't hold on any longer, and shouted, "Goodbye, I'm going", and then a native who had been sitting on the other side of the boat came over to where I was and gripped my wrists, so as to prevent me from slipping into the icy, black waters.

'He undoubtedly saved my life, for I could grip the boat's side

Joseph Tshite
(*Clothier*).

45

no longer. He then persuaded the men to stop rowing, the sailor near me shipped his oar, and with the help of others I was ignominiously dragged into the boat in a state of collapse. I can remember saying, "Thank the Lord" . . . and then falling in a sort of heap in the bottom of the boat.'

The boat was then rowed towards a light, which turned out to be a ship which was hove to, with ladders over the side. Hertslet was lifted aboard and carried to the galley where his clothes were stripped off and he was given some brandy to drink. He was thawed in front of one of the furnaces before being put into the Engineer's bed.

Matli was clinging to the Swazi's back when something touched his shoulder. 'When it happened the second time I caught hold of it and jumped on it. It was a flat board and I called to the Swazi man and I told him this was something where we could sit better. We heard some ship blowing and I started to shout.

'Then this man said I was foolish because I was calling the enemy. I told him that it was better to be taken prisoner or be killed than to die in these cold waters. Everything was dead silent and then suddenly we heard the roar of a boat. I shouted, but it was all in vain. I think on the boat were some men from the *Mendi*, because after some time the roar of the boat was heard again.

'I started to shout again and this time they heard me, because it came in our direction. When they were near us they hooked the board with something. I told them to start with the Swazi man, as he was dead cold and kept bending his head onto his chest. I had seen how some of the men had died, because the water knocked them out just on the back of their heads and then they would turn over with their hands and knees bent and would lie on the water with their backs up.

'The boat picked us up and we were taken to the ship. When they reached the ship, they tied this other man with ropes and pulled him up. I suggested to them that I would go up on my own. Not realising how cold I was, I tried to climb up the ladder made of ropes, but I could not make it and fell into the sea. A man came down for me and he had a diving suit on, then they tied me with a rope and pulled me up.

'We were then taken downstairs to a cabin that was filled with steam. In that room we found 12 Native men from the *Mendi* and one white man, a Mr Hamilton who was a sergeant, but he was not in the same cabin. That brought our total to 15 men who were picked up that morning. Then they brought us something to drink. Well I don't know whether it was brandy or whisky but I refused it as I have never had anything like that before. They tried to talk me into it, but I refused.

'They asked me if I couldn't see how nice the other men were feeling after a few drinks, but they gave up eventually and asked if I would like some cocoa. I said yes. The first mug they gave me I took at two full gulps. Then they gave me a second one with some rusks, and I felt that this one was hot. They then asked me why I did not take the second mug and drink it like the first one. I told them that this one was hot but the first one was like lukewarm water.'

Matli had been picked up by the *Sandsend*, a 3,814 ton tramp steamer. As he was one of the only blacks who could understand the crew, he was asked to assist in the ship's kitchen. Matli peeled vegetables and took coffee and rusks to his companions. Eventually the *Sandsend* transferred 23 rescued troops to the minesweeper *Balfour.*

Capt Henry Yardley
(*Clothier*).

Yardley was in the sea for over an hour. 'I had a lifebelt on. There were hundreds of boys around me after the wreck. They died from exposure. They all had lifebelts on. It was not freezing. It was a very cold, dark, damp, miserable night.

'The reason that I say that they died from exposure is that I eventually came across a raft with 14 or 16 boys hanging onto it. There was one on top of the raft and he expired while I was there. There were only two men in it and everybody wanted to get into it. I said, "Tow us alongside and everybody will be saved." I am afraid many of these boys expired before they got alongside. I was unconscious.'

One of the rafts, with a few survivors aboard, managed to reach the Dorset coast. Three white officers and seven white NCOs died. Of the 802 black troops, 615 died. Among the dead blacks were some prominent men such as the Pondoland chiefs Henry Bokleni, Dokoda Richard Ndamase, Mxonywa Bangani and Mongameli, as well as the Reverend Wauchope Dyobha.

On 9 March the members of the South African House of Assembly rose to pay tribute to the dead of the *Mendi*. It has been said that the black tribes in South Africa were aware of the disaster before they were officially advised by the government.

The survivors were to continue with their military service in France. One of the highlights was when some of them met the King and Queen of England at Rouen in July 1917. Matli recalled, 'One day we were all called together and we went to another ship. On the deck we met King George the V . . . and Queen Mary. The King addressed us personally and thanked us for the services we had rendered. He told us that we were going home within a few days, and when we reached home we must tell our Chiefs and fathers how he had thanked us.'

47

The corps returned home in late September 1918. They had enjoyed their stay in France, their first experience of living in a country without a colour bar. Some hid away and never returned to South Africa. General Botha disapproved of those in England who went about with white women and didn't want them in France. Matli shrugged, 'I do not know as to whether this was the truth or just rumour, but we came back and left many in England.'

Hertslet returned to his family in Cape Town early in January 1919. Mathumetse was to become a teacher and evangelist. He is remembered as a carefree, jovial man who died at Graskop, aged 73.

Mendi Day, 21 February, is still observed by some blacks. It is their equivalent of the whites' Delville Wood Day. The names of the *Mendi* dead are engraved on the Hollybrook Memorial, Southampton, for those lost at sea. 264 of the contingent who died in France are buried at Arques-la-Bataille, near Dieppe.

The South African Government gave formal recognition to their service in 1986, when a bronze plaque showing the sinking of the *Mendi* was among those unveiled at the museum at Delville Wood. In 1991 Mr Norman Clothier, author of 'Black Valour', the story of the *Mendi,* took a party, which included a Zulu prince, Pennel Zulu, to visit the site of the sinking and place wreaths on the water. The men of the *Mendi* and their death dance on the deck of the sinking ship will never be forgotten.

Galway Castle:

12 September 1918

During the First World War one of the most tragic, yet needless, disasters was when the *Galway Castle* was torpedoed. She was built by Harland and Wolff in Belfast in 1911, at the time that the legendary *Titanic* was under construction in the same yard. An intermediate steamer of 7,988 tons the *Galway Castle* was a sister ship to the *Gloucester Castle* and the *Guildford Castle*.

She was to be the principal troopship of the fleet which sailed between Cape Town and South West Africa, carrying reinforcements and supplies for General Botha's campaign. After the campaign she reverted to her normal role as a passenger ship.

According to Murray in 'Ships and South Africa' she regularly ran in the west coast service until 1914. 'Towards the end of that year she was to have taken her place in an improved Mauritius service, but owing to the war the new schedule was never put into operation. Shortly after the commencement of the "German West" campaign the *Galway Castle* was requisitioned as a troopship, and in command of Captain H Strong she carried many thousands of "Botha's Boys" between Table Bay and Luderitzbucht and other ports of south-west.

The *Galway Castle* in 1911 (*Murray*).

'She subsequently resumed her role of liner, but owing to the stress of wartime conditions she was promoted to the rank of mail steamer. On August 3rd, 1916, she underwent the unpleasant and comparatively novel experience of being attacked by German aircraft near the Gull Light-vessel in the English Channel, but fortunately none of the enemy bombs found its mark.

'On October 12th, 1917, when homeward bound from Durban, she grounded on the Orient Beach at East London but was refloat-

The *Galway Castle* aground at East London. Casings at the extreme end of her poop conceals her anti-submarine gun (*Murray*).

ed after some days. Her loss at this time would have been disastrous, as she was one of the few vessels remaining to the Union-Castle Line for its South African service, the great majority of the ships having by now been requisitioned for war purposes. She ran in the mail service until September 12th, 1918 when she was torpedoed ...'

'With Captain Dyer in command she set out in convoy from Plymouth on the morning of September 10th, 1918. Her civilian passengers numbered 346, among them being the Rt Hon Henry Burton, who had been in a mishap to the *Kenilworth Castle* three months before. In addition there were some 400 invalided South African troops, including a number of blinded soldiers who were being sent home. These, with the crew, gave the vessel a complement of close on 1,000 souls.

'At 7.30 am on September 12th, two days out from Plymouth, the *Galway Castle* was torpedoed by U-82. There was a terrifying noise of cracking steelwork caused by the breaking of the ship's back, and within a minute the *Galway Castle* was helpless. The splitting of the deck made communication between the forward and after parts extremely difficult, and it seemed as though the vessel would break in two at any moment.

'Everyone was immediately mustered on deck and the boats were launched as hurriedly as possible. Lowering the boats was no easy matter. Some were precipitated headlong into the sea and others were swamped, with the result that a considerable number of lives were lost.

'Destroyers meanwhile had rushed to the rescue and soon all the survivors were on the way to Plymouth, where they landed on Friday, September 13th. There was a heavy casualty list, for some 150 souls had perished in the disaster, among them a number of well-known South Africans. It was a tragic fact that no lives need have been lost, for the *Galway Castle* did not sink until three days later. No one, however, could foretell that she would remain afloat so long, while another torpedo might have struck her at any moment, with infinitely worse results.

'Few events of the war made such an impression in South Africa as the torpedoing of the *Galway Castle*. That a Union-Castle liner carrying mails and passengers to the Cape should actually have been sunk came as a rude shock to this country which had suffered so little as a result of the submarine campaign.'

The great tragedy of the *Galway Castle* sinking was that many of the men who had survived years of fighting in France were to die needlessly on their way home. Among them was Sergeant Percy McCarthy of Johannesburg. He had joined the 3rd South African Infantry Battalion at 18 years of age in November 1915 for service with the 1st South African Infantry Brigade in France.

Sgt Percy McCarthy.

McCarthy missed fighting at the Battle of Delville Wood as he arrived at Rouen six days after the battle ended. The young Lewis Gunner was immediately sent to the front. He was wounded in January 1917 and again in June. Promotion to corporal followed and in February 1918 to lance-sergeant. McCarthy then transferred to the 4th SAI (South African Scottish) Battalion.

On 24 March he was reported missing in action, but managed to return to his unit. Then on 13 April McCarthy was shot in his left hand and hospitalised for a month. On 23 June he was shot in the arm and leg during an attack, then evacuated and sent to England for treatment. By September he had recovered sufficiently to join the convalescent soldiers returning to South Africa on the *Galway Castle*. When it sank he was declared missing, then accepted as dead.

Among the nurses lost was Corrie Addison, a member of a prominent Natal family. Her duty would have been to attend to the sick and crippled soldiers aboard the ship. When it was torpedoed her task would have been to evacuate them and there is little doubt that it was while doing so that she died.

Her back broken, the *Galway Castle* slowly sinks (*Murray*).

Among the SA Scottish soldiers who survived was Private Ted Cooke. Originally from St Erth, Cornwall, he had enlisted early in the war and seen service in East Africa before volunteering for service in Europe. He had to undergo hospital treatment in England and when no longer fit for active service was shipped home on the *Galway Castle*.

One of the women passengers, Mrs Nursey, had her two-year-old daughter, Elsie, with her. As she abandoned ship she came into contact with the propellor and sustained mortal injuries. She managed to reach a raft with Elsie, where they were assisted by Ted Cooke. She told him that her husband was on active service and begged him to take care of her little daughter.

Pte Ted Cooke and
Elsie Nursey (*T Cooke*).

'Look after my child, and God will look after you', was her pathetic appeal. Cooke promised to do so. She asked him to take the valuable rings off her fingers, but owing to her terrible injuries he didn't do so. Shortly afterwards she died and was washed off the raft. After they were rescued Cooke kept the child, Elsie, with him until she could be safely handed over to welfare workers in England.

He had been unable to obtain the name of the mother or child, but was later contacted by Elsie's father, who brought her to visit him in Cornwall. He presented him with a gold watch, which is still a treasured heirloom in the Cooke family.

Elsie was brought to South Africa in her teens and adopted. She lived in Cape Town and served in the WAAS during World War II. She married Captain Leslie Pelteret, a former schoolfriend, in Cairo and they returned to live in Cape Town where they had two daughters. Elsie Pelteret has been widowed since.

Ted Cooke had served in East Africa with his father and younger brother. His elder brother was killed at Ypres. After the war Cooke worked on the gold mines and at sub-Nigel met Redvers Seaman another *Galway Castle* survivor. Cooke served in South Africa during World War II while a younger brother was in the SSB in Italy. Cooke retired to East London where he died in 1967.

Incongruously, a troopship heading north with South Africans was to be torpedoed in the same waters as the *Galway Castle*, also on 12 September, but 24 years later.

CHAPTER 4   # Adrift for 39 days

Surviving the sinking of a ship at sea can pale into insignificance beside the ordeal of surviving at sea thereafter. Anthony Large, from Durban, held the record among South Africans for staying alive while adrift on the ocean.

Laconia:

12 September 1942

On 29 August, 1942, Tony Large sailed on the *Laconia* from Cape Town for England. The 20,000 ton liner carried 2,000 passengers, which included 1,800 Italian prisoners of war. His father had been a gunnery officer in the old *Laconia* during World War I, and the present ship's commander, Captain Sharp, had served with him then. When the new *Laconia* called at Durban Mr Large senior had supervised some work on her for his shipping firm.

Large embarked at Durban. Before leaving he had been discussing with his family a philosopher who had taken poison, but couldn't remember his name. On reaching Cape Town he sent a letter home with one word in it, "Socrates!"

The Transport *Laconia* (*SA National Museum of Military History*).

Another South African on the *Laconia* was Norman MacDonald, 23, from Johannesburg. He had graduated from the University of the Witwatersrand with a BSc degree in Mining and Metallurgy, yet joined the Royal Navy in 1941 as a second-class stoker! MacDonald served in the Far East in HMS *Dragon*, which managed to escape from Singapore.

His ship took part in the battle of the Java Sea and had near misses from bomber aircraft. MacDonald was selected to attend courses in the United Kingdom, with a view to being commissioned, and duly embarked on the *Laconia*.

The U-156, which
under Kortvetten-
käpitan Hartenstein,
sank the *Laconia*
(*Stern*).

The *Laconia* was torpedoed when 700 miles west of the bulge of
Africa on 12 September, exactly 24 years since the *Galway Castle* suffered the same fate in the same waters. In a later letter to his parents Large wrote, 'I'm afraid Captain Sharp went down with the
ship when she was torpedoed. I hadn't seen or spoken to him since
just before Cape Town, because a day after we left I went down with
a bad go of tonsillitis and only left the sickbay on the day we caught
our packet. I wanted the ship's medical officer to take the offending
organ out, but mercifully he refrained and so I live to tell the tale.'

Large vividly recollected the sinking and his subsequent travails.
'We were all down in our messdeck talking and one of our party
had just arrived back from the canteen with some oranges. It was
unpleasant on the deck because of the darkness and wind.

'When the first torpedo hit us, on the starboard and at the other
end of the ship, we were sitting around quietly. By the time the second
torpedo struck, the messdeck was clear, and a hurrying stream of
temporarily panicky and shaken men poured out on to the decks
above. I lost contact with my party immediately and worked my way
forward towards my boat station.

'People milled in all directions but more slowly and purposely as
time went on and the panic wore off. Italian prisoners were everywhere. They cried and prayed for some miraculous assistance.
Subsequently I heard that many were shot when they tried to rush
boats. One, a tall, blonde man, attached himself to me and stayed
by me for a couple of days. His helplessness and apparent reliance
upon me, stiffened me up.

'The ship was listing fairly heavily to starboard and through the
darkness we coud see and hear boats going down. Deck rafts were
being manhandled and flung overboard. The sea was a long way
away and they turned over and over before crashing into it. Every

Tony Large (*Duffus*).

now and then someone would shine a torch or strike a light to see better what he was doing and a torrent of curses would descend upon him. We presented a magnificent target, but the submarines must have been well satisfied with their handiwork, for they left us alone.

'Soon enough I began to feel cold and realised that I only had on a pair of shorts and a shirt. There were too many people about, so the Italian, calling consistently on "Maria", and I worked our way further aft where we could see dimly a boat still turned in and apparently abandoned. We met a soldier of the ship's AA crew and when I asked him he got me an army greatcoat from his locker.

'Half a dozen of us rapidly swung out the boat and soon had her in the water. It was rougher than we expected and terrifying to be buffeted against the enormous expanse of the ship's side. We waited just as long as it took our lowerers to shin down the ladders and join us. The boat was a wooden one and well stocked.

'After a few minutes someone found the plug and checked the inward rush of water. I suppose there were 30 of us in the boat at this stage but after a very short time in the water we were loaded down to the gunwales. A count next day showed something over 60, a mixture of the services, civilians, Poles and Italian prisoners.

'As soon as possible we pulled away from the ship and when a few hundred yards off, lay to and watched her. After a long time she turned over on her starboard side, a great black mass, dipped slowly by the bows, floated vertically for a few seconds and suddenly slid under. Something blew up as she went down and we felt our boat shudder. No one seemed to feel any regret that she had gone, but we felt very alone.

'It drizzled intermittently all night and we did our best to get away from the numerous sources of noise. There were many raft-loads of Italians, and when they saw us they besought us to come over. A few of the more enterprising swam towards us, but loaded down as we were, we had to keep them off. It was a cruel business.

'Once we saw a U-boat, but he did not molest us. We pulled hard in the opposite direction, anxious to put space between us, minds full of atrocity stories and tales of ill-treatment.

'As soon as it became light we began to take stock of our position. There was nobody in the boat who knew exactly where we were, though we were generally supposed to be about two days out from Freetown. Several other boats were visible and occasionally we saw a U-boat. We presumed that in view of the time the ship had taken to sink, wireless messages had been sent out to the shore stations. Already we pictured Freetown spewing forth rescue craft of all shapes and sizes. It was a port that always appeared to be full to overflowing and in our simple-mindedness we assumed that soon enough we would be out of trouble and feeding on ham and eggs.

'We decided to stay put for the time being and spent the first day making ourselves comparatively comfortable. The weather was blistering hot by day and cold at night and I was glad of my great-coat.

'Next day opinion became divided as to our best plan of action. We began to squabble. There was a smart sou'-westerly breeze and many felt that we should be making use of it in the general direction of Africa. Others thought that we should stay where we were to give our rescuers a chance of finding us.

'Several U-boats were still in evidence and one closed on us. The commander, a hatchet-faced little man with scars on his cheeks, told us to stay where we were. French rescue ships, he said, were coming down from Dakar and would pick us up. He is supposed to have said, somewhat threateningly, that the nearest land was right underneath us.

'For some time the boats clung together in a little body, but after a while the red sails began to go up and they floundered off to the north-east. Dakar seemed a long way off to all of us and our boat was one of the first away.

'There was no unity in that boat; no common spirit strong enough to stop us bickering; no one personable enough to take charge. I am glad that I did not have to stay in her and endure all her occupants went through. She was well stocked with every type of emergency gear, but still not likeable. In so far as it was possible to make a comparison between boats, that one was "unhappy" and the other one "happy". Until weakness and desperation came out on top in the bad days when men began to die fast, our final crew was a comparatively well-knit entity.

'We sailed all afternoon and about sunset saw that our U-boat was chasing us. He reached us just before dark and once again the commander addressed us. He was furious that we had disobeyed him and set sail. He ordered us to heave to for the night. He said he would give us water in the morning and tow us to the rendezvous with the French. He was towing a boat full of Italians and told us to stay near them. This was not difficult, for they cried and complained all night.

'After sunrise the U-boat approached us and in the calm sea we drew alongside. He had British personnel on board – women, children, members of the forces and some Italians. From us he took a couple of men who were wounded and needed skilled attention.

'One was a British army colonel whom we had found the day before. He was hanging on to a piece of wreckage, smothered in oil and looking done in. His knee was badly smashed and he was delirious after his exposure. He attempted to assume command of the boat, but was too weak. There was much resentment that he should be given extra water because of his wound. He was helped

The U-506 with a deckload of survivors transferred to it from the U-156 (*Stern*).

down the conning tower and we didn't see him again. I presume that he drowned later on with the rest of his companions.

'The U-boat gave us a couple of gallons of water. It wasn't very much, averaging out about half a cup per man, but it was very welcome. The Italian boat was given the same ration. When the watering was finished he took us in tow and soon had two other boats, so that there was a string of four. We came directly behind him, then the Italians and then the other boats. The sea was calm and he made a good speed of about 10 knots. These boats are very stable and can be towed at 15 knots in a moderate sea.

'Everything went pleasantly until late in the forenoon when an American Liberator appeared. He circled round and then made off. Someone had been signalling from the conning tower and we assumed that we were safe enough. Five minutes later we saw him again. He was coming straight in to attack. The U-boat stopped and made no move to open fire. The Liberator came in very low with bomb doors open. None of us could believe what our eyes showed us to be true.

'He came in from the U-boat's port beam and dropped depth charges. They both overshot the mark. A German sailor came aft on the U-boat and cut the tow, but before there was any space between us the Liberator came in again. Everyone in the boat swore violently.

'By then our boat was about 25 yards from the submarine. One of the depth charges released in the second attack looked as if it were going to hit us. Instead, it dropped incredibly swiftly and gracefully, a great obscene silver sausage, and fell into the sea a yard from me. Somebody said, "Lord! Hold on!" and after an age we blew up.

'The boat lurched violently upward in a flood of evil-smelling water and I found myself in the sea, very surprised to be alive and unhurt. The bomber was coming in again and to get out of the water and away from the shock of the explosion I scrambled on to the bottom of the upturned boat.

'In the aircraft's third attack the bombs fell on either side of the submarine's conning tower. The pilot appeared to be satisfied, for he made off. We heard shouting on the U-boat and presently our own folk began to file out on deck. Looking very angry, the U-boat ran slowly forward and submerged. As it went down it fouled the lifeboat full of Italians and wrecked it. Those who had been in the U-boat, including women and children, were left in the sea some hundreds of yards away from us. The two remaining boats filled themselves to capacity picking them up.

'We were in a pretty grim position. About 20 of our boatload had survived the explosion and our boat was upside down with a large rent in the bottom. The sea had risen and we found it impossible to refloat her. What discipline there was had quite gone and our salvage attempts were wrecked by men who would not co-operate.

In *The Longest Battle* Richard Hough refers to this unfortunate occurrence and its consequences: 'The rescue operations were still proceeding, the French cruiser being instrumental in saving over 1 000 lives, when a Liberator flew over the scene, circled, flew off as if calling for instructions, then returned and bombed U-156, inaccurately as it turned out but with the immediate effect of cutting short the work of mercy.

'In spite of the most scathing inquiries no one has ever discovered where that bomber was based and whether or not it asked for and received orders. Its attack certainly led to the loss of many hundreds of lives. In all, 450 Italians of 1,800 were saved, and 1,111 of the 2,372 passengers (many of them women) and crew. A few, after appalling sufferings, reached the coast of Liberia in a lifeboat.

'When Doenitz [Grand Admiral of the U-boat force] heard this story he drafted an order which was despatched to all U-boats, in-

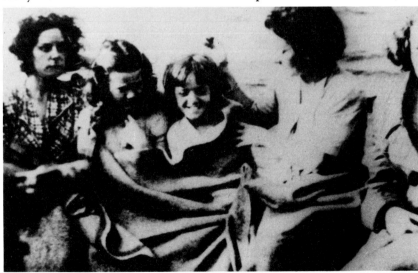

Women and children survivors of the *Laconia* (*Time–Life*).

structing commanders: "No attempt of any kind must be made at rescuing the crews of ships sunk. This prohibition applies to the picking up of men in the water and putting them in lifeboats, righting capsized lifeboats . . . Be harsh, bearing in mind that the enemy takes no regard of women and children in his bombing attacks on German cities".'

'At last we righted the boat and cleared it of the bodies inside – men stunned by the force of the explosion and then drowned underneath the boat. I still had my greatcoat on, over my lifejacket, and though it weighed me down, decided to keep it. The Italian who had clung so desperately to me, and who had survived all the indignation meted out to the members of his race, had now disappeared.

'The rest of us swam about the boat. She was gunwales down and we didn't have much of an afternoon. The sea was choppy and occasionally the boat would capsize, making us more and more exhausted. An infiltration by Italians began and we repelled them back to their own boat. It cost a lot of strength to strike a blow and the effort left one exhausted. We behaved like a lot of beasts fighting for survival.

'Someone found a can of water and sat waist deep in the water drinking. He was mad with acquisiteness, and though hit repeatedly would not give up his prize. The boat capsized and he lost it. The food lockers were under water and opened with difficulty. I rifled for myself a tin of pemmican (Dried meat paste pressed into cakes) and a few Horlick's tablets which I munched from time to time.

'As the day wore on there became fewer of us. The Italians seemed to drown easily. We began to get depressed and bitterly cold. We were numbed and careless with the eternal corkscrew motion of the boat; the sudden plunge, the scrambling for position, the precarious balancing in the wind and the feeling of insecurity that came just before we capsized again.

'An army officer who, God knows how, reeked of whisky, swam away from the boat and I watched him as his strokes grew weaker and weaker.

'Round sunset there came a miracle. Heaven knows what put us on her course, or how she could see such ill-defined objects as bobbing heads and waterlogged boats in the fading light, but a submarine came slowly up and hove to about 100 yards away. She was not as new or as large a craft as the others we had seen, and the men on board looked like Italians. They did not wave or beckon to us, but those of us still strong enough swam over to her. It was a long pull and an Italian sailor hauled me over the stern when I finally made it. Gradually about 20 of us collected, remnants of the two lifeboats and the men who had been on the U-boat. We were told to remain on deck.

'One Italian, an ex-prisoner of war, remained sitting apathetically in his lifeboat. He did not have the courage to move, nor the strength to hold the lines which were thrown over to him. As it grew dark we left him and made off. Periodically the submarine would stop its engines and idle.

'A *Laconia* steward whom we called "Satan" spoke Italian and through him we obtained some hot rice soup and some watered cognac. I was thankful for my coat. In the periods when we stopped I slept on deck, and only woke when the boat started again and seas swept over me. We hung on and prayed for dawn. There was a bustle once, up top, and an air of expectancy. A peculiar hush came over us all. A body was tossed over the side and the Italians crossed themselves.

'At daylight we were given coffee and cream crackers. Vile but welcome Italian cigarettes. "Satan" told us that we had to stay on deck, that the submarine would submerge immediately if it sighted anything suspicious, and that it would try and find the lifeboat out of which it had taken the Italians and leave us in her.

'He found the boat early in the afternoon and we packed into her. The submarine went off, fast and on the surface. We now numbered 51 – a Sicilian, half a dozen merchant seamen, four Poles, and an equal smattering of the forces. There were men returning home after having served their time out East; men in ill health; men going for courses; men who had never seen their children, whose families had been blitzed; butchers; bakers; candlestick makers – we were 51 males, thrown together by inscrutable destiny.'

In his later letter home Large expanded on what then happened, 'I got away in a boat and the next few days were really extraordinary. In this badly equipped boat (it had been swamped and most of the gear lost) 51 of us found ourselves with one and a half oars, no rudder, no mast or sail, and three gallons of fresh water, 700 miles from land.

'We rigged a mainsail (how I longed for *Three Brothers!* – a dinghy he and his brothers sailed) comprised of a raincoat lining and a dozen shirts. Our foresail was a blanket folded diagonally, the mast an oar. We used the half oar for steering. Aided by a steady prevailing wind we made about one knot forward and sideways in the general direction of the coast.

'We had to ration food and water very severely, and after a bit chaps began to get depressed. We managed to augment our food supplies with raw fish. There was a large shoal which followed us for days, and all that was necessary was to drop an unbaited bent nail over the side of the boat and wave it about. The fish, averaging five or six pounds apiece, did the rest.

'The procedure then was to cut the fish on the underside, just below the head, squeeze the blood into a tin, cut off head and get more blood, and drink it before it congealed. Get roe, if any, also liver and heart. Suck gills for blood and eyes for moisture, very like fresh water. We also skinned the fish and hung the stripped flesh to dry for the next day's consumption. You've no idea how good it tasted. One day we even tried to catch a turtle, but this was too ambitious and we exhausted ourselves for nothing. Another time a whale came within 10 yards of the boat, wondering whether we were worth a game or not, and scared the life out of us.

'Our ration of water was only half a tot a day and in spite of all warnings given, some began drinking salt water and urine. For a while they continued perfectly normally, but after a few days the stuff had its effect and they just gave in. Others died of exposure, depression and blood poisoning.

'There was a sailor, an English boy, going back to the UK. He was a magnificent figure of a man and had been a butcher. "Butch" followed automatically. His undisputed billet was right forward in the boat. In the daytime he sat there stark naked except for a piece of cloth wrapped around his head. He washed himself religiously every few hours and was one of our finest fishermen.

'He threw live and wriggling fish into the mass of men who lay in the bottom of the boat, already overcome by lassitude and watched the scrambling for titbits with malicious pleasure. Almost from the first he drank salt water. He drank a full pint morning and evening. He appeared perfectly normal for about a week and won many over to his philosophy.

'Combinations of Horlicks, pemmican, brine and urine were reputed to be harmless. Long before "Butch" went under himself his disciples began to go.

'One morning I woke up and "Satan" told me that a Pole was running rife with an axe. I was stronger than anyone at this stage, but still felt no enthusiasm about disarming him. The Pole was mad and was hitting at the bottom of the boat. This was fortunately steel and as yet he'd done no serious damage. I told him to hand over the axe and he threatened me with it.

'Somebody attracted his attention from behind and as he turned I jumped in and pulled the axe out of his hand. Later he obtained the axe again and we had to throw him overboard. He cried a little and then swam placidly away from the boat. There was no alternative. It was a bitter, hard little world where there could be no turning back from reality.

'One morning when we woke up even "Butch" showed the usual signs. He was silly, doped almost, and would not get up. He clambered into the most inextricable position in the boat and died there. This was a general tendency. Men seemed afraid to die in the open and pushed themselves into unimaginable positions from which we had a hard time extracting them. We grew callous of death. All it meant was that a body had to be lifted the agonizing few feet to the gunwales and dropped.

'There were exceptions who died nobly and who were greatly missed. Such was a Canadian who went over the side one day. He was discouraged and tired but he went over to give the rest of us a better chance. We managed to stop him once but later on he slipped over the side and floated quietly away. A grown man wept openly when he heard that "Canada" had gone.

'An English squadron leader doled out the water. When he became too weak to do the job I took the water round each evening at sunset. It was in a rectangular gallon can which had been provided by one of the U-boats. I used to take soundings of the water each day and reckoned out our future prospects.

'We never allowed ourselves very much. "Canada" had provided a tin which had once been a tropical film pack for a miniature camera, and somebody had scrounged a glass from the Italians. The best time to drink seemed to be sunset, but even in the cool placidity of those evenings the ration only came to half an inch in the glass and seemed dreadfully small.

'Some watched with round and wondering eyes as I poured, and some watched jealously. Some gulped the water, sweetish, rusty, beautiful stuff, in a single movement, and some took five minutes to sip it and ease it over their tongues.

'None tried to make me increase the daily ration. Things were getting pretty bad, but after "Canada" had gone I never confided in anyone. I told them there was plenty, but no one believed me. I told them that the destroyers would be here in the morning and some took courage. Occasionally someone would cry out, cursing bitterly, and a wave of despondency would run though the boat.

'One day in the heat of the afternoon when we were most exhausted, there was a loud outcry. The water can was lashed under the stern benches, where I perched and I woke to find a Cockney lad being accused of tinkering with it. He was a nice kid and I would not believe it. Then and there, with general assent, we decided that any person found stealing water or food would go over the side. The offense was too enormous to be envisaged.

'The Cockney denied the accusations vigorously, but was watched. Next day, about the same time, he was caught redhanded. He had a rubber tube and, dipping one end in the can, was sucking water through the other. This time there was no denial and mercifully he made no attempt to get away without punishment. He said he was very sorry, drank a lot of salt water from one of the tins and threw himself over.

'On the seventeenth night, when there were about 30 of us left –

and by this time none of us was strong enough to take the steering oar or do lookout – we sighted a ship. About half an hour before a fullish moon rose a merchant ship of about 4 000 tons passed us, about 400 yards away. This was the bitterest blow of all and people just gave up after that. Four days later there were only nine of us alive.

'We now had a day's ration of water left. I, at least, was too dry to eat any of our rations, except the chocolate, which I ate at night, taking an hour to get down one small piece – one inch by half inch by quarter inch. Our rations were three of these pieces a day, four pieces of Horlick's malted milk tablets, and a spoonful of Bovril pemmican. There were some biscuits in the boat, but these needed saliva and were out of the question.

'About the 21st day, with only nine of the total of 51 left, the wind dropped one evening and later, at about 2am, it rained. Yes, real, honest-to-God, life-giving rain, and for the first time in my life I appreciated it. It was not a tantalizing drizzle, but a gorgeous tropical downpour.

'I get excited now, as I think of it, standing out there shivering, feeling the strength coming back as I sucked water from thwarts and benches, from the sail, from tins, from anywhere. I must have drunk a couple of gallons that night as we filled our water cans and bottles.

'Four of the nine were too far gone to recover, and died, and one of the remaining five had a slight discharge from the ear and seemed to give up. He lived on for several days but would not eat anything.

'That left four of us, all RN ratings, and it strikes me as odd that out of the three services represented in that boat at the start, more or less equally, only navy should survive. The first and most interesting is Leading Seaman Harry Vines. He was a gunner on board the ship. In our boat he was in charge of navigation and seamanship, while I was in charge of food and water – "in charge" is a bit strong, but we had the last word.

'He's a vital, intelligent chap of 24 and is responsible for the gammon in my food list. Comes from Peterborough and was working in a grocery before the war. An ideal type to survive with, and it doesn't end there.

'Next is Ted Dobson, who is 27 and Regular Navy. He was in the *Enterprise* when we were fished out of the water after *Cornwall* had been sunk so we had a lot of common ground to go over. He's to be married as soon as he gets home to Lincoln.

'Next is Ted Riley from Liverpool who got sacked from his van-driving job for a laundry when a slump threatened and so joined the Navy.

'We four organised the food rations to give us about 25 more days, and now we fared quite well. After the rain, bowels had worked for the first time since the sinking and as we could not eat the biscuits a little bulk was provided daily. With the extra clothing we could rig up a sun shelter by day and keep warm at night.

'None of us knew anything about navigation. We used to time sunset and sunrise (when cloud permitted) each day with the mean time of three watches which continued to function throughout the escapade. Then with complicated (for our befuddled and unfed brains) calculations we'd work out how many degrees and the miles we'd sailed each day. I suppose that all the calculations were on the optimistic side, but it gave us something other than our extremely unpleasant prospects to dream about.

'It now rained fairly frequently and we scarcely needed to draw on the canned water, refilling bottles almost as soon as we'd emptied them. We were still very weak though, and used to have bad times bailing out after heavy rains. Once, too, we had an exhausting morning repairing our boom which had snapped. One always seemed to be climbing over thwarts and a four foot obstruction after weeks in an open boat on meagre rations is no joke.

'Our daily programme was something like this: if it rained, arise at dawn and bail out, try to dry clothes, look round for a ship (dawn and dusk seemed the most likely times, somehow). If it hadn't rained, up at about eight o'clock and breakfast as slowly as possible, breaking up biscuit into tiny pieces and eating them one by one.

'The awful agony I went through thinking of the food in that lovely parcel I was taking home (A 25 lb parcel of choice foods which Tony was taking to England as a gift to his aunt). After breakfast we would talk until the sun grew too hot. Then we would rig shelters with overcoats and try to sleep.

'Fourish, as the sun began to weaken, we would congregate to talk, read from the New Testament, eat at five o'clock and talk until nine o'clock. This was if the day was fine, but if it had rained we beetled for our shelters forward and aft (two in each).

'These days were not completely halcyon. Comparatively we lived like kings, and our chances of survival were bettered, but we lived too close together. Personal peculiarities and habits, however innocuous or minor, became matters of enormous importance. We were tremendously moody and it required great self-restraint not to come to blows over the most trifling matters.

'To amuse ourselves we used to spend hours delousing our clothes of the peculiar little white bugs that came to inhabit them. I was guilty of whistling Suppe's "Light Cavalry" *ad nauseam*. Riley whistled "A Whistler's Mother-in-Law" and nearly drove me crackers. Dobson would comb his beard for hours at a time. There was nothing at all to do but look, hope and talk.

'Vines terrified me one morning. He was a stalwart of unflinching character. It had poured all night and there was a foot of water in the bottom of the boat. The rest of us started our bailing, but Vines would not move. He sat there black as night and neither threats nor wheedling had any effect. Mercifully he threw it off and never looked back. I think he was a man who would feel ashamed to let the rest of us down.

'Anger was exhausting and depression was worse. The combination left us gasping for breath with a knotted stomach. Vines got all steamed up one day. There was an outburst from one of the party, who cried that he was fed up with the whole damn issue and was going. Vines told him succinctly to go now, before it was time to eat and drink, and not to forget to leave his watch behind. The man stayed.

'We were worse during the heat of the day. In the late afternoon when we had our session with the New Testament, had our meal and water, and told our oft-repeated tales, we became human and friendly again.

'One day it rained unceasingly and we were miserably wet and kept bailing out all through the night. If ever I develop rheumatism I shall know why. If it was fine we cuddled up under coats and slept out; if not, cursed and slept in. Actually, sleep is hardly the word; a more suitable word would be coma.

'That New Testament I mentioned, the property of an RAF sergeant who had died, gave me and the others, I'm sure, a lot of courage. After the rain I used to conduct our services and, odd and unorthodox though they were, they were still services. Disgusting how we turn to God only in distress. I must do my utmost to remain in my present state of mind.

'I was still confident that somehow, sometime, somewhere, we'd strike lucky. Then one morning we heard a 'plane, and though we didn't see him you can imagine the effect. Two days later – our 36th day in the boat – at about 11 o'clock a 'plane flew right over our heads and did not see us.

'On the same day we sighted new birds and oil fuel on the water. We had somehow got two days out in our reckoning and thought it was Sunday, whereas actually it was Tuesday.

'Next day we sighted a Sunderland in the distance and turned in feeling that at last we were getting near something. It rained at about 3 am and we beetled for cover and "coma'd" till dawn, when I felt the need to stretch and go out. At that hour there were very dark layers of horizon cloud, and one very black spot that might have been something. I called my companions out and we saw it dissolve into nothing. We felt very optimistic.

'I went back into shelter and the rain stopped. Again the spot appeared on the horizon, again I was called out, and again it dissolved. I had a bad knee and went back to shelter again. My companion stayed outside and called me back again five minutes later. This time I grumbled because it hurt like blazes to move, but eventually I got out.

'There on our four mile horizon were about a dozen pinpoints of masts, sticking up jet-black against the grey background. What's more, they were real masts, not the vague elusive things I had been seeing for the past five weeks.

'Convoy! I don't know where the strength came from, but I leapt up on a thwart to see better, and started waving madly with a blue jersey. We didn't dare wake the two who were sleeping forward because of the general depression it would have caused if the convoy passed us by.

'They were coming towards us and across, getting slowly closer . . . Harry and I talking and praying in whispers. Can see funnels and upper works . . . One ship turning either towards or away from us. Oh God! Pass one of those rain tins, Shorty (this is the thirst of excitement). Can see ships signalling to one another.

'Slowly she approaches and at last, when she's about a mile away, we can be sure. We wake the other two and they are unwilling to come out. "Don't joke about things like that", they say, but they do come out, and it's a pleasure to watch them.

'We collect ourselves and have a little service of thanks, gather up our precious souvenirs, all the gear and wallets, and wait, waving. She's an HM trawler converted from a fishing trawler, and she comes alongside throwing lines.

'We are mad with joy and start throwing stuff inboard – tins of pemmican and all. They shout to us to leave it all and come aboard. As we heave up I scramble for the side and hands pull me in. I take off my coat and lifejacket and sit on deck. A messdeck cup of tea, a Navy tot of neat rum, strange, astonished faces, strange voices, space – bliss. Then they dress our sores and boils.

'Then food! Sausage, tomato, bread and butter, South African grape jam, tea. They were all the spirit of kindness and put us in the chief's and petty officers' mess. They tried to make us lie down and sleep, but who could sleep in our happy, excited state? And have we not been on our backs 20 hours a day for at least $38\frac{1}{2}$ days?

'We wander about, longing to eat and eat meat, but we're on strict orders to go easy at first. She's a grand little ship and her name is engraved on my heart.

'We arrived at Freetown the following morning. Freetown was our dream port of the past weeks. We were only 80 miles from the coast when we were picked up. We talked together most of that night in spite of the rum and heavy sedatives they gave us.

'Next morning we went up to the hospital. It's a grand place situated high above the town, where there's a little cool air. Again everybody is very kind (the nurses cracked their last bottle of vintage

Tony Large jokes with a nurse at Freetown (*Duffus*).

Cliquot champagne for us) and we are put on a special diet. I am getting fit very quickly, and we're off to a rest camp farther up the hill in about three days time.

'I am not yet as fat as Mum would like me to be and still have odd bits of bone and rib sticking unbecomingly out, but the hospital and I co-operate very closely in making up for lost time. I can safely say that I never ate so much in my life, I'm to have a thorough check up on my heart as soon as I get up, but the old bird carried me through uncomplainingly and I personally consider the heart panic a lot of hooey. Three boils and a recovering knee. Otherwise OK. We hold the survivors' record for Freetown . . .'

Macdonald was picked up by a French warship three weeks after the sinking and was interned in Morocco. After the combined American and British landings in North Africa he was released and sent via the United States to South Africa. After being commissioned he served in the Mediterranean, mainly commanding MLs and MTBs in the Aegean Sea.

After the war he had a distinguished professional career and was a prominent member of ex-servicemen's organisations. He was Transvaal regional Chairman of the South Africa Legion when he died on 28 March, 1989.

Large surprised everyone with his appetite and his rapid recovery. He could have returned to South Africa on compassionate leave, but chose instead to continue with his training in England. One of the highlights of his time in the United Kingdom was when King George invested him with the British Empire Medal, 'For great fortitude and endurance during many days in a lifeboat after a merchantman was torpedoed.'

Large nevertheless felt, '. . . a little ashamed at having survived when so many others, far, far better people, went under. Still, I'm deeply grateful to God for letting me through like this and it's given me a standard to live up to.'

A few months later he was commissioned and left on HMS *Rother* as a sub-lieutenant. He was to visit the United States and was captivated by the country and its people.

Writing of Large's survival Louis Duffus pointed out that before the sinking he had suffered from tonsillitis, a weak heart and recurrent seasickness. 'What then remained to distinguish Tony from the forty-seven who died and even, in a smaller degreee, from the three who survived? I should say simply spirit. Some may call it religion. When everything else, hope, will-power, conscience and civilising veneer, had been stripped from the boatload of human beings, something granite was left in the soul of Tony Large . . .'

CHAPTER 5 Sea Terror

Nova Scotia:

28 November 1942

Many ships have been torpedoed off South Africa's coast, but never as many as in November, 1942. During that month 24 ships totalling 127 261 tons were lost in the southern approaches to the Mozambique Channel. According to Capt S W Roskill, in *The War at Sea*, 'It was the worst month in the Indian Ocean since Japanese warships had scoured the Bay of Bengal in the previous April.' Two of these ships were the *Nova Scotia* and the *Llandaff Castle*.

The fortunes of war are such that tragic events often have small beginnings. So it was for Alda Ignisti, whose life was to change when a young second-lieutenant, Robert Taylor, was ordered to report to Cairo. According to Taylor, 'One day an order appeared in Part II Orders requiring all Commanding Officers to make a return of men serving under their command who were in civilian lives either civil servants, magistrates or policemen. In this way my own name was submitted to General Headquarters Middle East Command.

'Shortly thereafter I was summoned to Cairo to be interviewed by some very formidable looking figures indeed. One of them was Brigadier Lord Rodd and another, who subsequently became an old friend, was a Colonel Adshead.

'Sometime later my regimental HQ received an order saying that 2nd Lieutenant R M Taylor RA would be struck off the strength of his unit forthwith and posted to OETA (Occupied Enemy Territory Administration) Eritrea with the rank of lieutenant. I had no idea what this might entail and neither did anyone else, but I was universally congratulated by my colleagues on leaving the dump I was in and a very fortunate departure it proved to be, because that very same unit within 12 months was mopped up in Tobruk and there were not enough survivors to reform it.

'By train and river steamer I went to Khartoum and presented myself at headquarters there. This was at the time when Gen Platt was assembling a force to attack Italian East Africa from the north, while at the same time Gen Cunningham with South Africans and East African forces was making an attack from Nairobi and the south.

'I was not a member of a combatant unit at that time, having been posted to OETA and therefore was never actually in the fighting, but followed along behind it and in this way entered Asmara one day after the city had been occupied, after a particularly bloody battle at Keren some 60 miles short of Asmara.

'The Italian authorities had declared Asmara to be an open city in order to avoid destruction and the British troops marched into a city which showed very little signs of war.

2/Lt Robert Taylor (*AT*).

'International law requires that a country occupying another country by force of arms ahould become the power administering the civil government and this was what OETA, which I had just joined, was all about. The advance of the army beyond Asmara was swift and decisive and coming up the other way Cunningham also made rapid progress. It was not long before Addis Ababa fell and the whole of Italian East Africa was in British hands. This vast area then had to be administered by the British.

'I found myself cast in the role of finance officer and I speedily acquired the rank of captain. One of my assistants was a Lieut Frank McFadzean, who after the war became well known in financial circles and eventually became the head of the Shell company. He is now the Lord McFadzean of Kelvinside, but he and I became great friends at that time and we still are.

'Our principal job was to create a treasury, as the British understood it, for the country of Eritrea. Things were pretty chaotic. We couldn't understand Italian and the Italians didn't seem to understand us, which I suppose was not so very odd. I managed to make some headway with learning the language and one day I said to the captain commanding our security branch, Capt Zervudachis, that I wished he could find us a decent interpreter and he said, "Well Bob, I think I probably can if you will just wait a day or two".

'In a day or two he produced Alda. She was a young and attractive woman of about 28 years of age, who had been born and brought up in South Africa of Italian parents. Her father had been a civil engineer who came to South Africa to find work in building the railway system in Zululand.' Alda Cecilia Lorenzino was born at Ermelo, Transvaal, in July 1914.

'As is the practice of so many Italians, he had set up business on his own as a sub-contractor and had done quite well for a time until he took on a difficult tunnel contract and went 'bust' on the job. Shortly after, he died of Blackwater Fever, leaving his widow with five young children, of whom Alda was the second in seniority.

'She married at the age of 18 an Italian [Gastone Ignesti] who took her with him to Eritrea, which was one of the jewels in Mussolini's crown. Unfortunately, and not as a result of any enemy action, he died of a tumour on the brain. Within a few days of his death Italy declared war against Britain. Alda was trapped in Eritrea, together with her young daughter, who at the time was about eight years of age.

'Having been brought up in South Africa, her English was better than her Italian, but she had a grasp of the colloquial Italian, which no books could help us to master. I remember pointing to an advertisement in the daily paper, which was advertising what was on at that time in the local cinema. It was plugging a film called *Tre Regazze in Gamba*. Now 'Regazze' means girls, 'gamba' means leg, so what on earth could 'three girls in leg' mean?

70

Gastone Ignesti,
Valcheria and Alda (*A Taylor*).

'I asked her and without batting an eyelid she came back in perfectly understandable English, the name of the film was *Three smart girls*. This was good enough for me and I realised that we had found the interpreter we needed.

'She had also gone to a secretarial school in her home town, Durban, and therefore with her command of the language and with some ability to take dictation and type and look after files she became a secretary in this little treasury we were trying to build up.

'She used to work mostly for my boss, Lieut-Col Fuller, but I used to take every opportunity of seeking her assistance to do this or that for me. As I have said, she was young, she was slim and attractive, she had a lovely pair of legs and a most enchanting tail, which used to wriggle when she walked, and altogether I found myself tremendously attracted to her.

'The attraction must have been mutual, because she did not demur when I suggested that I should take her out for dinner one evening in one of the numerous nightclubs, which this occupied Italian city still had in full operation. Mark you, things were a bit tricky. She was an Italian citizen and British troops had been forbidden to fraternize with the enemy, but she was so obviously British in everything she said and did that the powers that be winked an eye at our association. Nobody raised any objection as our meetings became more numerous and our outings an established and accepted fact.

'This proved somewhat difficult for her, because her in-laws did not altogether see eye-to-eye with this habit of going out with a British officer and being so frequently in our company.'

The U-Cruisers

On September 17, 1942, a German submarine, the U-177, sailed from Kiel. Her orders were to round the Cape of Good Hope, do what damage she could, and then to hunt allied shipping in the Indian Ocean. U-177 was one of the first four German U-cruisers, a new class of U-boat. Each had six torpedo tubes and 24 torpedoes.

The commander was Kapitänleutnant Robert Gysae, 31, who had a reputation of being a cool-headed and dedicated officer. Once clear of Portugal he remained on the surface as much as possible for speed and to load his batteries. He ploughed south through the Atlantic swells before rounding the bulge of North Africa and heading for the Cape.

The British Admiralty's long-felt anxiety regarding the concentration of ill-defended shipping rounding the Cape of Good Hope was justified by events. The enemy's earlier attempts to use submarines in these waters was foiled when their supply ships were intercepted. A long-range U-boat cruiser was then developed.

The submarines had a radius of action of 48,000 kilometres and had considerably increased bunkers and higher surface speed. Their displacement was 1,616 tons surfaced and 1,804 tons submerged with full loads. The Type IXD1 was designed to transport limited amounts of essential materials to and from the Far East. The military version was Type IXD2 and was also intended for the Far East operations.

The range of these U-Cruisers was more than doubled to give them the widest radius of action of any German submarine. They were the culmination of U-boat design and were the largest and fastest built.

The U-177 (*RK*).

By 21 September the Submarine Tracking Room had, with prescient accuracy, given warning that a southbound movement of U-boats was imminent. All shipping was routed further west, away from the African coast. East-bound traffic was sent to Durban instead of Cape Town and orders were issued that west-bound ships which had to call at Cape Town were to be escorted. These measures were to save allied shipping from unnecessarily heavy losses.

On 7 October, almost three weeks after the Submarine Tracking Room's warning had been given the first U-Cruisers arrived off the Cape. They were long-range cruisers of the IXD2 Type and were U-177, U-178, U-179 and U-181.

Obtaining passage

Robert Taylor became worried about Alda's future. 'As the weeks and months went on, during which our association became more permanent and more recognized, I began to worry about her future.

'It was 1942, the war was only just beginning in reality. Surely the British army wouldn't leave me in Eritrea for the duration. I had to be moved on somewhere, sometime, to something else and something more in keeping with what I had been trained to do during my six months at Shrivenham OCTU.

'Accordingly, I began to investigate the possibilities of finding some way of getting her back to Durban, where her mother and family lived. I knew she would like this and if I could get it done before I left Eritrea, this would be a load off my mind and a good thing for her.

'I spoke to Capt Zervudachis, who was the head of security branch, and it was not long before he came up with a good idea. There were scores of thousands of Italian prisoners of war in Eritrea. They had surrendered to the British army in droves and feeding them and keeping them in Eritrea, a country which produced very little food and in which many of the necessities of life had to be imported, was proving a great strain to the military authorities, who had so many other competing claims of the war upon their scarce resources of transport and material.

'They were, therefore, being sent away to other PoW camps in East Africa and South Africa. Zervudachis came up with the idea that we should send Aldo and her little daughter, Valcheria, on one of the ships transporting them. This took some organising, but eventually through our secret channels we discovered that a batch of prisoners was being prepared for shipment to South Africa and that a ship called the *Nova Scotia* was coming to Massawa to pick up some 1,200 of them.

'More secret and personal negotiations took place and Zervudachis and I contrived that Alda, with her daughter, should join the ship as Secretary to OC Troops and in this way they would be taken to Durban. One night, in late October 1942, I drove down the mountain from Asmara to Massawa, taking Alda and Valcheria with me. We stayed that night as the guests of the Senior Political Officer in Massawa, Col Miller, who made us very welcome.

**Wednesday
3 November**

Among the troops awaiting embarkation at Port Tewfik was a Jewish lawyer, L/Bombardier Nat Herman, 38. He had served as a gunner in the 7th Field Regiment of the South African Field Artillery in North Africa. Herman recalled his leave orders, 'It was early in November, 1942, when we received our movement order to return to the Union from the Middle East. For a few days we remained in the Transit Camp at Port Tewfik awaiting a ship to transport us to South Africa.

'After receiving numerous warnings and threats about divulging information of military value, either by communication to our people at home, or the enemy by some unknown means, we were told that we were to leave on short notice (as is always the practice of the army)

Nat Herman (*RK*).

on a Tuesday morning. We were also told the worst possible news for men returning from leave – we should be required to undertake prisoner-escort duty from Eritrea.

'The men to embark were selected from those kicking up their heels in the Transit Camp, through another of those unknown systems in vogue in the army from time to time immemorial. All the men had seen considerable service outside the Union; some had been away for fully two and a half years, had been through the East African campaign and had been members of either the First or Second Division – including those who had been able to get away from Sidi Rezegh or evade capture at Tobruk.

'A few were being sent as Instructors in Tank Warfare for the Sixth Division, now being sent to replace the lost Second South African Division. A few were battle casualties or boarded men who were leaving the Middle East for good.

'Before leaving for Eritrea, we embarked about 1 000 American soldiers, including some 60 odd nurses who had just arrived from America, and who were being sent to form lines of communication in medical, signalling and other non-divisional units in North Africa.

'During the afternoon of the 3rd November, 1942, we South Africans went on board the troopship *Nova Scotia*. We were relegated to the close quarters of the hold, which portion of the ship had previously been used for transporting animals and even human freight. We just had to pig it.'

The Furness Withy freighter *Nova Scotia* had been built in 1926 for the Liverpool-Halifax route. During World War II she was assigned by the British Ministry of War Transport to the East African theatre. The 6 796 ton freighter would carry South African troops, weapons and supplies to Suez, then on the return journey transport Italian prisoners-of-war to South Africa.

Nat Herman was not impressed with the conduct of American troops. 'Early the following morning the Americans came on board and seized the best part of the ship for themselves, just because they were Americans and entitled to it; we simply suffered in silence. As this story has little to tell of this portion of our voyage, or any incidents, except one, which occurred in the very early stages.

'I will say that once one got to know the Americans they were very friendly, quite interesting and very proud of the fact that they came from the States and that each and every one of them came from a different state.

'One morning I was leaning idly over a deck rail looking at the sea, when an American soldier touched me and called me aside. It appeared that as he was strolling on the promenade deck he hap-

The Furness Withey freighter *Nova Scotia* (*RK*).

pened to look through an open window into a cabin. To his pleasant surprise he saw the reflection in a mirror of a nurse having a shower bath.

'I was invited to take the opportunity of making an inspection, which I refused, but within a matter of seconds there was a queue and a steady stream of Americans passed the open window until the good lady had completed her ablutions, blissfully ignorant of the intense interest she had aroused among her fellow passengers, who were pleased to have had some variation from the usual routine.'

Monday 8 November

Herman recalled their arrival at Massawa. 'The Americans disembarked at Massawa in Eritrea some five days later. We remained in port for about two days and just before our departure some 750 Italians of a nondescript type were marched on board. I was told that they included the worst characters and criminals ever to have left their home country. How far this is correct I am not in a position to say, as I am unable to endorse the authenticity of this statement.

'These men were immediately shepherded into the holds, which we had now vacated, and were ensconsed in the cabins which the Americans had now given to us. Owing to the cramped space of the quarters, many of us chose to sleep on the deck.

'Several high ranking Italian officers were marched on board; but as the authorities did not know whether it was proper for them to share quarters with their own men, and they saw no reason why they should share the officers' mess with enemy prisoners of war, they were promptly marched off again. What the reaction of our men would have been had these Italian officers been privileged over the South Africans, I would not like to say, because at that stage of the war many had very open and bitter feelings. They were suffering from war weariness and a hankering to get back to their people, a subject which was of major importance in South Africa and in the Middle East.

'In due course details of the assignments were made known. The larger body of men were given guard duties, working one day on and one day off, as their duties were more onerous for reasons which I will go into more fully later.

'On the first night at Massawa an Italian made a desperate bid to escape. It was dark and a shout arose 'Man overboard'. I was near the side of the deck where this occurred and went to the ship rail. The man who had fallen or jumped into the sea seemed to be making satisfactory progress from the ship into darkness.

'One of our officers rushed to a guard who was already posted on duty on one of the points of the ship and ordered him to shoot and added, 'But don't shoot to kill'. All that could be seen of the fugitive was his head bobbing in the sea, so how one was expected to shoot without killing him I still have to learn. The searchlights were turned on to this man, the guards blazed away and missed and he got away into the darkness and made it across the bay.

'In the meantime a military police van rushed to the opposite side and the unfortunate Italian, completely breathless and exhausted, simply walked into their waiting hands. He was brought back wet and dripping and placed in the guard room of the ship. In many respects he was, at that time, more fortunate than some other Italians I had seen attempting to escape from a POW cage in the field at night, for they were shot in their tracks. More than one of our men was overheard to say that this man deserved to get away.

'There was a blackout in the early hours of each night and there was very little to keep the men amused when off duty. The usual 'housey' and poker schools immediately came into existence when the ship left port. These men played below deck from the early hours until late at night, unless on duty or fatigue. The novices to the five card game were, in due course, eliminated, leaving the old hands to gamble with their money.

'It was impossible to know everyone on the ship, especially as the men came from practically every unit of the South African forces. I did know a few personally, however. Some were from my own unit and some from my home town.

'The NCO's who were allocated to guard duty were expected in the middle of the night to move a guard or two from their posts in the hold at half hourly intervals, owing to the excessive heat and closeness. Men who were assigned to that post at night were, however, reluctant to leave their posts if they were heavy smokers as it was the one and only place on the ship where one was permitted to smoke. I was surprised to find how few men wished to leave the hold for that reason.

'As I was one who held the worst rank in the army, that is 'one stripe', I did not have to walk a beat or do sentry duty, but was required to see to the changing of these guards. On the nights I was on duty, the NCO with me asked if he could be on duty in the midnight hours. I gladly obliged because I suppose he and his pals had a chat and a smoke while I simply slept.

'One of the Jewish soldiers succeeded in bringing a monkey on board ship. Where he got the monkey and whether it had travelled with him through Africa, I do not know. Nor can I imagine how he expected to get it past the Customs and Immigration Officers at Durban on arrival. He did tell me that it was to be left on the ship for the crew, but this may have been eyewash for I have no doubt that given the opportunity he would have smuggled the monkey out in his kitbag.

'The monkey did create a diversion by breaking loose one day and causing damage in the capain's cabin. The monkey, when pursued, climbed on every precarious position on the ship, including the side of a lifeboat and nearly fell into the sea. Eventually it was enticed onto the ship and a mirror was held in front of it. Fascinated by its reflection, it allowed itself to be recaptured.

'Another of the Jewish soldiers, who shared the same cabin with me, was being returned to the Union, 'bomb happy'. This soldier walked about the ship armed to the teeth, in full battledress, webbing, waterbottle, gaiters and clothing. There was no reason for him to dress like this when off duty and even on duty he need only have been lightly clad, except for identifying uniform. I mention this because he would have had a possible chance of being alive today had he been dressed otherwise.

'Three women and a child also embarked on the ship at Massawa and Aden, evacuees from these areas.'

Captain Taylor delivered Alda and Valcheria to the harbour. 'The following morning I put them on board the *Nova Scotia* and said good-bye. I do not know exactly when the ship sailed, because of course such movements were very hush-hush. However, it sailed shortly thereafter and that was that for the time being. She, or rather they, were on their way home.

'There were some other women on board, members of the forces, principally ATS and FANY. The ship stopped at Aden to take aboard a contingent of nurses who were proceeding to South Africa. Of course they were required to augment the ship's medical facilities in view of the large number of people who were being carried. There were some 1 200 [sic 765] prisoners of war on board, apart from the normal crew and accompanying military personnel.'

**Sunday
14 November**

The *Nova Scotia* edged out of the little coral harbour of Massawa, crowded with Italian prisoners, returning soldiers, internees and

Alda Ignesti and Valcheria at Massawa (*A Taylor*).

civilians, numbering almost 1 000. At the same time, some 5 000 miles to the south, the U-177 was rounding the Cape of Good Hope, her lookouts scanning the skies for any patrolling South African aircraft.

Cpl George Kennaugh
(*R Kennaugh*).

Among the returning South African soldiers was Corporal George Kennaugh, 36, of the 3rd SA Reconnaissance Battalion. He had stepped on a landmine near El Alamein and got burnt, to which he owed his repatriation to South Africa. In civilian life Kennaugh had been a carpenter. He had the useful ability to remain calm in trying circumstances as was demonstrated in 1929.

At the time he had been 23-years-old and worked on the eighth floor of Union House in Johannesburg. He was turning a heavy-laden winch when it suddenly slipped, jerked his arm upwards and broke two bones. The force of the blow hurled him backwards and over the edge into the open lift well.

Kennaugh recalled pulling his twisted arm straight as he fell. The hope that he wouldn't die flashed through his mind, then he rounded his shoulders to prepare for the impact. He crashed into a pile of sand and miraculously survived. After two months in hospital he returned to play as hooker for the Diggers' second rugby team.

Herman found that his job as escort to the POWs interrupted the pleasant voyage. 'Our actual duties were not onerous, but boring and monotonous. On one occasion, on a round of inspection, I found a rifle resting against the side of the ship, but no sentry. The Italians were walking about quite unconcerned. I located the sentry a short while later and asked him what the deuce he was up to. He casually informed me that neither he nor the Italians were in the slightest bit interested in his rifle. There was not much possibility of anybody attempting to make a getaway on the high seas, nor were the Italians likely to try and capture the ship.

'From my own impression of the prisoners, although they may have been desperados, I came to the conclusion that there was sound reason in what he said, so I did not place the man on report or under arrest. We were all sick and tired of the job.

'Lifeboat drill took place at a fixed hour and we were assigned to certain posts on the ship. In addition to my casual guard duties, I was in charge of a fire picket and a raft. I did not for a moment believe that there were sufficient rafts on the ship to carry all the persons on board in case of a sinking. The few lifeboats were placed under the control of the ship's crew.

'Most of the men were entirely ignorant of what would be required of them in case of emergency except for one point, which was emphasised throughout the voyage and at all times, that no one was permitted to move about the ship unless carrying a life-jacket on his person.

'There is one other incident I remember, namely a church parade, which ranks only second in the army to an OC's parade. On the allotted day, a Sunday, we were told to fall in and the men, according to their religious denominations, asked to fall out. Those on guard duty were only too thankful to escape this doubtful pleasure.

'The members of the Church of England and the Dutch Reformed Church, making up the bulk of the men present, were marched off. The remaining soldiers, being a few Jews, agnostics and other freaks, were told they could be dismissed and hold divine service when and where they pleased. As it happened, only another Jewish soldier and I attended the parade and this friend of mine, to my surprise, marched off with the C of E soldiers.

'Sometime after the parade, when we were together again, I met this NCO, who shared my cabin, and said, 'Lionel, what on earth made you fall in with the C of E men?' His reply was, 'I thought that the Jews and others were going to be caught for fatigue, so I reckoned that it would be better to go to the church parade'. So, actually, he was the one that was caught.

'About three weeks or more after leaving Port Tewfik, we were warned to post special submarine lookouts. We were never told what the actual dangers were, what the war situation was, or whether there had been any sinkings. This secrecy throughout the first two or three years of the war, in opposition to the real intention of security precautions, was, I believe, a contributory cause of the death of many men.

'At a later stage in the war men were told what was happening and given reasons. I do know from my own experiences in the war, in the battle area, on the field and at the base, that we were nearly always kept in ignorance of what was happening, where we were going, why we were doing things or what we were expected to do.

'In this instance, had the men been directly warned that there had been numerous sinkings and that there was considerable danger in these waters, they would have been more prepared for what actually did occur.

'What was also extremely unwise was the fact that we were without convoy. We were travelling at a very slow speed, although zig-zagging all the time. In short, we were a sitting target for any enemy vessel.'

The *Nova Scotia* had completed the trip a dozen times. There was no known submarine activity in the area so few precautions were taken. With no convoy, sea or air cover the freighter would have to rely on its four-inch gun aft and the two anti-aircraft guns flanking the bridge.

**Friday
27 November**

On the morning of November 27 the U-177 captain, Robert Gysae, sighted a ship cleaving through the swell. An escort destroyer was nearby, and Gysae decided not to attack. That night he chased a small convoy, but lost contact in the darkness.

Alda served as secretary to the *Nova Scotia's* captain. She worked late on the 27th as she didn't want to be held up when disembarking the next day. Captain Hender appreciated her hard work and regularly had her seated at his table in the dining room.

**Saturday
28 November**

At 6.12 am Captain Gysae sighted smoke bearing 27 degrees. 'Enemy coming nearer fast', he recorded in his log, 'She is zig-zagging strongly around 210 degrees. She is a medium-sized passenger ship doing 14 knots'.

In the sites of the periscope was the *Nova Scotia* – unescorted and virtually unarmed. Apart from the British crew, there were 765 Italian prisoners of war, 134 South African soldiers and three women and a child aboard.

Herman looked forward to arriving in Durban. 'On the morning of Saturday, 28 November, we knew that we were nearing the end of our voyage. We had not been officially told anything and duties continued with the same monotonous regularity. The thought uppermost in the mens' minds was when they were going to dock at Durban and we all felt pretty sure that it would be within 48 hours.

'It was a dull day and at about 9 o'clock that morning I decided to go down to my bunk in the cabin to relax for a matter of three quarters of an hour before going on deck for lifeboat drill, which took place at about 10 o'clock. I expected to be on duty that night from 6 pm for 24 hours and hoped that it would be my last duty.

'I had just had a discussion with one of the corporals on the ship, who had throughout the voyage been very enterprising and was returning as an instructor. He had a good army record and had been mentioned twice in despatches for service in the field.

'The men had decided to make a collection as a token of appreciation to the cook and kitchen staff for the excellent fare they had provided on this ship. The food throughout the voyage had been good and the fellows thought this would be a fitting gesture.

'I had arranged to meet this friend as soon as I came on deck. I was in my cabin on a top bunk, dressed only in bathing trunks and was wearing my identity discs, which I had worn throughout the war. None of us was permitted to be without them in the Middle East or on this voyage.

'There were two other men in the cabin at the time, also resting. I did not know whether they had been or were going on duty. One did not worry about things of no real interest, there was nothing to amuse oneself with on the voyage.

At 7.30 am Corporal George Kennaugh dozed off on deck. 'I had just taken a swim in the pool on deck. I lounged lazily in my swimming trunks beside the pool. It was hot and overcast. I was returning home to Johannesburg on leave, having been burned by a landmine explosion near El Alamein. During the voyage my task was to share the guard of prisoners.

'My thoughts drifted nowhere in particular that sultry morning. I had finished guard duty at 7 am and now dozed fitfully.

At 8.31 am U-177 submerged. Captain Gysae's log recorded: 'Through periscope I see she is strongly armed (three guns, many machine-guns, wireless direction finding gear, control tower) and warship paint with camouflage over paint.'

Believing that the *Nova Scotia* was an auxiliary cruiser he radioed BdU-Befehlshaber der Unterseebote (Commander in Chief U-boats, Admiral Karl Doenitz). BdU's staff queried Gysae's evidence.

Alda finished breakfast and came up on deck to have a cigarette. Valcheria was with her, 'We had a peaceful trip until we reached the Mozambique Channel. After breakfast I decided to go on deck to have a cigarette, before going into the cabin to finish my work off so that we could be free that evening in Durban.

Kapitänleutnant Robert Gysae (*RK*).

It was 9 am when Capt Gysae, suspecting the *Nova Scotia* to be a camouflaged auxiliary cruiser, decided to sink her. As the hands of the *Nova Scotia's* clock approached 9.15 and with only 1 000 feet separating her and the U-boat, Gysae gave the order to fire his three bow torpedoes . . .

The U-177 Log reported: 'Spread of three fired tubes I, III and IV (running depth three and four metres; distance 380 metres), Three observed hits – engine room, bridge and for'ard. Midship starts burning immediately. Then the dense, thick smoke drifting over the periscope blots out everything.

'Hydrophone effects show that the auxiliary cruiser has stopped engines. After periscope is cleared the ship shows a pronounced list to port. The deck is teeming with humanity, some with, some without lifebelts. Midships, with bridge, wireless room, passenger quarters and lifeboats are blazing fiercely. Due to the pronounced list the guns cannot be served any longer.'

Out of the hazy blue of the ocean torpedo tracks sped toward the *Nova Scotia*. Two explosions rent the hull, throwing up tall columns of water. One burst through below the bridge while the other torpedo hit the engine room quarters. The ship rolled convulsively then listed to port. Some of the oil bunkers burst into flame and the bridge area was engulfed in flames.

According to Herman, 'One South African positively affirms that he saw the torpedo approaching the ship in a double line, like a tramline leaving a track in its wake. He had no time to do anything. He went into the sea fully dressed, with his boots on, after the ship had been hit and swam out to the only wreckage he could find, which was the side of the small wooden swimming pool on the ship. He had three or four Italians with him and he was picked up on the fourth day by a British destroyer, the sole survivor, as the Italians had all died.

Sapper Ivor 'Tinker' Bass, 24, of the 4th SA Field Engineers was having coffee with the South African guard sent to relieve him, when the torpedoes struck. 'We were standing on the deck and heard a huge explosion as one or two torps hit the ship. The *Nova Scotia* gave a jolt. We saw the sub come up and tried to man the guns aft. The ship gave another lurch.

Sapper Vic Davidson, 27, had served in Abyssinia and the Western Desert, 'We knew we were nearing home. We were already packed and ready to go ashore. I had come off guard duty at 6am and was actually sitting down on a hatch cover getting my kit lined up when the first torpedo hit the engine room, and the ship blew up. I was flung against the ship's railing, injuring my spine.

Sergeant Henry Gierke, 41, was leaning on the ship's rail, smoking and dreaming of his homecoming, when the topedoes struck. The next minute he was a badly injured man, desperately trying to jump from a tilting deck into an already overcrowded lifeboat.

Gunner Eric Manson of the Transvaal Heavy Artillery felt refreshed after his morning shower. While standing on deck he asked a member of the ship's crew, 'Do you have any idea where we are?'
'The Zululand coast is over there', the seaman replied, pointing across the ocean. Manson had instinctively looked in the direction the man was pointing. 'I can distinctly remember seeing the white foam of a torpedo running across the ship's path. Then came the terrible explosions. Next thing the ship heeled over and flame and smoke belched from the funnel. I leapt overboard immediately and tried to get away from the ship.
'I managed to find a piece of driftwood, part of one of the temporary swimming pools which had been erected on the *Nova Scotia*. This I shared with an Italian prisoner of war.'

Corporal Kennaugh was jerked awake. 'I was certain we would go down. My first thought was not to make for a lifeboat, but to recover my cash from below. I had won a useful amount playing crown and anchor. I didn't have much time. The deck was a madhouse, with hundreds of shouting passengers jamming the rails.

'Many of the Italian prisoners who had been confined below were dead or dying – destroyed by their allies' torpedoes. Several oil bunkers were on fire, engulfing the midship area and the bridge in flames. Most of the deck, particularly the part nearest to the engine room, was wet with oil, seeping from below. Fires were breaking out. The three lifeboats on the port side had been blasted away by the explosion.

'I ran below and saw the head of one passenger floating on the oil. He had been blown to pieces. In shock I abandoned all thought of recovering my money and struggled up the companionway to the deck. I was told later that one crewman, in despair at the nightmare on deck, walked back into his burning cabin and certain, quick death.

'Other crewmen worked frantically to launch the three starboard lifeboats. Two were launched successfully but the third dumped its occupants into the ocean when the lines lowering it broke at one end. For an instant the boat dangled in the air, then, on being cut free, filled with water and sank.

Alda and Valcheria were thrown to the deck by the force of the explosions. 'Valcheria was beside me when the first torpedo struck. In a few minutes fire broke out. Officers appeared and told us to move to the other end of the ship. Meantime the prisoners of war had started throwing lifebelts and rafts into the sea. One lifeboat was lowered, but was obviously damaged because it did not last long in the sea.'

The boats on the port side had been destroyed by the explosions, so the crew worked frantically at launching the three starboard ones. The one that was launched dumped its occupants into the sea when the ropes on one side parted. It filled with water and lay wallowing in the waves.

One of the men dumped into the sea when the rope snapped was the badly injured Sergeant Henry Gierke. For him and hundreds of others, a fight for life had started – a fight that few won.

According to J D Ratcliff, a journalist who interviewed survivors, 'On deck the confusion was indescribable. Hundreds of Italians jammed the rails, afraid to jump, blocking the way of those who wanted to do so. Horribly burnt men ran about wildly, screaming with pain. Incongruously, one man searched for his false teeth – blown out by the explosion.

'A squat old Italian seaman had been sitting against a rail smoking his pipe when the explosions came. He rose and quietly surveyed the situation. Then he got a length of rope, tied one end around

his waist and the other round the rail. He had made his decision:
he would die quickly . . .'

Nat Herman was one of the unfortunates caught below decks when
the torpedoes struck. 'I had been resting for about half an hour
when, in the midst of my doze, I heard a terrific explosion and the
whole ship shook. It didn't need much to tell me that this was no
minor incident, or that a saucer had fallen off the table. I knew
that it was extremely serious. The nature of the explosion, and the
fact that I had been with the artillery, made me think that we must
have struck a mine.

'The cabin was plunged into darkness, all the electric lights having
gone out. I jumped off the bunk and for a moment thought of getting my wallet and paybook out of my shirt and slipping it into my
bathing trunks. But I realised well from experience that in matters
of life and death worldly goods mean nothing and that any
momentary pause or hesitation might mean my end.

'Consequently, just as I was and barefooted, I seized my lifejacket
and rushed up the alleyway in order to get to my position either at
the raft or on the fire picket. As I turned a corner I nearly collided
with a soldier rushing to his cabin and I found myself dashing
headlong at the end of the corridor into a pillar of flame.

'The oil tanks had evidently exploded and caught alight and the
whole ship was on fire, instantaneously one might say. I got the
biggest fright of my life. My heart stood still. I felt that I was completely trapped and there seemed no hope of escaping from the
ship. I may mention one thing, by the way, when I was in the
Middle East returning to the base and was being examined by a
doctor after "collecting a packet", I jokingly told him, when he congratulated me on a miraculous escape from death, that I never
went "up north" or into the Libyan desert with a single ticket, and
that my return ticket although invisible, was grasped firmly in my
hand. The thought in my mind at the time, strange though it may
seem, was that this time my return half had gone to hell.

'No one, perhaps, can picture the horror and fear of finding
oneself in this terrible predicament. One can only pause and think
of those many who made a mission over Germany on bombers that
were set alight and plunged to earth physically uninjured, but
unable to extricate themselves. What their thoughts must have
been in that state of helplessness, although the end came swiftly,
were similar to the thoughts that went through my mind at the time.

'I heard someone shouting "The porthole" and slipped back to
my cabin and from a side view I saw a man forcing himself through
a porthole in the adjoining cabin. As I got into my own, I found
that one soldier had prised the porthole flap open. Although I was
on my third troopship, I had never given any thought to portholes.

Most of the latter were firmly barred because of blackout precautions. They could only be opened to allow ventilation and how the one in our cabin actually opened I do not know to this day.

'I heard someone shouting, "Slam the doors!" Even now I have no clear recollection whether the door of our cabin was closed or not – the danger being flaming oil that would flood and set the cabin alight. How far this could have been prevented is a matter for conjecture. In matters like these, fractions of a second count, and any hesitation might have meant the loss of one's life.

'In this position it was a case of every man for himself. I saw the first man get out of the porthole and our second cabin-mate began to follow. Although this may sound easy, it needed a terrific physical effort. This man succeeded in getting out and grasped a rope. He then shouted for a lifejacket, which I endeavoured to find, but without success, owing to the semi-darkness of the cabin. I shouted to him to get a move on, as I was in just as desperate a hurry to get out of the stricken ship and avoid being incinerated.

'I could feel the ship canting over and settling rapidly. There was no doubt that she had been struck in a vital spot. She had received a direct hit amidships on the port side. My cabin was on the starboard side. Had it been on the bow or port I should never have survived. Men in the washrooms below deck never got out. They were hopelessly trapped, for there was no means of escape. The only exit being through the alleyways which were burning fiercely. They never had a chance. Others must have been killed outright by the blast, or crushed. At least their end was swift.

'One man afterwards told me he had just left the washroom and was walking along the companionway when the explosion occurred. He saw the burning oil rushing towards him, but got on deck in time. As far as he knows, he was the only survivor from that part of the ship.

'The second soldier who managed to get out of the porthole was sliding down the rope into the sea. I never saw him again. I was told that he was seen to get onto a raft with some other men but what happened to this raft I do not know.

'My greatest concern was to get out of the ship and take my chance as quickly as possible in the sea. I immediately commenced getting out of the cabin in the same way as the other cabin-mates, not knowing what was on the other side, when I found myself wedged firmly in the porthole. I had, in my anxiety, hung the life-jacket on my shoulder for the reason that, in the open sea, one did not know how long one might be floating around, or what prospects there were of being picked up.

'I was a fairly good swimmer and quite fit at the time. I got back into the cabin, placed the jacket on the bunk and began to squirm through the porthole. How bigger men than myself managed to get through in the other parts of the ship remains an inexplicable mystery to me. At least ten survivors owed their lives to escape in this manner.

'I somehow managed to struggle through, during which time I cut my back and bear the scar to this day. I then released the rope to which I at first clung and hung onto the porthole to pull out the lifejacket from the bunk. The ship was already on a slope and I hung the jacket loosely over me.

'Remembering the fate of so many men who had been on the *Repulse* and *Renown* when sunk by the Japanese, I hurled myself as far out as I possibly could in order to avoid hitting the side of the ship. It was not an elegant dive. I landed flat on my back with a terrific wallop. The lifejacket, which ordinarily should have been fastened tightly, was very loose and I was partially winded. I went down like a stone and came up gasping for breath, pitch black from head to toe from the oil that was now on the surface. It got in everywhere.

'My first thought was for a lifeboat. There wasn't one to be seen and the only thing I did see was a piece of wood floating from the side of the ship, carried away by the waves. I did not ask any questions because there was no one to ask. I swam out to the wood which was drifting away rapidly.

'As I said earlier, the delay of a second – and these were fleeting rapidly by when I was in the cabin – might have meant the missing of this flotsam. When I got to the wood I found that I had succeeded in bagging the smallest type of raft on the ship, it being about the size of an ordinary wooden bathmat, with rope on the sides, and intended only for clinging to until succour arrived.

'As I had no competitors, I promptly got onto the raft and sat on my haunches, which was better than clinging. Before I had learned, however, to keep my balance, I fell into the sea again. I was in a panic as I thought I was going to lose this piece of wood. I managed to retrieve the raft somehow. This time I was more successful in my efforts at balancing myself.'

Staff-sergeant C J Smit also escaped through a porthole, 'I used to be quite well-built, but I was so desperate to get through the porthole that I literally scraped the flesh clean off my shoulders. I remember pulling a chap named Erasmus through the porthole as well. He was also badly scraped, but at least he got away. There was a third person in the cabin, who was too fat to get through the porthole. He burnt to death.'

Alda tried to protect Valcheria as they groped their way aft. 'Confusion reigned and as we were running aft a second torpedo struck. Again a fire broke out. People were running around in all directions. There was no time for lifebelts. A British officer instructed: "You'd better jump into the water. I'll take the little girl. Jump after me."

'He jumped with Valcheria and I saw him put her in the lifeboat. She had a red jersey on and was plain to see. That was the last I saw of her. At that moment the ship listed dangerously and it was time for me to jump. I did so, but the suction of the ship going down made it difficult for me to get away. I had to struggle to swim away from the sinking vessel which was sucking people in. Thank God I was a good swimmer and managed to get away.

'I'm a small woman, less than 5 ft tall, and weighed under 100 lbs then. But I was determined to survive. I swam with all my might and was relieved to find myself in the sea with others around me. My aim was to reach the lifeboat, but high waves prevented me from seeing anything.'

Mike Summerville, a lance-sergeant of the Air Liaison Officer (ALO) Unit, who had been seconded to the RAF from Second Division Intelligence, recalled, 'At about 9 am I was in the orderly room when I heard a sudden crash, a massive impact as three torpedoes slammed into the ship. The *Nova Scotia* listed immediately and began her last voyage to the bottom.

'A thought flashed through my mind, 'Where's my lifebelt? I haven't got it.' Flames were leaping up around me and I quickly decided to go below. I knew that if I could not find my lifebelt, I would have no chance at all. As I made my way further down into the ship I managed to find a lifebelt in one of the cabins.

'Rushing up to the deck, I discovered that all hell had broken loose. There was absolute chaos. Men were running around desperately trying to leave the ship. At that moment the British ship's officer who was OC troops dashed towards me cursing, "The Bastards!" I always remember that very clearly.

'Somebody told me that the ship's cook or barber, I can't remember which, had locked himself in his cabin. He had lost all hope and was prepared to go down with the ship. I looked down towards the foredeck and could see a crowd of men jostling to try to reach the lifeboats. Ultimately their efforts were in vain; some of the lifeboats had been blown away.

'For some reason I climbed to the highest point aft. I was alone, high up, with the ship listing dangerously. To this day I cannot tell you why I did not follow the herd instinct and go with the crowds. This is a natural reaction, an expected response. I still cannot say why I wished to remain alone.'

'The ship was going down fast. I clung to the rail, petrified. While constantly peering over the rail and looking at the sea, about five storeys below, I mumbled silent prayers, promising the Lord that if I ever got through this I would never, ever, do anything wrong again.'

'Luckily for me I remembered the lifeboat drill. If you have to jump overboard you must keep your lifebelt in your hand. Keep it down, otherwise you will break your back. Suddenly I made up my mind and jumped. I went down, down, down. When I came up the surface of the sea was coal black, covered with oil. Thank goodness I could still see. I wasn't the best of swimmers and I must say I wasn't very optimistic.

'Fighting my way through enormous waves I tried to reach a raft measuring about three metres square, that was jam-packed with South Africans. Men were everywhere on the raft itself and hanging onto ropes on the sides. As I approached one of the men shouted, "Hey! The raft is full." Anyway, I managed to squeeze on board.

'Moments later somebody shouted, "We had better get away from the ship when it goes down. It will pull us down with it." I don't know how we managed to get away, but we did it. I can't remember the details but we must have paddled frantically.

'Just then an Italian swam towards the raft and was told, "The raft is full." The man held on to the ropes on the raft and I tried to pull him on board. I could see that he was getting weaker and weaker and couldn't last in the water. Suddenly he disappeared. Only afterwards did I realise that he had been taken by a shark.'

Nat Herman was later to hear of others' experiences, 'A number of Italians panicked on the deck and an Australian told me that he was obliged to use the sharp edge of a raft axe upon them. The fatalistic outlook of some is indicated in the story of the cook who came up on deck, took one look around, probably considered the situation hopeless, merely shrugged his shoulders and then walked back into the ship.

'Of the poker players, only one, whom I knew very well, was saved. At the time of the torpedoing he was sitting on deck with another South African, playing chess. The first thing he experienced was a shower of oil pouring down on him, which caused him to slide across the deck.

'Another South African, on the port side, found himself blown into the sea, causing him to lose his false teeth. Nearly every man had a different experience. I could tell quite a number of such stories, but this would make the narrative too long.'

The ship was settling rapidly and Tinker Bass realised that it was doomed. 'The ship gave another lurch and went onto its side. An English soldier shouted, "Throw the rafts into the water for the Italian prisoners". We were all too afraid to jump.' Yet jump they did, singly and in groups men leapt into the oil-blackened sea.

Their lifejackets brought them swiftly to the surface, to wipe oil away from their eyes before striking away from the hull and hauling themselves up onto rafts. 'The rafts were close to the ship. We were all mixed together on the rafts, South African soldiers, Italians and Englishmen.

'The raft I was on was overcrowded, with about 40 men [aboard]. Some were holding onto the ropes around the edges of the H-shaped raft. Some men were in the water in lifejackets and others were holding onto debris.'

George Kennaugh was still on board, clinging to the rail as the deck steepened under him. Seven minutes after being hit the *Nova Scotia* listed heavily and began to sink. To avoid being sucked down with the ship he climbed over the rail and threw himself into space. 'On hitting the ocean I started to choke on the oil-blackened water and struggled to get air into my lungs . . .'

Bombardier Nat Herman, floated on a raft the size of a small bath-mat, 'The raft was now drifting away from the ship, when I heard a shout from somewhere in English, "There she comes!" and I saw that sinister and loathsome monster of the sea rising slowly out of the water – a submarine. The conning tower and superstructure of the submarine began moving slowly towards the ship.

'Our ship had been fairly well armed with light ack-ack guns and carried a sizeable gun at the stern, approximately 3.7″ or 4″ calibre. The submarine must have been fairly certain of itself, otherwise it would not have risen to the surface. The only question that puzzled me was whether it was a German or Japanese submarine and what the next move would be.

'They were leaving nothing to chance and their guns were mounted and ready for action. I was afterwards told that several South Africans had made a dash with the naval gunners to the gun at the stern in a desperate and determined effort, if possible, to sink the submarine, despite the fact that the ship was going down fast. As the stern was rising sharply out of the water, they were apparently unable to depress the gun and get a bead. Had they been successful there is not the slightest doubt that they would have sunk the submarine.

'It was fortunate for me and a few others, as it subsequently transpired, that this effort failed. The threat to other ships at sea still remained and although I treasure my life, it would have been better to have sunk the submarine than to have left it to continue its depredations in the Indian Ocean.

'The submarine proceeded slowly round the ship, which was now blazing and smoking, and came round to within about 30 yards of where I was floating.

Herman watched the U-boat suspiciously, 'I saw the submarine turn a sharp right angle and submerge. The ship now presented a dramatic sight – identical to those pictures which many of us saw in the cinemas during the war. The flames were shooting sky high and dense volumes of smoke were rising. The ship was canting over sharply and her stern began to rise out of the water, exposing the rudder.

'Men were jumping off in all directions and I was told that there were South Africans hanging on to the bitter end and crying, "I can't swim!" and refusing to let go. Possibly they had mislaid their lifejackets, or they were plainly afraid. The ship went down perpendicularly into the sea and that was the end.

'After the ship had gone down, odd bits of wreckage or rafts, on which men were sitting, could be seen drifting away from one another rapidly. The sea was still covered in oil. From the time the ship was struck until she went down was a matter of seven or eight minutes and it seemed a lifetime.'

Vic Davidson was among the last to abandon ship. 'The ship was sinking. I took off my boots and whipped off my shirt. I went to the lifebelts and put on my Mae West and as the water came over the side I dived into the sea. Then I swam like hell till I got about 100 yards away.

'I turned and saw just the rear end of the ship sticking up. You could see the propellers. I saw that the bridge was still above water and it was just one mass of flames. A few chaps were still jumping as the ship went right down. Everything was one big mess of oil, which had caught alight and we had to swim to keep away from the flames.

'Three torpedoes hit the ship. The first hit the engine room and the second must have gone somewhere near the front, because of the way the ship just tilted and went down nose first. In about five minutes it was all over. She was gone.'

Ratcliff summed up the next dramatic moments as the ship's stern rose higher. 'Five minutes had elapsed and *Nova Scotia* had one remaining minute of life. Scores of men still jammed the after rail. As the stern rose in the ship's last seconds, a dozen men grasped at the stilled propeller – and all were sucked down into the great vortex.

'Oil-blackened human misery dotted the now lonely, empty sea. For this pathetic human driftwood the long tortuous fight for survival began, a fight that would end in defeat for the vast majority.

'A score of men, including *Nova Scotia's* commander, Captain Hender, struggled with the lone, water-filled lifeboat. A young British seaman asked what their chances were. "None, I'm afraid,"

Hender replied. As far as Hender was concerned, this was an accurate estimate. Badly burned, he must have died quickly.

'Despite frequent fights that nearly always ended fatally for the combatants, there were relieving moments of generosity. Corporal Andrew Biccard, of the Cape Town Highlanders, tried to board a tiny raft which barely had room for the two Italians already there. They tried to push him away. Then one noticed he had a rosary around his neck. They were fellow Catholics! Biccard was pulled to safety.'

Kennaugh stared aghast as the ship slipped under. 'Suddenly the *Nova Scotia* was gone. With a sickening, squelching, sucking sound, the great hulk was devoured by the waves. Fragments of driftwood were belched back from the depths. Oil-smeared survivors fought to climb onto rafts, lifeboats or dinghies or to grasp at driftwood.

'I was able to seize an oar which had fallen from one of the lifeboats and tied my wrists to it with the cord from my swimming trunks. Another survivor also grabbed the oar. He told me that he had been wounded in the stomach.

'While we floated aimlessly on the anthracite-black ocean, U-177 surfaced about 400 yards away from a mass of bobbing bodies. The commander stepped from the conning tower onto the deck. Survivors screamed and yelled, some giving the Nazi salute.

'The U-boat submerged, resurfaced further away and crew were seen taking photographs. The shouts died down in shocked disbelief as we saw two German crewmen begin to unlace the submarine's gun-covers, but they withdrew at a gesture from the U-boat captain.'

Tinker Bass recalled that the U-boat had appeared again 30 minutes after the sinking. 'I saw the captain who had a neatly trimmed blonde beard. The German sailors started to man the guns, then a man shouted loudly, "Italiano!" There was no shooting.'

While floating in the oily water, the injured Vic Davidson thought that he would be shot. 'The submarine surfaced among the wreckage and sailors manned the guns. I thought that they were going to machine-gun us in the water, but they didn't. It seems that when they realised it was a prisoner-of-war ship they had sunk, they indicated that help would be sent. Then they went away.'

Gunner Eric Manson also thought that they were going to be shot. 'Meanwhile the U-boat surfaced, and some of its crew started to take off the covering from the machine-gun on the boat's deck. Thinking that the Germans were going to gun us down, the Italian POW and I tried to get as far as possible from the main body of the survivors.

The Type IX U-boat
'Seekuh' (Sea Cow)
conning tower, similar
to that of the U-177
(*Stern – Bundesarchiv*).

This turned out to be an almost fatal move, as we cut ourselves off from the main group which was picked up by the Portuguese.

'I remember seeing some of the Italian POWs trying to clamber aboard the U-boat. The Germans stamped on their hands to stop them getting onto the submarine.'

Nat Herman was to swear at Captain Gysae, 'There were four Europeans on deck, including a youngish man in naval uniform and a man with a short beard. They called out to me and asked what the name of the ship was.

'By now my biggest fear was over. I was in a thoroughly truculent mood, so I used an army expression and told them exactly what to do. I wasn't sure whether they were now going to open up on me or not. In any case we were all going to drown, so it made very little difference. I had no intention of spending the rest of the war in a German prisoner-of-war camp, or of being tricked out of my piece of plank.

'I saw a South African I knew floating on a similar raft nearby. As the submarine had now continued its circle, I asked him what he thought I should have done. He told me he would have done the same thing. The fellow then said that he was going to look for a pal of his and by sort of manoeuvring with his hands, managed to paddle away. He never found his friend, but he himself was saved. As for his friend, we met six hours later when he was floating on another raft in company with a number of Italians.

'The submarine completed a circle and I then saw for the first and only time in my life that horrible salute "Heil Hitler".

'It appears that there were a few rafts drifting about containing Italians and they began shouting to the Germans on the submarine, "Italiano!" and giving the Fascist salute. The Germans responded and it was obvious that the submarine commander received a tremendous shock when he found that he had torpedoed a prisoner-of-war ship carrying his allies.

'He then raised a hand to pacify the Italians, or reassure them, and it was apparent that he could not possibly leave them to drown. How he proposed getting help was not clear to me at the time.

'The submarine then completed its circle and approached me a second time at a distance of about 25 or 30 yards, travelling at a moderate speed. They then shouted to me again, asking for the name of the ship, and as it was obvious that it was their intention to deliver the information to someone, I this time gave the name.

'They then shouted to me in English to come "On board" and I felt that I was literally and metaphorically between the devil and the deep blue sea. I refused. At the same time the Germans required someone for information purposes and as I was not sure what their next step might be, or whether they might use force or intimidate me, I took off my discs and attached them to my raft. I had no intention of being identified either as a soldier or anything else at all, as I wasn't too sure what my position was.'

'In the meantime there was an Italian floating on a raft nearby and he was very keen to go on board. Nor would I have blamed him in his situation. A rope was therefore thrown to him and, as I had ignored the invitation, the Italian was pulled in. Whatever information of military value he could have given would not have gone very far towards helping the German war effort.

'I might have been liquidated through a torpedo tube after they had got all the information they wanted from me. There is, after all, only limited living space on a submarine. As soon as the Italian was on board the submarine completed its cruise, for it had been searching for the captain of the *Nova Scotia* without success.

'They were apparently in a desperate hurry to get away from the scene of the tragedy before any allied warship arrived. No radio message had, in fact, been sent – the radio of our ship had been blasted out of commission and also the emergency transmitter. Possibly the radio operator was killed. The captain did get off the ship and onto a raft or lifeboat, but was never picked up.

'There were no lifeboats about. One or two that came off the ship capsized. Too many men attempted to get into one and it merely tumbled over and over again. Of the 40 men clinging to it, only two South Africans were eventually saved. They were sitting on the keel when found.'

L/Sgt Summerville recalled, 'We floated around aimlessly. The situation seemed hopeless and there appeared to be no future. The only saving grace was that you shared the company of your fellows – you could say that we were companions in distress.

'From out of nowhere the U-boat surfaced and I could see men dressed in white about 100 metres from the raft. The captain shouted out in German, "Does anyone speak German?" At that stage we were more concerned about saving our lives than the possible danger presented by the U-boat. If I had been asked to board the U-boat I would have done so. Let's face it, the prospects on a raft, in the middle of the ocean, are not very good. I recall that a few people were taken on board the U-boat.

'My most vivid memories were of the enormous size of the breakers, they seemed to be six metres high, and the hopelessness of our plight.'

A bearded U-boat officer, wearing a white uniform and presumably Captain Gysae, spent five minutes photographing the scene.

The log of U-177 recorded: 'In the water there are hundreds of survivors drifting in their lifebelts, or on rafts or rubber boats. Insufficient life-saving equipment. Try to find out the name of ship by asking survivors. No success as they all shout and yell at the same time. But I see that Italians are floating in the water. Strong indications of panic. To clarify the position I make for a raft to take on one survivor; but from all sides they come swimming to the boat. As two of them reach the boat at the same time I take them both on board.'

The two were a cabin boy and an Italian seaman. Months later they were put ashore at U-177's new base at Bordeaux. Others tried to scramble on board but, threatening to swamp the U-boat, were pushed back into the ocean. Before pulling away the captain shouted repeatedly in English: 'I am sorry . . . I am terribly sorry . . . I will radio Berlin . . . Help will be sent . . . Be brave . . .'

At 10 am U-177 moved off 'on account of the danger from the air'. Two allied aircraft had flown overhead, but they were too high to take in the situation.

Nat Herman searched the sea near him, 'I looked around, but there was no one near me. One rescued South African told me that he saw me sitting on my raft and going over the waves as if I were riding a horse in a steeplechase. It was the only amusing sight to him during the whole time he was in the sea. He was right. In no time I became violently sea-sick. The sea dashed over me and at times it was hot and at times cold. I got bilious and I had a terrible feeling of nausea. I experienced every conceivable form of discomfort, including violent cramp and heartburn, from the position I was sitting in and the chilling wind.

'It was a question of time how long one could stand up to this kind of shock and exposure – I was drifting around aimlessly, hoping for the best. I can certainly say that there were few worse places on this earth than sittting sick, naked and all alone on a piece of wood in the Indian Ocean.

According to Ratcliff, 'Hundreds of those in the water disappeared within a few minutes. Some fought on until overcome by exhaustion; others were choked by the slimy oil. By the end of the first hour the crest of horror had passed. From now on death would be more selective, and in many respects far more terrible.'

Rescue was, nevertheless, still a long way off for the exhausted men clinging to pieces of wood or drifting on rafts and small boats.

Alda had failed to reach Valcheria's lifeboat. 'I swam for what seemed like hours. In the distance I could see a lifeboat with a little red blob on it. Valcheria was wearing a red jersey and was plain to see.' She swam with all her might and urged herself on with the words, "There she is. You have to get to her." The lifeboat then disappeared and Valcheria with it.

'I went around searching, searching. By this time I was exhausted. The submarine surfaced and picked up a survivor or two and then disappeared. I then found a raft with eight people hanging on. Someone shouted, "Hang on here," indicating the ropes tied to the raft. I joined them.'

Herman rode his small raft in the choppy water, sitting rigidly upright to keep from falling off. 'After some time, it may have been some hours, I drifted into the vicinity of a large raft carrying Italians. It was crammed full. I shouted to them, or they shouted to me, and I managed somehow or other to manoeuvre myself next to this raft. I felt that it would be better to die in company.

'As for the Italians, their position was peculiar. There was no South African with them, they knew nothing of what was happening or where they were and they probably felt that if there was a soldier with them he might be in a position to help them. There was no hope of their getting back to Italy. They could, of course, easily have thrown me overboard and acts of violence did occur on other rafts.

'I got on the raft with them and lashed my own raft to it. They asked me when I thought help would come and I said, "Soon". Although I knew just as much as they did, I thought it would make them happy. They probably imagined that I had some inside information.

'A little while after that, another raft, identical to my bathmat, came nearby with two men sitting on it. They were both Italians. The Italians on our raft refused to allow them to join us. We were already overcrowded and the raft was low down in the water. Those in the centre, where there was a drop, were sitting in water. I was sitting flush on sea level, with the water sometimes passing over my lap as we drifted in the waves.

'I called the Italians, lashed their raft to ours and pulled one Italian on board myself, despite the fact that my colleagues didn't wish me to do this. Willy nilly I became skipper. This Italian was shockingly burnt, probably from oil [fire]. The other Italian was now sitting on the other raft lashed to us and I made him understand, somehow or other, that I would get him on later.

'A little while after that, another one of these rafts drifted nearby containing a South African soldier and an Italian. I managed to get them to our raft, but could not get them onto it because it was too crowded and the sea was rough. Unfortunately, the South African was extremely deaf. He could not hear my instructions at a distance of 12 or 15 feet on account of the wind and his hardness of hearing. He lashed his raft to ours and was with me for a number of hours, until the violence of the sea broke it loose.

'I was helpless to tell him what to do, so the raft drifted away and he disappeared. We could barely take another person on, but I thought that if he could manage to come round to my side, I might have given him a bit of space, though we were all sitting on our haunches. This South African, I am glad to say, was saved. He and the Italian were the last to be picked up. For sheer grit, determination and courage this fellow deserves every admiration and praise.

'On this, my first day on the open sea, my only thought was of safety and every half hour or so I stood up on the raft, with two Italians holding my legs to support me, in order to see if there was any sign of a passing ship. Unsupported, I should have simply fallen into the sea.

'All the time the raft was bouncing on the waves, as the sea was choppy. Frequently we were drenched and we were always sitting in the water. The weather was changeable. At times it was hot, with intermittent sun, and then dull. This made everybody feel pretty miserable.

The tension and stress of the overcrowding on the rafts led to some fighting. Tinker Bass recalled the life and death struggle on theirs. 'At about midday we heard the Italians say, "The English must go!" It was the survival of the fittest and we had to fight for our lives. There was a fight on the raft and the Italians were thrown off.

'Those in lifejackets and those holding onto floating wreckage were swept away by the current. There were then about 20 men on the raft. We picked up three Afrikaans men who were on a small raft. While their raft drifted a man was washed off and we all wondered who would save him. Fortunately he was washed back on again.

'I was determined to stay alive, although we did not realise how serious the danger was.' They were soon to find out.

Alda lay exhausted on the raft. 'I had been swimming for a long time in the icy cold water. All I was wearing was a pair of slacks and a top. By this time it was getting dark. I don't know if my imagination was playing tricks on me, but I thought I could see land or lights in the distance.

'More people joined the raft and the number of shipwrecked increased to 11. We spent the night hanging on. Still there was no sign of rescue. I cannot remember how we passed the night, but occasionally one person would let go and then we got him back and helped him to hang on.'

'One of the castaways was a nurse – a tough girl who smoked cigars, but who was very nice. The nurse kept falling off. "Come on, hang on," I urged. "Hang on as long as you can." I was getting very tired and could not hang on to her as well as save myself.'

The noise of the ship sinking, followed by the thrashing of men in the water and the smell of blood from the burnt and injured attracted the ocean's predators. Sharks began homing in on the scene from miles around.

Nat Herman was among the first to see the menacing fins. 'That afternoon whilst I was sitting on my haunches meditating, I heard a shout from one of the Italians. I cannot remember what word he used, but I saw a shark heading for the raft. I suppose it was about 12 ft or 14 ft long. A little while after it was joined by another shark. We immediately lifted our feet, which had been dangling over the side, and had to manoeuvre to cling onto the wood, out of reach.

'From that time on, until we were eventually saved, the sharks never left us. They were constantly coursing round and round the raft within an arm's throw and frequently swam below the raft and out on the other side. We had two pieces of wood attached to the side of the raft, intended for use as oars, which were released and these the Italians used to "shoo" them off, but this did not deter them from coming back again.'

Corporal Kennaugh and his friend, Dougie, clung to the oar, seemingly safe. 'Meanwhile, a new horror faced us survivors. A shout sent a chill of terror racing along my spine. "Sharks!" It was a cry repeated many times during the long hours ahead; a cry of despair, panic and, sometimes, of agony.

'My companion and I were still hanging onto our oar, but our will to live was all gone. "I can't go on," my colleague kept repeating. "I can't go on. It's easier to die than to live like this. I pleaded with him to carry on fighting, but to no avail.

'He seemed to be determined to let go, so I asked him to leave me his lifejacket. As he was loosening his lifejacket he suddenly screamed and the upper part of his body rose out of the water. He fell back and I saw the water had become red with blood and that his foot had been bitten off.

'At this moment I saw the grey form of a shark swimming excitedly round and I paddled away as fast as I could. Then a number of sharks congregated around me – I estimated their lengths at between six and seven feet. Every now and then one would come straight for me – I splashed hard and this seemed to drive it away.'

Tinker Bass was relatively safe on the large raft, but he couldn't shut out the sounds of men being savaged by the sea monsters. 'In the late afternoon and evening we heard men scream as they were taken by sharks. I did not see sharks rise from the water and attack the men – but we heard their screams. Sharks constantly swam around the rafts and we could see them through the slats swimming underneath.'

Herman watched the fins circling them, 'Quite apparently, they were waiting for someone to fall off and this was bound to happen sooner or later if we had not been saved. The limit of human endurance is soon reached and actually there were many men on other rafts who became victims of the elements through sheer exhaustion, shock and exposure. The sharks, too, claimed victims who were clinging to rafts or floating in the water.

'We had nothing to eat or drink the first day, so that by dusk we were feeling more than sick and miserable. Still, we had no sign of

Detail of a painting
Sharks by Rosemary
Clark.

any assistance. There was only one other raft in the vicinity, the rest had simply disappeared, and though I felt that no SOS could have gone out, "hope springs eternal in the human breast". I was determined to stick it out as long as I could.'

The Italian prisoners also clung tenaciously to life. According to Ratcliff, 'Hope for those who survived that first hour lay in the pieces of driftwood or whatever else could be found to cling to. Sergeant Lorenzo Bucci managed to make his way to a floating hatch cover to which a dozen other Italians were clinging. By nightfall Bucci and his companions on their improvised raft found themselves at the centre of a grisly drama.

'A lone swimmer would appear, then suddenly throw his arms into the air, scream and disappear. Soon afterwards a reddish blob would colour the water. Sharks had arrived – and death in its most gruesome form now took over.

'Even in the Indian Ocean, there has never been another shark attack of such proportions.

'Survivors in the water fought savagely as they struggled for places on the rafts. Now Bucci's raft was approached by two oil-blackened men, a South African and a Sicilian who paddled towards it on a piece of planking. Bucci and his companions made it clear that the intruders were not wanted: their situation was already precarious enough.

'The South African pulled out a sheath knife. "I don't want to kill you", he said. "I want to save you. Our chances are best if we stick together." Hostility wilted. The South African pulled off his belt and fastened his plank to the hatch-cover.

'The new arrivals had an explanation for their escape from the sharks. "I suppose we are rather unappetising dishes with all this oil on us," said the South African. From time to time a man's grip would loosen and he would float away. The South African, a strong swimmer, dragged each one back.'

Vic Davidson was supported only by his Mae West. 'Then I saw a hatch cover floating past with four South Africans on it. I knew one of them well. He put out his foot and I climbed onto the cover. It was floating about 18 inches below the surface.

'There were sharks all round. There seemed to be hundreds of them and barracuda were biting at whatever parts of our bodies they could get at. Big chunks were taken out of my legs.

'Late on Saturday a proper raft drifted near us. It was made of empty drums joined with pieces of wood, and there was no one on it. Two of the chaps on our hatch cover decided to try to get to the raft. I just saw them splash over the side and then there were two red blobs in the water – and they were gone. The sharks had got them. The sea was alive with sharks and dozens of men were taken.'

The short tropical sunset was followed by a night of misery. Kennaugh had somehow survived the sharks, 'I had now been in the water for 12 hours. My wrists were still tied to the oar and were tired and throbbing, whereas my body was cold and tired. Drifting along hour after hour I thought of some of the good times in my life. It was the wrong time to feel tired or despondent.

'The night was a terrible time. The *Nova Scotia* sinking, choking oil slime, shark attacks, thirst and hunger had been bad enough, but it was the night I feared. If a ship approaches from afar there is a good chance that it will not see you. The same applies to aircraft flying overhead. In these circumstances you have to will yourself not to get tired, not to give up. Give in and die, or fight on and live – this was the simple choice.'

Kennaugh lost track of time. He then saw a large Afrikaner drift by on a 44-gallon drum. The two men then began bumping into a raft occupied by Italians. The prisoners-of-war screamed and hit at them with lanterns, which had been fastened to the back of the raft.

The Afrikaner, whose stomach was raw from having been rubbed against the barrel, shouted at Kennaugh, 'You were a guard commander last night and you can't let the bloody prisoners do this to us.'

'What can we do?' replied Kennaugh. The Afrikaner then decided that action was more effective than words. He scrambled onto the raft and tipped it and it's occupants into the sea. Kennaugh managed to loosen the cord from his wrists, climbed onto the raft and grabbed one of the lanterns. Using this as a baton he flailed it about at some of the Italians swimming around.

'He later remarked, 'It was war and the Jerries and Ities were out to kill us, so we had to fight for our survival.' They succeeded in taking over the raft and allowed some Italians back on. Drifting through the swells they picked up 22 South Africans and several members of the British crew.

According to Kennaugh, 'Attached to the side of the raft was a torch which, once loosened, floats in an upright position and automatically lights up. I had learnt about this while I was on the ship, so made use of this knowledge when darkness came. I attached the torch to a stick, which someone held aloft on the off-chance that we might be seen by some ship at night.

'The day had been bad enough, but the night was infinitely worse. It was impossible to sleep as the sea was constantly breaking over us. We were tossed about at various times. When this happened we were all but tipped over and a moan would rise from the Italians.

'Late that night the moon came up and I was able to guess the approximate time, because only four days before I had watched the moon rising whilst on duty and remembered its hour. I reckoned that it was about 12.30 or 1 o'clock in the early hours.'

One of the survivors later recalled during a newspaper interview: 'With no food or water and having nothing but the clothes I was wearing when the ship was torpedoed, I drifted from one piece of wood to another. In the late afternoon I got onto a small raft with five Italians. We drifted about hoping for the best.

'When night came I lashed myself to a raft and was so exhausted

I went to sleep. When I awoke I found that only one Italian and myself were left out of the party of six.'

Kennaugh became numb with exhaustion, 'I lost track of time. Night seemed to merge into day. The water on our raft was running out. Two men on the raft died. They just petered out. We threw their bodies into the water. Sharks just nudged the bodies and rolled them about. I can only assume that by then they had eaten their fill.'

Ratcliff wrote of the perils during the hours of darkness, 'During the long night, a tiring Italian asked permission of the others to climb aboard the plank and rest. There were no objections. A wave washed over the plank and he disappeared.

'Another man climbed into his place. Half an hour later a second wave washed over the plank and he, too, was gone.'

'James Latham, *Nova Scotia's* bo'sun, had dived overboard soon after the explosions. A ladder floated nearby. Latham climbed on, strapped his knees to it with his belt, and stretched out on his back, hooking his arms through the rungs above his head. As the day wore on he went to sleep, and when he wakened he was gazing into a starlit sky.

'Sensing some motion beneath him he looked down through the ladder rungs and saw the phosphorescent outline of a shark swimming along with him. Eventually the shark disappeared and Latham dozed off again.'

The *Nova Scotia* had been sunk about 30 miles from Cape St Lucia and 180 miles south-east of Lourenço Marques. Ratcliff pointed out that the U-boat couldn't use its radio in the proximity of the sinking. 'It would have been suicidal for Gysae to send for help immediately. They were only a few score miles off the South African coast, and patrol planes would soon be bombing them. Accordingly he cruised out to sea for an hour; then, against regulations, he surfaced and radioed Berlin asking that help be got to the men in the water.

At 4.43 pm the commander reported to BdU (U-boat command): 'Sank auxiliary cruiser *Nova Scotia* with over 1 000 internees from Massawa . . . Two survivors on board. Still about 400 on boats and rafts . . . Moving away because of the air.'

U-boat command signalled back at 7.37 pm: 'Continue operating. Waging war comes first. No rescue attempts'.

According to Ratcliff, 'When the radio message from U-177 was received in Berlin, a coded appeal for help went out to the German Embassy in Madrid. The Lisbon Embassy was to inform the Portuguese Government – a neutral country – and ask for aid to be

Capt José Augusto
Guerreiro de Brito (*RK*)

sent from Mozambique, the Portuguese East African colony nearest to the spot where *Nova Scotia* had sunk.

The message requesting aid for the survivors was received in Lourenço Marques at 9 pm. Ratcliff wrote, 'The Portuguese training ship *Afonso de Albuquerque*, a 1 400 ton frigate, had put in at Lourenço Marques the day before. Since it had planned to stay in port only a day or so, the ship was provisioned immediately and the oil and water tanks were filled.

'This forethought was to be of life-and-death importance to the *Nova Scotia* survivors. At 9 pm on Saturday, 12 hours after the sinking, a message crackled into the frigate's radio room.

'Captain José Augusto Guerreiro de Brito was hastily summoned from a restaurant in the town. When he boarded *Albuquerque*, de Brito was handed a message: PROCEED IMMEDIATELY FULL SPEED TO PICK UP SURVIVORS. SHIP SUNK 9AM TODAY. LATITUDE 28°30'S, LONGITUDE 33°E — 180 MILES SOUTH LOURENÇO MARQUES.

**Sunday
29 November**

The *Albuquerque* put to sea at 2.30 am. Captain De Brito calculated that the survivors would have been swept south of the site of the sinking by the strong Mozambique current. He reached his projected search area by 6am and his numerous lookouts scanned the vast ocean expanses, but saw nothing . . .

Alda somehow clung to life as others around her died. 'The night passed and by morning there were only three of us left. The two British stokers and I were weak and cold, so we decided to lie on our tummies across the raft. I was in the middle, hanging on by my chin, my arms around each man. I couldn't let them go, as I was afraid of being left alone. We were very tired, but I dared not go to sleep. Sharks had not worried me, though there was a lot of red blood amidst the oil which had leaked from the ship.'

'When dawn came', wrote Ratcliff, 'James Latham began paddling with his hands – why or where he knew not. He passed a raft. On it was a friend, John Halligan, a pantryman, and six Italians. Latham lifted his head, bowed slightly, and said a polite "Good morning" – as if he were greeting an acquaintance on deck on a pleasant day. Despite their plight the men on the raft had to smile. Then Latham paddled away.'

Vic Davidson and the two South Africans with him, Jan and Koosie, clung to their hatch cover throughout the night. He realised that one side of his body was paralysed. Davidson noticed that one shark in particular was accompanying the hatch cover. 'He seemed to be with me all day on Sunday. He swam round and round the

103

cover, and every time he came round I could see the white balls of his eyes moving.'

Eric Manson found himself alone, 'My Italian companion weakened rapidly and in the dawn of our second day, he slipped away from the driftwood. I never saw him again.

'There were plenty of bodies floating near me at the time. Most were in a vertical position as they still had lifebelts on. I had no lifebelt. What was more terrifying than anything else was watching how some of these bodies would suddenly jerk in the water and then the water would redden around them as the sharks got to work.

'At one time I looked down to see two big white shapes below me. I knew they must be sharks because I could just see the tail of one swishing back and forth. I climbed on top of my driftwood and knelt there for hours. Everywhere I drifted the white forms followed.'

Nat Herman was to have a busy morning. Eventually we saw the sun rise in the dull weather. There had been occasional drizzle and the sun broke through fitfully.

'Never in the days of my youth had I ever thought that I should dwell upon the words of Coleridge in "The Ancient Mariner" –

> Alone, alone, all alone
> Alone on a wide, wide sea
> And never a saint took pity on
> My soul in agony
> The many men, so beautiful!
> And they all dead did lie:
> And a thousand, thousand slimy things
> Lived on; and so did I.

'On the second day the thought of food and drink was uppermost in our minds. The raft upon which we were settled contained sealed tinned canisters, which had water and biscuits in them, but the heavy weight on the raft submerged these below the level of the sea. The question arose how to raise the canisters above water.

'We decided to move nearly all the men onto one side of the raft, despite the sharks, and eventually managed to tilt one side above sea level and unscrew the cap of the water canister. I was asked which rations should be issued and, as I did not know how long we were going to remain on the raft, in these circumstances I felt that we should go very carefully with the water.

'A metal cup was chained onto the canister and I imagined that I had about one third of a cup of water, which was all the ration each man had. We opened another canister and found biscuits in it, which had become pitch black, musty and mouldy and absolutely unfit for human consumption. I don't suppose that these canisters and the contents had ever been checked or examined from the day the ill-fated troopship went on war service.

'A couple of Italians attempted to eat the biscuits and so did I, because I felt that I had to have something to sustain me, but they were absolutely unpalatable.

'We went back into our original positions and so the day wore on. We either sat down or stood up. I suppose most men had been praying and on the second day they openly gave way to their feelings. One must understand that these men had had their spirits broken. I also gave way to prayer, but not so openly. Some of the Italians began complaining and moaning and I shouted at them to keep quiet, telling them that if they didn't like it they could get off the raft.

The *Albuquerque* lookouts spotted the first survivors at 1.12 pm. Ratcliff recorded, 'A deck officer's voice blared over the loudspeaker: "Raft three miles north-east." *Albuquerque* raced towards it at full speed through the choppy sea.

'A rope ladder was put over the side, but most of the 18 men on the raft were so weak they had to be carried aboard.

'On deck, survivors were stripped of their oil-blackened clothes and given a searing glass of *aguardente*, a rough Portuguese brandy. Then they were taken to the showers to be scrubbed. Painfully swollen and inflamed eyes were swabbed; those with flagging pulses received injections.

'Although the remaining large rafts were sighted, lookouts had also spotted dozens of lone survivors clinging to driftwood. De Brito reached a bitter decision. For the time being the two big rafts would be disregarded, as the men aboard were better situated and had

The rescue ship
Afonso de Albuquerque
(*Hawthorn Leslie Ltd*).

greater chance for survival. Attention would be given first to those with the least chance. Thus the men on the large rafts saw the ship disappearing and thought all hope had gone.'

Herman feared that they would be swamped that afternoon. 'At one time in the afternoon the weather became extremely dull and a terrific storm seemed to be creeping up on us from all sides. I did not think we would survive it. We seemed to be in the middle of a cyclone, but the storm simply passed over us and left us unscathed.

'In the middle of all this our two sharks suddenly disappeared. I heard another shout and saw one of the hugest specimens that could ever have lived in the Indian Ocean. It was well over 20 feet and one toss of its tail would have turned the raft over. If the smaller sharks were frightened, imagine our own feelings. The shark, fortunately, left us shortly afterwards and we never saw it again. The smaller ones returned in due course.

'Late in the afternoon I saw a ship on the horizon during one of my periods of scanning the ocean. It was difficult to estimate its distance. We had tied shirts to our two oars with the idea of trying to rig up some form of sail. They were quite useless for any purpose, because whichever way we pulled, the current seemed to take us in another direction.

'I had not the remotest idea in which direction we were travelling, as we appeared to turn round in circles, completely at the mercy of the waves and the currents of the Madagascar Channel. I personally had no confidence whatsoever in these contraptions. I might add that the currents were alternately warm and cold.

'We were so far away from the ship, that we could not possibly have been seen, even with our waving of the shirts, hidden as we were between the waves.

Alda also had visions of being rescued. 'We were covered in oil and burning from the hot sun. During mid-afternoon we caught sight of a ship. It seemed to be quite close. We had to make sure they would see us, so I took off my shirt, found a piece of wood in the sea and made a flag. While my two companions held on to me, I stood up and waved it as madly as I could.

The *Albuquerque* stopped near Tinker Bass's raft. 'At 4 pm on the Sunday we were picked up by the Portuguese sloop. Earlier a plane had flown overhead, but it did not see us. When the men saw the rescue ship they became excited and we feared it would turn over. The captain of the sloop sent out a lifeboat which took us back to the Portuguese ship.'

Alda's efforts to attract the attention of the ship's crew was in vain,

A *Nova Scotia* lifeboat
being picked up (*RK*).

as it was for Herman. He recalled, 'In the sunset we could still see
the ship moving about. Presumably it was busy picking up survivors. About that time an aeroplane, flying at a fairly high altitude,
passed overhead. It did not bear the markings of any allied force
and I assumed that it must have been sent by this ship, which as-
sumption was later proved to be correct.

'After darkness we could see the full lights blazing from the ship.
This was an extraordinary spectacle, accustomed as I had been for
the past few years to black-outs and I could not, at the time, fathom
the reason why this ship was so exceptional.

By sunset the *Albuquerque* had rescued 122 men. The sun set at 6 pm
and the two lifeboats and the motor launch continued searching in
the darkness before they would be ordered back at 7.30 pm.

Alda's waving had failed to attract the rescue ship. 'By nightfall we
had given up hope, when suddenly a boat came up beside us. That
was after 36 hours. We were taken on the boat and they looked
around for more survivors, but there were none. They then took us
on board the ship and to the hospital ward.

'They didn't know I was a woman because my hair was plastered
down. The oil and tar burned us badly.' The oil-soaked clothing
was stripped off the survivors. 'While they were busy cleaning us up
with brandy they discovered that I was a woman.

'Then I was taken to a cabin and looked after beautifully. I was given a gown and a bowl of soup. I asked if a child had been picked up. It was difficult to make them understand, as I didn't speak Portuguese, but with a mixture of Italian and English they got the message. Those survivors who had seen us on the ship knew what I was talking about. The reply was "No".'

The *Albuquerque* turned on its two searchlights and swept the ocean throughout the night. By midnight six more survivors had been picked up, then the search was stopped for the night

Herman and his fellow survivors faced another night at sea, 'In the meantime the one Italian who had been picked up was in a very bad state. He was now delirious and attempted to drink sea water, which I prevented, and so the second night closed on us.

'It was wet, it was cold, some of us were sick, some were becoming lightheaded and we were all still covered in oil. I was already developing sores from the buffeting and the rubbing of my naked skin on the raft and these marks I still bear as a memento.

'The memory of Robert Louis Stevenson's description of the sufferings and discomfort of the principal person in his book *Kidnapped*, a set work at school, brought home to me then how graphically and truthfully he had written this story. I had plenty of time to contemplate. I can only say that we all went through similar experiences, probably worse.

'It was impossible to sleep and if you did fall into a doze, you were sharply awakened by a wave pounding on your back. We prayed for the dawn, for then at least the raft could be manoeuvred so that we were in the trough of the waves. Against the waves they almost succeeded in tilting the raft completely over.

Monday 30 November

Davidson lost one of his companions, 'The sea was hellishly rough all this time, and on Sunday night we lost another man. His name was Jan and he was washed off the cover during the night. When dawn came there were only two of us left of the original five – myself and a young South African called Koosie.'

The search was resumed at dawn and at 9.50 am a large raft was spotted. When seen the previous day it had 15 men aboard, but then held only 12. They were taken aboard.

George Kennaugh sat on his raft in a stupor. 'Then, on Monday morning, we sighted a ship's flag on the horizon. It was the *Afonso de Albuquerque*. We learned later that the sloop had been picking up survivors since Sunday evening.

'I had been in the water 40 hours when the *Afonso* arrived but, probably through exhaustion, was calm – even indifferent. A couple of men on the raft stood and waved excitedly and fell into the ocean. We pulled them clear. Despite heavy seas the crew of the ship hauled us on board, one by one, with the aid of a rope.

'We were given coffee, brandy and blankets. Several times during the rescue the crew had to use hooks to drive off the sharks.

A raft holding three South Africans was seen. The raft had been designed to carry six and at one stage 13 South Africans had been aboard. One of the three to survive was Sgt Henry Gierke, whose half-paralysed body had to be lifted off the raft by the Portuguese. Captain de Brito took a photograph of them on the raft and a copy was later given to Gierke.

Nat Herman's group had been missed in the dark. 'Our torch petered out during the night. Had it kept alight, I think there might have been a reasonable chance of our being seen and saved. The ship had disappeared and in the daylight there was absolutely no sign of it whatsoever.

'The following day we had another ration of water, carrying out the same procedure as before. By now it was becoming increasingly difficult to swallow. Our sharks were still with us. The sick Italian was now unconscious. He had been mumbling words in German and Italian and a little while later he died. He was next to me.

'I discussed as best I could with one of the Italians, who spoke a few words in broken English, what we were to do. As I was no companion for a dead man and he was no companion for me, we decided there was no alternative but to consign the body to the deep, where the sharks promptly seized it and bore it below the surface.

'One raft, which had been near us during our two and a half days on the water and seemed to be drifting in the same current, carried about the same number of Italians as that on which I was. This raft also had two South Africans. At times we kept within speaking distance and at other times drifted away altogether. Eventually, however, we lost sight of this raft.

'At about 10 o'clock in the morning of the third day I saw a ship again. The ship appeared to be very much closer than the one seen the day before and was moving slowly about the ocean from one place to another. I was completely satisfied now that it was picking up survivors.

'Gradually we drifted or the ship came nearer and finally it was so close that it could be identified and I saw that it was a Portuguese man-of-war. It left us alone and went somewhere else. The Italians began cursing, because they thought that we were now being abandoned, but as I had insisted on the waving of their shirts for at least half an hour as an SOS signal, I was sure that we had been seen.'

Herman's raft was then spotted. According to Ratcliff, 'A lookout now spotted the last big raft; it was flying a blue shirt as a pathetic flag of appeal. At the same time another lookout sighted a small raft with two men aboard. Which first? This time, with the sea growing rougher by the minute, De Brito decided in favour of the greater number and picked up the 17 aboard the big raft.'

Nat Herman was thrilled. 'The ship turned back, approached us and stopped and I saw that she was waiting for us to drift a couple of hundred yards towards her and so we did, running right up against the side of the ship. For the second time I took off my discs before going on board. This time I threw them into the sea. I had had these discs ever since I had left the Union, but did not want to become an internee. There was no means of identification in my naked state.

'I did not know my legal position on being found in mid-ocean, or whether I should actually be subject to internment, nor did I know who had been saved. As we were later told, the Portuguese had received a message, either through Lisbon or Lourenço Marques, from the submarine commander some 18 hours after the *Nova Scotia* had been sunk. This was to enable them to pick up the Italians. The ship only arrived at the scene of the sinking 18 hours later. It was about 185 miles from Lourenço Marques. It was yet another day before we were found. The aeroplane we had seen was from the ship.

'On getting on board I found a number of survivors. I asked whether the South African, who had been with me, had been picked up. I was told that he had not yet been, but that they would

Life-jacketed survivors on a small raft watch for sharks (*RK*).

110

keep a look-out for him. An hour or so later, whilst I was lying on a table in the sickbay, I was told that he had been saved. He was the last man to be picked up. Although the ship cruised round for several hours, not a sign was seen of any other survivors.

Alda woke from a sleep of utter exhaustion late in the morning. Fortunately the captain was a small man and she was given a shirt and a pair of shorts of his to wear. To her despair there was still no news of Valcheria being picked up.

The rescue of the last survivors was recorded by Ratcliff, 'At 1.20 pm the small raft, carrying an Englishman [sic South African] and an Italian, was spotted again. When *Albuquerque* had turned away from them hours earlier to go to the big raft, the Italian had given up and dived overboard. The Englishman swam after him and dragged him back.

'Now, safe aboard the rescue ship, the Italian thanked his saviour effusively. The Englishman replied: "In the water we were both human beings struggling to keep alive. Now I am once more an Englishman and you are an Italian. We are enemies." With that he turned and walked away.

Staff-sergeant C J Smit was then rescued, 'As far as I can remember, I was the second last person to be picked up. I think that a chap called Middleton was the last. I spent three days in the sea before being picked up. I can vividly recall seeing the lights of the search ships each night. We called out, but the wind was blowing against us, and I suppose our voices were just drowned out.

'Eventually we were picked up by the Portuguese frigate, *Afonso De Albuquerque*. The captain had been taking pictures of the survivors in the water, and I have a full set of these. Some of them show me and former Sergeant H Gierke.

'Captain de Brito reached another difficult decision at 4 pm. A bad storm was brewing and hope of further rescue seemed remote. Moreover, he had the immediate responsibility of getting dozens of sick people to hospital as quickly as possible. With 183 survivors aboard, he headed for port.'

One more rescue was to take place. According to Davidson, 'Koosie passed away on Monday afternoon. It was about one or two o'clock when I noticed he was dead, and I was all alone. By that time I had completely given up all hope of being saved. But on Monday evening I saw the lights of a ship, and a Portuguese cruiser rescued me and took me and other survivors to Lourenço Marques.'

Herman summed up the results of the rescue, 'In all, 42 South Africans had been saved out of 134. I was the 41st and the last but one survivor to be picked up. One woman had also been saved and over 100 Italians. Nearly 750 people had lost their lives. We were extremely well treated by the Portuguese sailors, whose sympathies were openly with us.

Eric Manson was still adrift. The two sharks had disappeared from underneath his driftwood early on Monday morning, but a new peril awaited him, 'My skin was peeling off by this time and I was beginning to lose all concept of time and space.

'I saw an aeroplane fly overhead once and I think I saw a ship on the horizon, though this may have been my imagination, which was starting to play tricks on me. Eventually the glare coming off the sea blinded me. Everything turned white and I couldn't distinguish between sea and sky.'

Tuesday 1 November

The *Albuquerque* docked in Lourenço Marques at 10 am. Most of the survivors could walk ashore, but dozens had to be carried.

George Kennaugh recalled their reception at Lourenço Marques. 'The next day we landed at Lourenço Marques. Sandwiches were spread on tables near the quay and a field kitchen supplied hot coffee and wine.

'The death toll was estimated at 750. The survivors numbered 190. But for those who did live, the memories of that ordeal will endure forever.'

For Eric Manson the ordeal was not yet over, 'Day and night seemed to come and go without my knowing which was which. Then I suddenly felt hands under my armpits and felt myself being lifted up. I was rescued by a British destroyer that had been sent out to look for the U-boat which had torpedoed the *Nova Scotia*.

'As I lay recovering in the hospital room of the destroyer I heard depth-charges going off as the destroyer hunted the U-boat. I thought I'd have to go through it all again, and my nerves just went to pieces.'

It was to take some months before he got his eyesight back to normal. While recuperating at the Potchefstroom military hospital Manson was told by the military authorities that he had been the last man to be picked up.

Nat Herman realised how lucky they had been. 'The following day we were landed at Lourenço Marques and "put in the bag".

'Most, if not all, were in a shocking state of collapse. Many of the men went through far more suffering than I did and in greater discomfort, but fortunately they had been picked up 12 or 18 hours earlier. In Portuguese territory we were kindly treated until we got successfully away, but that is another story. Some of the South Africans returned to see further action in Italy, or to service within the union.

'The oil took nearly 14 days to remove and it was months, even years, before I recovered completely from the shock, exposure and resultant ill effects. I got home after some further discomfort and returned to duty in the Union about three and a half months later.'

Alda Ignisti (*AT*).

Alda became a celebrity. 'News had reached Lourenço Marques that there was one woman survivor on board. When we docked there were hundreds of people on the quayside calling for me.

'The difficulty was getting me ashore without being seen. We eventually made it from the lower deck. We were whisked into a car and taken to the South African Consul's home, where I was bathed and changed and given some clothes. I was moved from one house to another to avoid reporters.

'I was very badly bruised and my skin horribly burnt from the sun and oil. I tried not to look at myself in the mirror, but in spite of it all I was in fairly good shape. I visited some of the survivors in hospital, asking all of them if they had seen my child, but I had no luck.

'The Portuguese were wonderful and did all they could to help me. Clothes and money were sent to me. After a few days it was felt that something else had to be done. The consul, Mr Scanlan, therefore organised a cocktail party at his home and invited some Portuguese dignitaries. I had to be present and after the Portuguese had seen the state I was in they also decided to do something about me.

'A picnic was arranged close to the South African border. We had lunch and after I was shown the way, I walked over the hills to the border, which really was not very far. I arrived at Komatipoort where I was met by people who expected me. A train was waiting. I was ushered into a compartment and locked in so that no one could reach me. I had VIP treatment all the way and eventually arrived in Pretoria, where I met up with some of my family.'

During the week following the sinking of the *Nova Scotia*, 120 bodies were swept by the inshore current onto Durban's beaches. On 4 December bodies were found at sea and brought to Durban. More bodies were driven onto the beaches over long stretches of the Natal and Zululand coast.

On Monday 7 December an Italian prisoner-of-war was found on Mtunzini Beach, Zululand, wearing only a pair of underpants. He was suffering from shock and exposure, having spent seven days and nights at sea on a raft without food and water.

The interned South Africans had Malcolm Muggeridge to thank for their subsequent escape from Mozambique. The mission of the later editor of *Punch* was to get information about British convoys sailing to North Africa up the Mozambique Channel and where they were being torpedoed.

When Muggeridge was posted to Mozambique as an unlikely Intelligence Officer he didn't know where the place was. 'I did, in point of fact, read up the entry in the *Encyclopaedia Britannica* on Mozambique, and learnt – it is the solitary fact remaining with me – that Gladstone could have bought it off the Portuguese for a million pounds, but decided the price was too high.

'His parsimony was ill-judged; it would have been a good buy, Delagoa Bay providing an excellent harbour, which Durban notably lacks.'

His first impression of Lourenço Marques 'was of a rather run-down Mediterranean resort with bathing beaches, picture post-cards, souvenirs, cafes, restaurants and, at night, cabarets and casinos; except that the sun was hotter and the air more humid.'

At the Polana Hotel, overlooking the sea, he was able to observe his opposite numbers – the German Consul-General, Leopold Wertz, and the Italian Consul-General, Campini, who were totally different in appearance and temperament. Wertz was 'blonde and pink and spectacled and earnest' whereas Campini was large and theatrical. given to 'extravagant gestures and rhetorical flourishes'.

Muggeridge later learned from captured Abwehr archives documents that he had been portrayed as an 'intrepid spymaster with a chain of agents, extending over the whole of Southern Africa', whom Wertz was nonetheless able to pulverise. To this Muggeridge said, 'Diplomats and intelligence agents, in my experience, are even bigger liars than journalists, and the historians who try to reconstruct the past out of records are, for the most part, dealing in fantasy.'

The British Consul General and members of his staff treated Muggeridge 'as a kind of pampered interloper whose activities were not to be taken seriously.' Equipped with his typewriter, code-book, invisible inks and cash he was assigned to try and stop the enemy from 'getting information about our convoys sailing to North Africa up the Mozambique Channel, where they were being torpedoed by German submarines.'

A long, coded telegram from double-agent Kim Philby, then in MI6, told him that he should try to infiltrate the Campini apparat rather than the Wertz one, 'since the personality of Campini, to judge from his boastful, high-flown style, seemed the more vulnerable of the two.'

Muggeridge prowled about the hotel corridors and peered in through windows 'though the only discovery I made was that Dr Wertz wore a hair-net in the privacy of his room – an interesting, but scarcely significant item of intelligence.'

As a British secret agent he recalled the damage wrought by the

German submarines, 'This was happening on a large scale, greatly assisted by the ease with which a message could be sent from Durban to Lourenço Marques, giving details of allied shipping passing through the port. The task was daunting and I scarcely knew where to begin, seeing I had no local contacts and my knowledge of Portuguese was sketchy to say the least.'

Muggeridge was able to bribe a senior Lourenço Marques police official, Inspector Y, who proved to be well worth his pay. The British Consulate arranged for the South Africans to be taken to Swaziland, then a British colony, and the Inspector was able to ensure 'that there were no traffic hold-ups and misadventures along the way'.

He reported that all troops aboard the *Nova Scotia* had disappeared without trace in shark-infested seas. 'At the Consulate-General we heard of the catastrophe and I went along with the rest of the staff to receive the survivors when they came ashore, wet and shivering and bewildered; some of them, especially the lascars, babbling incomprehensively and letting out strange, anguished howls which merged with the cries of the scavenger birds the scene had attracted.

'It was an eerie spectacle; a moonless night, pitch-black, the sea stormy and, apart from flickering lights, only the white of the breakers to be seen as they came roaring in.

'The survivors, as belligerants landing in a neutral country, had to be turned over to the Mozambique authorities and put in the Assistencia Publica, a place of such squalid horror that even rebellious seamen planning to desert to Lourenço Marques, after a sight of it, returned meekly to their ships and the boatswain's whistle.'

Muggeridge managed to get a message to the South Africans, 'If they would arrange to take a stroll along the road to the Swaziland frontier on a particular Sunday afternoon, I'd hope to have some cars going in the same direction and would stop and give them a lift.'

He sought the assistance of the South African business community in Lourenço Marques, but they resisted, fearing trouble with the authorities which might damage their businesses.

It was the taxi-drivers of Lourenço Marques who eventually saved the day. 'By chance' about 10 taxis happened to be driving in the direction of Swaziland that day. The South Africans were given a lift by them to the frontier 80 kilometres away.

Muggeridge recalled their arrival in South Africa, 'In no time they were in Mbabane, the capital of Swaziland, and thence whisked away to Johannesburg and home. The taxi-drivers would accept no more money than the normal fare, though the risk they ran was far greater than the South African businessmen would have had to face.

'It is true, of course, that, thanks to Inspector Y, the risk was far less than they supposed, but I doubt if they knew this. I really believed they would have done the job for nothing, so delighted were they to have a chance to serve the allied cause.

'Thenceforth they were all my firm friends. Years later, when I was banned from entering the Union of South Africa, the story of the escape of the interned soldiers was resurrected in the South African press. I was very happy to learn that some of those who took the Swaziland road had survived the war and remembered their deliverance from the Assistencia Publica.'

As regards his performance as an Intelligence Agent in Lourenço Marques, Muggeridge concluded, 'It looked so much better in telegrams than when actually happening . . . was considered to have been impressive and earned me a certain prestige.'

According to Ratcliff the 14 survivors of the 114 of *Nova Scotia's* crew were free to leave Mozambique when well enough to travel, and went by train to Durban. 'As combatants the South Africans were subject to internment, but the Portuguese put no severe obstacles in their way to freedom across the nearby Transvaal border.

'Surrounded by enemy territory, the Italians had nowhere to go. Given a small allowance by their government, they settled down to live the pleasant life of the town, getting jobs to supplement their income.

'For most of them the homeward journey did not begin until 1946; several had long been thought dead by wives and relatives. A few decided to stay in Lourenço Marques.

As far as Vic Davidson could recall, there were 14 British troops who survived, more than 100 Italian prisoners and 23 South Africans, ten of whom were badly injured and taken to a Portuguese hospital. The other 13 were interned in a Lourenço Marques barracks. The South African Consul and two other South Africans – one of them a woman – visited the Springboks in hospital.

'The woman warned us that Lourenço Marques was full of enemy spies and that we should talk to nobody. The Portuguese themselves were wonderful to us, especially the sailors. I will never forget that were it not for them I would not be here today.'

He then told of the escape of the South Africans, 'We were told in secret by a South African that arrangements were being made to get us back home. On the ninth day after our arrival in Lourenço Marques I was told by a South African woman that an attempt would be made that night to get the uninjured South African troops out of Mozambique.

'She told me that the 13 uninjured men would give a party that night for the Portuguese who had saved them, and that during the party the 13 men would "do a duck" and make for the Lourenço

Marques museum, where apparently a number of taxis would be waiting to take them away.

'I was told that those of us in hospital would have to try to make our break the following night. Each of us was given a little card with the number of a bus on it. I remember that it was bus number two. When the time arrived we were to board this bus to the museum and present our cards to taxi drivers near there.

'The next day, our 10th in Lourenço Marques, we were told that we had to make it out that night. It was our last chance and if we did not take it we would probably remain in internment for the rest of the war. We were told that it was up to us to find some way of getting out of the hospital and into the town, where we would be able to catch the bus to the museum about 10 pm, as arranged. The other 13 had successfully made their escape the night before, we learned.

'Getting out of the hospital was not easy.' At that stage Davidson was able to move about on the arm of a helper, dragging one leg. His group devised a ruse whereby they asked the doctor for permission to visit a town barber as a group.

'The doctor said he didn't think two of us were well enough to leave the hospital – myself and another man. But eventually he agreed that we could all go, provided a male nurse accompanied us. At exactly 9.45 pm we hit the breeze. We asked the first person we saw outside the nightclub where to catch the number 2 bus. We boarded the bus, got off at the museum and saw the taxis.

'I went up to one and showed the driver my little card. In two taxis we were driven to a club in Lourenço Marques where we found the woman who had helped us before, and her husband. We spent the night there and at dawn the two taxis called to take us away.

'We were all wearing civilian clothes bought for us by local South Africans. We drove to the border of Swaziland, where we saw the British flag flying and a Swaziland policeman waiting for us with a three ton truck. We were just about home.'

On 6 December, 1942, 35 South Africans and two Englishmen, one a seaman and the other a medical dispenser, were handed over to the British authorities, then taken to Ermelo. They were: Sapper I W Bass, 24, of Springs; L/Cpl A P Biccard, 46, of Parow; Sapper J E Carstens, 45, of Woodstock; Pte B N Cheswell, 41, of Johannesburg; Cpl M G P Claase, 29, of Krugersdorp; Sapper V C Davidson, 29, Johannesburg; Sapper C M Dempers 45, Noorder Paarl; Bdr D E Erasmus, 38, of Potchefstroom; Gunner P R Frylinck, 30, of Ferndale; Sgt H R W Gierke, 41, Johannesburg; Pte R C Harburn, 36, Volksrust; L/Bdr J A Herman, 38, of Pietersburg; Pte R E Hill, 24, of Witbank; Pte D M Hodgkinson, 31, East London; Gunner E C Hunter, 19, Discovery; Pte P B James, 30, Elgin; W H Johnson, 32, Cape Town; Cpl G Kennaugh, 36, Johannesburg; Driver S C Knutsen,

37, East London; Sgnr L J Liebenberg, 20, Johannesburg; Sapper J
H Mathews, 36, Roodepoort; Pte W T Middenwick, 26, Escourt; Pte
C J Meyer, 24, Middelburg, Tvl; Sapper D D Mahoney, 25,
Liebenberg, Tvl; Trooper J C Parton, 54, Johannesburg; Driver
Jakobus Pieterse, 23, Nylstroom; Cpl W H Rachman, 35, Pretoria;
Spr H V Retief, 42, Moorreesburg; Gunner P J J Snyman, 23,
Johannesburg; Gunner G E Stevenson, 46, Springs; L/Sgt M Summer-
ville, 35, Durban; L/Sgt C J Smit, 22, Johannesburg; Driver W L
Tredennick, 29, Wynberg, Cape; Pte G J van Tonder, 46, Riversdale;
and Pte T M Warren, 22, Benoni.

The two Britons with them were Seaman Brian Buchanan, 21, of
Glasgow and Sgt-Dispenser Holland, 27, of Mansfield, Nottinghamshire.

Malcolm Muggeridge ensured that the taxi drivers weren't victimised:
'It was not really a hazardous operation at all; the Portuguese I
think, were really only too glad to see the last of their unwanted
guests, and when the Germans made their inevitable protest the
blame was put on the British Consulate-General.

'All the same, the taxi-drivers took a decided risk; not, let me
add, for money. They had a deep, abiding loathing of the Nazis and
all their works and were overjoyed to have an opportunity to express
it. I think of them with affection, gratitude and admiration.'

News reaches Asmara

Captain Taylor had no idea of what had happened. 'For a time,
perhaps ten days to a fortnight, I heard nothing more. Nor did I
expect to hear anything because communications in wartime were
not easy. But one evening Frank McFadzean came into the Mess
with a very serious face, which was quite unlike him because we
were usually rather cheerful, and taking me on one side said, "Bob,
I've got some bad news."

' "Oh!' said I, not guessing at what might follow, "What's that?"
He said that the *Nova Scotia* had been torpedoed and the loss of life
was very heavy. There was nothing I could do, but I had good
friends and in the course of the next couple of days, news was
received through security channels that some 100 people had been
picked up from the *Nova Scotia*, including a single woman.

'Just one woman survivor out of the whole ship's complement. It
took me some weeks longer to discover that that woman was Alda
and some time after that before I learned her story.

'Back in Asmara, of course, I knew nothing about all this [the
details of Alda's escape]. My sole piece of information was that she
was safe and in Lourenço Marques. Then what I had been expect-
ing for some time, which was the real reason I had sent her back to
South Africa, happened. Posting orders came through transferring
me to another country.

'I had hoped that my next move would take me somewhere nearer the fighting, but this was not to be. Other people in OETA had the same idea and although I was quite senior in rank, I was the junior of those who had the right to make these decisions.

'What had happened was that the chief man in Nairobi managed to get himself posted back into the Western Desert. This left a vacancy for a top man in Nairobi, which the man in Somalia was transferred to fill. This left a vacancy in Mogadishu which somebody from British Somaliland was sent to fill. This left a vacancy in British Somaliland and I was sent to fill that, this time with the rank of major.

'I stayed in Hargeisa, British Somaliland, for seven or eight months and then the game of transfer started all over again. This time I was sent down to Mogadishu, but by this time I had re-established proper contact with Alda. She was living with her mother in Durban and picking up the threads of her old life again.

'Despite enquiries and a great deal of newspaper interest in her story nothing was ever heard again of Valcheria and it must be assumed that she perished at sea with the lifeboat she was in.

'There was one good thing about my moves from Asmara: all of them were in a southerly direction. If they were taking me further away from the war they were taking me nearer to Alda. My posting to Mogadishu took me only some 500–600 miles away from Nairobi, which in its turn was only about 1,800 miles away from Johannesburg. We were making progress.

'We kept up a voluminous correspondence and I asked her to marry me. Before this could be done we had to change her nationality again. She had been British, but on marriage to an Italian she had lost that nationality and become an Italian. It was quite impossible for me to marry an enemy citizen during the war.

'Alda, therefore, had to go through the process of re-naturalising herself in South Africa and this took a little time. Eventually the formalities were completed and she became a British citizen and a citizen of South Africa once again.

'The way was now clear, but there was still a considerable distance between us and how was this to be bridged? Obviously one way was ruled out – that was by sea. The coast was still dangerous and nothing would have persuaded her to embark on another ship at that time.

'There was a long and very difficult overland route through Southern Rhodesia and Northern Rhodesia and the Belgian Congo by a combination of rail and river steamers, up through Lake Tanganyika and eventually to Nairobi, but this was not a journey to be attempted by a lone woman. One day she hit upon the idea of flying and asked her mother whether it would be all right. Of course, her mother had no idea at all whether it would be all right, or all wrong, but she agreed that it was worth a try.

'There was at that time a little airline called RANA, Rhodesian and National Airways or Air Services. It flew little eight-seater De-Havilland Rapide Biplanes and it was finally organised that Alda would take a trip in one of these to Nairobi. While she was doing that, I would take some leave and wait for her to arrive in Nairobi.

'So, one morning she pitched up at the appointed hour at Germiston airport, near Johannesburg, to catch this small aircraft. Unfortunately, someone had overbooked it and she had to give up her seat to a small schoolboy returning to school in Nairobi. There was no way in which she could tell me this. I met the plane on arrival in Nairobi and she was not on it. I thought she had changed her mind.

'There were only two flights a week and three days later I had a message from Nairobi Airport to say there was a young lady there looking for me. This was Alda. She had managed to get on the next plane. Let me explain that this journey was not like flying from Johannesburg to Nairobi today, in a matter of four or five hours. This little aircraft took three days and they stopped twice overnight *en route*.

Robert Taylor and Alda Ignisti are married (*A Taylor*).

'We were married in Nairobi at the District Commissioner's office on 16 May 1944. After a short honeymoon at the Outspan Hotel at Nyeri, I took her back with me to Mogadishu overland. The trip took five and a half days and we slept in the bush on camp beds, under the stars each night. We got there without undue difficulty and there we remained for about a year.

'I was then transferred to Nairobi as the man in charge of OETA finances in East Africa with the rank of full colonel. Of course she came with me. After a short while in that job I was transferred to Cairo in a similar capacity for the Middle East Command. On this occasion Alda went home and stayed with her family until such time as I could send for her.

'This took a little time, but she joined me at the end of 1945 and our daughter, Valerie, was born in Cairo in July, 1946. I chose the name Valerie for her, because it was the nearest sounding name to Valcheria, who had been lost. I used to tell Alda she was a replacement for her.

'It was now peacetime and thought had to be given to our post-war existence. I was a civil servant and all the time I had been in the army my job in the home civil service had been kept for me. Indeed, in those early days when I was only a bombardier, or something like that, the civil service made up the difference between army pay and my civilian pay, which came in very useful. I didn't greatly fancy going back to the home civil service and this is the beginning of another story.

'If, as was the case, Britain was told to administer another country's colonies, naturally she set about the job in exactly the same way as she administered her own colonies. All these Italian colonies of Eritrea, Cyrenaica, Tripolitania and the Dodecanese Islands were being run by the end of the war in exactly the same way as numerous British colonies such as Kenya.

'For the last few years I had been closely involved in the administration of all these Italian territories and in the process had become known to quite a number of people in the colonial office, who were supervising and helping what we were doing.

'I had acquired not only a knowledge of British colonial methods, but also a taste for them, and before I was demobilised I wrote to the colonial office, offering my services in some suitable capacity in a civilian role. After I had returned to England at the beginning of 1947 with Alda and Valerie, I received an offer from the colonial office to go to Fiji for two years as the economic adviser to that government.

'Conditions at that time in Britain were very poor indeed. We had no house of our own, no furniture worth talking about, the winter was bitterly cold and the shops were empty of anything to buy, although we had quite a lot of ration coupons and quite a bit of money to spend.

'On receipt of this letter I said to Alda, "Alda, would you like to go to Fiji?" Without batting an eyelid she said, "Yes" and then paused for a moment and added, "Where is it?" And so in April 1947 we set sail from Tilbury Docks on the Shaw Savill boat *Waiwera*, bound for Auckland, New Zealand, via the Panama Canal. After a while in Auckland we managed to get on a flying boat, which took us to Suva in Fiji, where I took up my new job.

'The following year the colonial office invited me to become Financial Secretary of Fiji and asked me to agree to being trans-

The author's wife, Barbara, with Lady Taylor in London in November 1992.

ferred permanently from the Home Service to the Colonial Service. This I gladly did and that is how Alda and I started out life together in the colonial service, which was to take us after four more years in Fiji to Lusaka in Northern Rhodesia and to Salisbury in Southern Rhodesia – but the rest of the tale is pretty well documented and very well known and there is no need to enlarge on it here.'

Robert and Alda Taylor later moved to Northern Rhodesia, where he was financial secretary. After federation they lived in Rhodesia for 15 years. Taylor was created a CB, then knighted in 1962 as a KMG. From 1976–83 he was chairman of Thomas Tilling and lived in London. He died in January 1985. Lady Taylor has continued living in her London apartment and visits her sister in Johannesburg annually.

In concluding his article Ratcliff wrote, 'Captain de Brito of the rescue ship, a retired vice-admiral, later lived in Lisbon. Kapitänleutnant Gysae became a captain on the naval staff of the West German Ministry of Defence in Bonn.

'*Albuquerque*, the ship of mercy, met a sad fate. In an incident off Goa in December 1961, she was scuttled by her crew.'

According to one of the defenders of Goa the *Albuquerque* had been on her last rescue mission. Permitted to take food to the starving garrison she had been going dead slow in the approaches when guns opened up and at point-blank range blew her to pieces. Captain de Brito was among the survivors.

George Kennaugh in later years (*RK*).

Nat Herman practised law in Germiston, where he was knocked over by a car in November 1963 and killed. He is buried in the West Park cemetery. In 1969 Vic Davidson was working as a mechanic in Durban, while Eric Manson lived on an army pension in Richmond, Johannesburg. Smit became a driver with a firm of road tanker operators. George Kennaugh was killed in May 1989, when run down by a motor car.

Whatever the eventual fates of the survivors of the *Nova Scotia*, while they lived they would never forget the horrors they had experienced in the worst sea disaster ever off South Africa's coast.

CHAPTER 6 Order out of Chaos

The U-177 was to sink another transport two days after the *Nova Scotia*. Thanks to her having sent distress signals and having launched more boats the loss of life would be considerably less than the *Nova Scotia*.

Llandaff Castle:

30 November 1942

The 10 786 ton *Llandaff Castle* was an intermediate steamer built by the Workman Clark yard at Belfast in 1927. Almost identical to the second *Llandovery Castle*, she was the only Union-Castle liner to be built at that yard. The main differences were that the *Llandaff Castle* had more open deck rails and more promenade space due to the stowage of boats and disposition of the ventilating cowls.

The *Llandaff Castle* was 471 feet by 62 feet and her twin screws could push her to a speed of $13\frac{1}{2}$ knots. During the war she was used on the run from Durban to the Middle East and back. On her previous voyage she had run aground at Massawa and after being towed free by tugs had picked up commandos at Mombasa for the invasion of Madagascar.

Vic Harms, 23, was a chef on board who recalled that the soldiers each carried a red umbrella, yellow scarf and a bag of hand grenades. 'I learnt that the umbrellas would be opened after the landing and, holding onto the scarves between them, the commandos would guide aircraft to targets. The ship's captain, Captain Castle, died and was buried in northern Madagascar.' Harms was one of his pall-bearers.

One of his Durban Light Infantry assistants in the galley was a chartered accountant and nephew of Sir Robert Gibbs, chairman of the Union Castle line. Unused to the coal stoves in such ships, he penned the following lines about his position:

> We board the Llandaff Castle and sailed away up north
> What trials and tribulations will destiny bring forth
> No sooner had we left the shores when loudly came the shout
> Fatigues, fatigues my merry men, what's all this sitting about
> Headquarters Number one platoon, you always fear for dirt
> Report to the galley and the chef, you will not need a shirt
> Down to the bowels of the Llandaff we wandered as were bid
> It wasn't cool down there, like hell without a lid
> Some started peeling spuds and beans until they felt too sick
> My mate and I were assigned to a chap called Vic
> He was not too bad a lad, nor Bob, nor Slip, nor Slim
> Old Charlie, he was a lad alright, but now we come to him
> Him was the big white chief, that walked around all day

123

They gave you jobs to follow jobs, but no one dared to say a nay
Once we had settled down and got on sea dog's legs
Vic Harms broke the news to us, the troops got scrambled eggs
No sooner had we started to break this fruit – a 1,000 more or less
I began to wish that I was Hess
When I joined up long, long ago men were in my employ
But now to aid democracy, I work as a larder boy.

Vic Harms (*VH*).

Harms came from the Isle of Sheppy, near the mouth of the Thames in Kent, was married to Alice and had two sons and a daughter. Early in the war he had been caught in a London blitz and when he arrived at his ship, the *Dunbar Castle,* he found that one moored in front and one behind had been sunk. They sailed in convoy shortly afterwards.

As a tourist pantryman at the time, he was below the watermark when the ship hit a magnetic mine. 'Everything was dark and I couldn't find my way out. The water was rising rapidly when I saw someone with a torch ahead and thanked my lucky stars as I made my way out. Then I saw that it was the cook, who had been set alight by the stove. I got out by the companion way with the water up to my chest and within 10 minutes she was gone.'

When she left Suez the *Llandaff Castle* carried 400 Greek passengers besides some troops. The Greeks were islanders from Khios who had been displaced during the war and had wandered throughout the Middle East. They were then *en route* to Tanganyika to make a new life.

When the ship called at Mombasa she took on more passengers, mainly from the Far East. The Greeks then disembarked at Dar-es-Salaam. The *Llandaff Castle* then had aboard 280 crew and passengers, some of whom had been evacuated from Singapore to Ceylon, where, after the blitz they sailed for Africa.

Corporal Harry Brotton, 22, of the Prince of Wales Volunteer Regiment, sailed from Greenock, Scotland, on 23 March, 1942, to Madagascar, where a combined operation landing took place on 5 May. During the Battle for Diego Suarez he was blown up by a Vichy mortar, then evacuated by hospital ship to Mombasa General Hospital.

'From there I was sent to Nairobi to recuperate', Brotton recalled, 'I stayed there for three weeks, then returned to Mombasa by train and embarked on the *Llandaff Castle* on 19 November. It was bringing officers' wives and children from Egypt. Also on board were Italian women and children being shipped from Somalia to Zanzibar, where they disembarked. Some of us slept on deck.'

The Greek steamer *Cleanthis* was attacked by a Japanese submarine on the morning of 30 November, about 190 miles north of Lourenço

124

Marques. The ship was shelled and machine-gunned and her captain, Stiros Kavanzis, was killed. When the crew took to the boats they were machine-gunned. After 53 hours afloat 22 of them, 13 of whom were wounded, were eventually picked up 90 miles north of Lourenço Marques.

That day the voyage of the *Llandaff Castle* was uneventful, nevertheless a sharp watch was kept from the bridge. At sunset the officer on watch saw a trail of bubbles heading towards the ship from the west. The wheel was hastily turned to port but before the ship could respond a torpedo slammed into the starboard side.

The ship heeled over to port, then slowly righted itself as oil poured from its ruptured tanks. According to the Rand Daily Mail, 'The 10 786-ton vessel keeled over, then righted herself, and the passengers began taking to the boats.'

Harry Brotton knew that they had been mortally hit. 'On the 30th we had just had supper when two torpedoes hit the ship. It listed to one side, then two torpedoes hit the other side and seemed to tip the ship back.'

Harry Brotton (*HB*).

It was 7.30 pm and some of the passengers were having dinner. Among them were Mr and Mrs P Gleadell, who rushed to their cabin to fetch their children, two little girls and a baby boy of three months. They each grabbed a girl while a steward took the baby, then set off for their boat station.

The children remained calm and when being handed down into a boat the elder girl, aged four, smacked the ship's rail and said, 'Naughty boat, to break'. Once in the boat the Gleadells realised that the steward and baby were missing. Mr Gleadell climbed back onto the ship to look for them.

Vic Harms was in a quandary. 'I happened to be amidships and was undecided which way to run, fore or aft, so went forward into the mess. The port boats couldn't be lowered as she was listing too much to starboard. Numbers 1, 3 and 5 boats were out of action so I jumped out of No 5 and swam over to No 7 boat. All of the crew who jumped from the damaged boats were picked up. Number 7 boat now held 45 survivors, and had only 6″ of freeboard.'

Harry Brotton found himself in the same lifeboat, 'We abandoned ship and the women and children were taken off by the sun deck. I jumped about 20 feet from the deck into the sea. It was full of oil and my hair became caked with it. The U-boat then put another torpedo into the ship. I was then picked up by one of the lifeboats. I saw the ship's engineer swinging on a rope and banging his head on the side of the ship.'

'There was no panic,' according to the *Daily Mail*, 'and the boats got away in an orderly fashion. Some passengers climbed onto rafts and others swam to the boats. Ten minutes after the first torpedo had struck the starboard side there occurred a violent explosion to port.

'One survivor said that apparently the U-boat had changed position past the ship's bows in order to avoid the gun aft. "This explosion rocked our lifeboat which was alongside at the time," said the survivor, "and a huge cascade of water threatened to swamp us. Many were thrown overboard by the shock of the explosion and we had difficulty in picking them out of the water because of the fuel oil. Some jumped overboard."

'The second explosion struck No 3 hold, but even then the ship showed no sign of going down. Nobody expected the second explosion and when it occurred there was a wild scramble over the side by those who had remained on board.

'A few minutes later a third explosion caught the vessel amidships. This time she seemed to lift her stern for a few seconds. Then it settled. Her bows came up and she slid out of sight.'

The U-boat

According to Brotton, 'It took about three-quarters of an hour for the ship to sink. The ship went down stern first. Shortly afterwards the U-boat surfaced, then came to within 10–15 feet of us.

'They had a machine gun trained on us and one of their officers began shouting through a loud hailer. He called for the ship's captain, first officer and engineer. We lay on the bottom of the boat and kept quiet. Our crew consisted mainly of civvies serving in the merchant navy.

Vic Harms added, 'Dusk was falling as the U-177 surfaced alongside us. The commander wanted to know the name of the ship and where the captain was, but he got no reply from any of us. However, he did stop the sub's engines to allow us to drift by.'

The nearest person to the submarine was the *Llandaff Castle's* master, Captain C J Clutterbuck. He was on a sinking raft and when asked to come aboard shouted that he couldn't manoeuvre the raft. When asked the name and tonnage of the ship various voices shouted back, '*Queen Mary, Nonesuch, Arundel Castle*' and other unmentionable names.

The Rand Daily Mail reported a survivor's experience: 'By this time it was almost dusk', added the survivor. 'Suddenly, quite close, the U-boat surfaced, and what a whopper she was. I heard a voice call out in perfect English: "Come alongside". We made no move to do so, but apparently there was a raft alongside, and the survivors on it were asked the name of the ship and the tonnage.

'I believe somebody was asked what the survivors intended to do, and they replied: "Make for land as soon as possible." The U-boat's searchlight then flashed over each boat in turn. I thought that was the end and that the next moment we would be machine-gunned, but nothing like that happened.

'We heard the U-boat's motors start up, and she slipped quite soundlessly beneath the surface. There was nothing we could do after dark but hang about.'

The U-boat moved off towards the south-east and submerged. A flashlight on the ship's motor-boat then began flashing a morse signal, 'Come'. The boats converged on the light and then picked up those on rafts. The seven boats were tied together with their painters and drifted throughout the night.

The wireless room on the *Llandaff Castle* had been put out of action by the first torpedo, so no distress message had been sent. One of the lifeboats fortunately had a small emergency wireless transmitter and emergency signals were sent every half hour.

Dawn at sea

The sea was calm during the night, nevertheless two boats had drifted off. At dawn a heavy breeze and swell soon had the passengers feeling seasick. One of the five remaining boats held 50 people and all suffered from the cramped conditions.

The survivor continued, 'At dawn the next day the captain brought all the boats together and we were made fast to one another. One boat had an emergency radio aboard and signals were sent out every 30 minutes. The survivors did not suffer from hunger or thirst, for there were sufficient rations on board. The weather was mild at first, but later a heavy swell set in and many were seasick, while all suffered acutely from cramp owing to the confined quarters.'

The Gleadell's baby was then found. 'Early in the morning a three-month-old baby, which had become separated from its mother in the confusion, was located and handed over from boat to boat until it reached its mother, none-the-worse for its adventure.'

Captain Clutterbuck ordered the five remaining boats to set sail and the small convoy headed west, towards land. Rations of dry biscuits and water were handed out and in the heat of the day canvas awnings were erected to shade the women and children. The small boats sailed on and the transmitter sent out its half-hourly signal. This was picked up by naval craft off Durban, who sent an aircraft ahead to advise them that help was on its way.

The survivor recalled their first joyous sight of possible rescue, 'At about 4 pm a plane approached, causing much cheering for we were convinced we would be rescued before nightfall. We had been setting a course due west all day and were then in sight of land but this was still a long way off.

'By night, however, no rescue vessels were in sight so the captain ordered the boats to heave to, for it was not intended to approach the shore owing to uncertainty of what the landing conditions would be like. Moreover, in the dark the boats might have struck reefs or submerged rocks.

'At dawn the following day two rescue vessels were seen some distance astern, and the boats put back in that direction.'

They were picked up by a Royal Navy destroyer. Sailors in the rescue ship made clothes for the children, and one naval officer undid a parcel he had ready to take home and distributed powder and lipstick among the women.

According to the survivor, 'We were picked up, given hot baths and drinks and cared for extremely well before being landed at Durban where everything possible was done for us.

'Charity can be cold, but Durban's charity and kindness is as kind as its sunshine', two survivors agreed. They had been evacuated from Singapore, caught in the Ceylon "blitz" and torpedoed off Africa. "People have been unbelievably kind and generous and we will always be grateful to them." '

Mrs Gleadell, mother of the three-months-old baby, who also had two young girls, lost everything she had brought from India and Ceylon. She anxiously awaited news of her husband. The survivors were taken on a tour of the shopping centres and one Durban store gave Mrs Gleadell a layette for her baby son.

Then news was received that one of the missing lifeboats had been found. After being 68 hours adrift it was found by a naval vessel. Mr Gleadell was among the 25 survivors. He had missed the steward on the sinking *Llandaff Castle* and had eventually been forced to slide down a rope to the lifeboat. He burnt his hands in doing so and was hospitalised on reaching Durban.

The remaining boat In the last boat Brotton recalled what had happened after the U-boat submerged, 'We saw that other boats were roping themselves together. I took stock of our passengers, about 49, which included women and children. A cook with us who weighed 15 stone had been sunk in the Atlantic twice. We rowed a while then rigged the mast and hoisted the sail. It was night, so we put out a sea anchor and steered by the stars. We knew that if we went west we were bound to hit Africa somewhere.'

Vic Harms was also aboard. 'In spite of our efforts to keep two or three lifeboats together we were separated during the night by a heavy swell and as dawn broke we were on our own. For two nights and three days we battled continuously to bail sea water from the boat and keep it from sinking. The ship's quartermaster took control of our boat and was outstanding. The only life we saw was a coastguard plane which flashed a message none of us could understand.'

'There was a little girl who was unconscious in the boat. We wet her face and combed her hair and talked to her until she regained her senses.'

As their lifeboat approached the coast Brotton was party to a dispute. 'After a day we saw a river mouth and some thought that it might be the border between Mozambique and South Africa. Some of the soldiers wanted to go north, to be interned, whereas the women and children wanted to go south.'

The boat's commander decided to land south of the river mouth, so let the boat drift southwards on the Mozambique current. Harms recalled, 'We got our first sight of land on the third day, but the quartermaster decided not to try a landing as it would soon be dusk and we wouldn't be able to see a reef or rocks. It was only on the following morning that we were able to negotiate the coral reef and make a landing. I jumped overboard with the painter but found that the water was deeper than I had thought. Others followed and we pulled the heavy-laden boat ashore.'

Vic Harms and three of the fittest men then set off to find help. Harry Brotton was with the party that remained. 'We had eaten water biscuits and drank Nestlé milk, so had enough strength to begin walking. We saw a Zulu warrior in full regalia on top of a sand dune, who then disappeared. The children were placed in the sail between some oars and carried by us in turn.

'We walked for two days, then were seen by a passing aeroplane. They dropped us supplies by parachute and we were happy to find chocolate, corned beef and condensed milk in the packages. I was barefooted so suffered from thorns in my feet. After a long journey we arrived at an Indian's trading store. He telephoned the authorities and we were then trucked to Durban.'

Harms and his three companions got completely lost in the bush. 'Fortunately we had with us a Cape Coloured who spoke Zulu. We stumbled on some Zulu huts and were given some water in banana leaves and they made a shelter for us, where we slept that night.

'During the second night I was called by a black and saw about eight Zulus waiting for us. They then took us to a German mission station, where we were given tea and sweet-potatoes. I wrote a letter that we were four of 40 odd survivors and gave it to a Zulu messenger. We slept there that night.

The Zulus then gave us some familiar rations, which they admitted they had found at our deserted lifeboat. We had walked almost a complete circle. A police jeep then came and fetched us during the day. They had received my letter. As we pulled off the Zulus threw some dead chickens into the vehicle. They'd apparently overheard me saying that I'd like to wring the necks of the chickens I saw strutting around.

The policeman gave us some of his clothes, on the understanding that we'd return them. People came to greet us at the villages on the way southwards. We heard that the main party of 41 had passed that way and that they had all given the little girl toys and frocks. Apparently as they approached a village the sailors would take her frock off, so that the villagers would take pity on her and give her clothes!

'We were the last to reach Durban. I was met by my adopted family, Neil Dewar, his wife and three daughters. They had replaced my lost wardrobe and even had photographs taken of some I had given them, to replace the originals I had lost.

Bodies on the beaches

Harry Brotton was among those from the *Llandaff Castle* who received medical treatment. 'I was hospitalised and my feet treated, then released after a couple of days. Later, while walking along the beachfront we heard that bodies were washing up and that the soldiers were there to keep the public away.'

The public of Durban went out of their way to take care of the shipwreck survivors, as Harms experienced. 'On the following Sunday my adopted family, Mr and Mrs Dewar of Umbilo, helped me to attend a very sad ceremony when a large number of our allied servicemen were buried with full military honours in Stellawood Cemetery, Durban. The little girl who had survived was reunited with her mother and they later went to live in Australia.

'Here I might mention that the Union Castle Steamship Company stopped all our wages on the day we were sunk, and it was only due to the wonderful love and generosity of the South Africans that we were able to pull through the months of waiting for a return to the United Kingdom.'

When Harms returned to England he did so in company with Bosum Latham of the *Llandaff Castle* and with James Rothon, bosun of the *Nova Scotia*. During the sea trip they had plenty of opportunity to relive the horrors they had experienced.

Vic Harms recalled a song which went, 'We sing about the army and navy and air force too, but we never sing about the men who manned the mercantile marine.' They had no uniform and one day, although he wore his merchant navy badge, a young lady said to him, 'Pity you don't join up.' By then he'd already been in two ships which had been torpedoed. One of his mates said, 'Just ignore her.' He did, but he never forgot.

Harms later returned to live in Durban. In 1987 he had a reunion luncheon in Durban with Stan Gair, the captain's 'Tiger' (sole steward) and Frank Rigby, the former tourist class boss.

He and Gair had been pallbearers at Captain Castle's funeral after the invasion of Madagascar. After sitting around in Durban, Frank Rigby had volunteered for the Durban Light Infantry and went 'up north' with them. When crossing to Italy on the *Isle de France* he saw that Archie Weir, who had also survived the *Llandaff Castle*, was one of the crew. Instead of going below with the rest of the soldiers Rigby was given a cabin by his erstwhile shipmate. Frank Rigby returned to settle in Durban.

130

Mary and Harry
Brotton today (*HB*).

Vic Harms today.

Harry Brotton was sent to Bombay and thereafter Burma, where he served until the war's end. He was at Chittagong when the Atom Bombs were dropped on Japan. He returned to England and settled in Colchester, the oldest town in England.

While visiting his stepdaughter in Pietermaritzburg in 1991, he and the author travelled together with their wives. They stopped at the Van Reenen's Pass church, where they read a plaque to 'Llandaff Mathew', who died in a colliery saving the lives of others on 28 March, 1925. This triggered Brotton's recollections of that terrible day, almost 50 years before, when the *Llandaff Castle* met its end.

Vic Harms served on merchant ships until the war's end, then became a meat wholesaler in his home town. He visited Durban with his wife and introduced her to his 'family' there. One of their sons served in the RAF for 30 years. Alice died after 47 years of marriage to Vic. He then came to South Africa, where he married the Dewar's youngest daughter, Ivy. She died four years later. Vic stays in Durban and keeps busy playing bowls for the MOTHs and sketching.

A sequel to the landing of the *Llandaff* survivors on the Zululand coast occurred four years afterwards. During an official visit to the Northern Zululand coast, the Administrator of Natal met the local induna, Mpahleni Zikali. He was told by Zikali that they had never been rewarded for assisting the survivors.

As a result the Union Castle Company presented the induna with three cows, twenty pounds in a savings account in his name, and cash. Other members of his tribe were given blankets and a spit-barbecue. After Zikali had told his story to the Administrator he had presented him with a compass, which had been found on the lifeboat, and commented, 'I no longer want this watch which doesn't keep time.'

Former shipmates meet in Durban in 1987: Stan Gair, Vic Harms and Frank Rigby (*Home Front*).

Klipfontein:

8 January 1953

In 1953 a passenger liner, the 10 544 ton motor ship, the *Klipfontein*, hit a rock south of Lourenço Marques. One of the Holland Afrika Line, she made regular runs around Africa. The ship left the harbour at 5 am on Thursday, 8 January, and travelled southwards at a steady 17 knots, carrying a complement of 118 crew and 116 passengers. At 1.15 pm she was travelling less than a mile from the shore when she struck a rock.

According to one of the lady passengers, 'The force was so great that the water from the swimming-bath was thrown out like a tidal wave and came cascading down the companionways in a welter of foam.

'The ship shuddered, the engines stopped and the ship began to settle by the bows. The officer on duty came up to the passengers, telling us to remain where we were, not to panic and all would be well. Within a quarter of an hour, however, the crew began to take the covers off the lifeboats and we were told to collect our handbags, passports and lifebelts only and to take up our boat stations.

'Meanwhile the angle of the boat was increasing rapidly and the electricity was cut off. We adjusted our lifebelts calmly and quietly and were allotted to out lifeboat positions. Now began the business of lowering the boats.

'The first to be tackled was one amidships. Three seamen were in the boat being lowered when the rear davit broke, throwing one man into the sea, the others managing to hang on.

'The drizzle had now caught up with us, the sea was not rough but there was a heavy swell. Lifebelts and a rope ladder were thrown out to the man in distress, who managed to get safely back aboard.

'Meanwhile Nos 2 and 3 lifeboats got safely away 60 people in one and 45 in the other, babies and toddlers each in his or her little lifebelt. Our boat was No 5 and on the after deck very close over the propellors. The boat was lowered to deck level, but the stem of the ship was by now rapidly settling, the stern rising higher and higher out of the water, which made the lowering of our (after) boat both difficult and dangerous.

'However, we managed to climb into the boat which was suspended at a sickening angle over the seething, boiling wash around the rudder and propellors. The rope jammed and we were eventually lowered in a series of jolts.

'At last we were sea-borne but now had to take aboard the seamen detailed to our boat. They slid down the falls monkey-fashion with the lifeboat being continuously and severely dashed against the ship's side, fortunately with no fatal results. The last to board No 5 boat was the chief steward, who before coming down threw us an ample supply of cigarettes to keep up our morale.

'At last we were away. We pulled a fair distance from the doomed vessel and rested there, waiting for the other lifeboats to assemble.

132

At 2 pm an "SOS" had been sent to the Union Castle liner *Bloem-fontein Castle*, which was two hours sailing time behind us. She was steaming at full speed in our direction, so all the time this activity was going on we knew that help was at hand.

'For two hours and ten minutes the *Klipfontein's* crew battled to keep all the lifeboats together and heads to wind. Although the sea was calm the swell seemed tremendous to us in our small craft and the waves like mountains so that half the people, including some seamen were violently ill.

'While we awaited the *Bloemfontein Castle* we watched with sad eyes the death of another good ship. We now learned we had struck an uncharted rock which tore the bottom out of the vessel. By this time she was settling very quickly and the stern was right out of the water.

'Slowly, and it seemed painfully, the ship turned on her side, water rushed in the funnel, the sea bubbled and boiled, the stern rose high above the water and then as if the struggle was too much, at 4.25 pm she slid quickly and quietly to her watery grave, three hours after receiving her death blow. Can you imagine for one moment our feelings of sadness, loss and utter desolation?

'We now had to attend to the serious business of rowing our small craft over to the *Bloemfontein Castle*, now hove to a mile or so away. What a mile that was! The sea was covered with oil with which we were generously spattered. We were wet, oily, cramped, but quite cheerful and there had not been the slightest signs of panic.

'I must pay tribute to the officers and crew of the *Klipfontein* who were marvellous, quiet, courteous and efficient. Throughout our ordeal at no time was an order given except in an ordinary speaking tone. We were the third boat to be rescued. The method was as follows – *Bloemfontein Castle* would lower one of her lifeboats into which the occupants of one of ours scrambled.

'It was then pulled up to deck level and off we walked, dirty and bedraggled, to be greeted by an officer who bowed and said, "Welcome, ladies, and travel the Union Castle way!" This dry humour caused a laugh, tension was broken and we were immediately at our ease.

'The officers and staff of the *Bloemfontein Castle* were wonderful. The beautiful Smoking Room had been turned into an emergency reception base where blankets, tea and whisky were handed out to everyone and I can assure you we badly needed all three. Then hot baths and dinner. By now it was 8 pm.

'At 9 pm a Service of Thanksgiving for our safe deliverance from the dangers of the sea was held in the Lounge, after which we retired. I still feel tired, numb and in a daze. All we have, swept away before our eyes in a matter of three hours in this year of grace 1953, leaving us with what we stand up in and our handbags and passports the sum total of our worldly possessions!'

A Dutch Shipping Court of Enquiry found the ship's master, Captain J H Oosterhuis, guilty of careless navigation and probably hitting an obstacle marked on the Portuguese coastal chart. No 'uncharted' rocks were subsequently found.

After striking the rock the *Klipfontein* had drifted to within four miles of Zavora lighthouse, before sinking in 190 feet of water. Among the cargo was 1,500 tons of electrolytic copper bars, which was being shipped to Marseilles in France. A salvage vessel *Twyford* sent divers down, who laid explosive charges along the port side of the wreck and split the holds open. Over 1,000 tons of the copper was then recovered with a remote-controlled grab.

In 1968 a Johannesburg orthopaedic surgeon, Dr H Reitz, was granted sole rights by the Portuguese authorities to do further salvage work. He located the wreck and removed more of the valuable copper. One of his leading divers, John Dench, recalled that the wreck had become well covered with marine growth and the home of huge schools of Kingfish and Barracuda and some 500 pound Groupers. The jagged steel plates left from the explosions and strong currents presented a hazard to the divers and made the cargo difficult to find.

During the evacuation of the sinking ship the only mishap had been a twisted ankle suffered by one of the women passengers when boarding a lifeboat. The behaviour of the officers and crew had been exemplary, in marked contrast to that on the *Oceanos*, 38 years later.

CHAPTER 7 Miracle at Coffee Bay

Ever since the sinking of the *Birkenhead* it has been established seafaring tradition that in times of danger the credo of 'women and children first' would apply. The world was shocked to hear that when a Greek passenger liner foundered in a gale off Coffee Bay, Transkei, the captain, officers and most of the crew abandoned almost 600 passengers to their fate.

Oceanos:

4 August 1991

The coastal voyage on the passenger liner MTS *Oceanos* was to be a memorable experience for the 361 passengers and 184 crew, mainly Greek. The ship was built in 1952, was 150 metres long, 20 metres wide, and displaced 7,554 tons. Painted cream with a blue funnel, the cruise liner had six decks and was on charter to TFC Tours of Johannesburg. The operators and the TFC entertainers totalled 26.

The ship's commander, Captain Yiannis Avranas, 51, was a good socialiser who appeared to be confident and decisive. He had a strict schedule to keep and intended slipping moorings at East London at 4 pm on Saturday, 3 August, 1991. She had arrived from Cape Town two days earlier and a 'wedding of the year' had been held aboard.

Mr Winston Sahd of Queenstown hired the ship from Thursday to Saturday to celebrate the wedding of his daughter, Linith, to Chris Maytham. The newlyweds then went on honeymoon to the wild coast.

The wedding had been arranged by a travel consultant, Mercia Schultz, who recalled that a waiter had jumped overboard after a squabble over a bottle of champagne. A doctor had described him as mentally unstable. 'I think their whole crew were', she added,

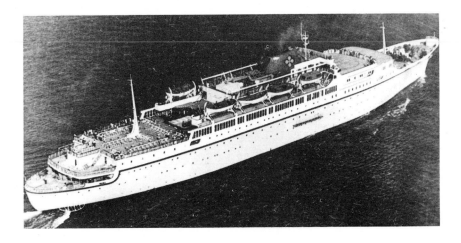

MTS *Oceanos* (*TFC Tours*).

'They had no idea of the procedure involved in abandoning ship.'

A former master of the *Oceanos*, the French Captain Jean Vachon, said, 'The *Oceanos* was fit for the break-up yard years ago. But greed kept it afloat as a cruise liner, when in fact it was just a patched-up wreck.' It was launched in 1952 as the *Jean-Laborde* and operated in the Indian Ocean until 1970. It was then sold to a Greek shipowner and renamed the *Ancoma*.

'It was almost immediately resold to another Greek, and its name was changed to *Mikimai*, until purchased by a Panamanian who renamed it *Eastern Princess*. Finally, the former *Jean-Laborde* again changed hands and became *Oceanos*. The fact is that a vessel usually has a maritime life of say 30 years. In other words, by 1991 *Oceanos* was just a poor, feeble sea creature.

'It was criminal to have allowed it to sail in one of the most dangerous seas in the world, and in the southern African winter at that. But in my opinion there is an even worse criticism to make. The transformation of the interior to change it into a luxury cruise liner had the effect of making it top heavy. The *Jean-Laborde* was designed as both a cargo ship and passenger liner . . .'

Despite threatening weather, with winds at sea exceeding 30 knots, he decided to leave. The stretch of coast leading to Durban, 270

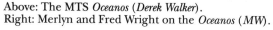

Above: The MTS *Oceanos* (*Derek Walker*).
Right: Merlyn and Fred Wright on the *Oceanos* (*MW*).

136

Lorraine Betts (*Reader's Digest*).

nautical miles north of them, was notorious as one of the most dangerous in the world. Over 80 years earlier the liner *Waratah* had disappeared without trace while steaming southwards from Durban.

On the *Oceanos*, Lorraine Betts, 35, was the TFC cruise director. She had been born in Kenya and educated in the Seychelles. Betts had catnapped during the past two days of intense work. She had impressed on her team that although the passengers were on holiday, they were there to work. Her 87-year-old grandmother, Maria Smyth, was also aboard.

Among the passengers were Fred Wright, 84, and his wife, Merlyn, 67. They had both served during the Second World War, Fred in the Transvaal Scottish and Merlyn in the Women's Auxiliary Air Force.

In June 1942 when Gen Erwin Rommel's Afrika Korps broke through the Gazala Line and headed for Tobruk, Sergeant Fred Wright was part of a rearguard detachment at Acroma Keep. For two weeks they defended their position with mortars, a captured German 88 mm and an Italian two pounder gun. At one stage he and an officer went to the Germans to organise a truce for evacuation of Indian POWs who were in the firing line.

Their determined stand kept the Afrika Korps from using the main road and earned Fred a Distinguished Conduct Medal. He was later wounded at Sollum and captured, then spent almost three years as a prisoner-of-war. For his leadership in the camps Fred was mentioned in dispatches.

Their trip on the *Oceanos* was Fred's birthday gift to Merlyn. She later recalled the heavy seas which the ship encountered: 'Sunday 4 August was definitely to be a day with a difference. We had been on the *Oceanos* from Durban to Cape Town and on the way back to Durban had disembarked at East London to allow for the Wedding of the Year to take place. We returned to the ship on Saturday 3 August and sailed out of East London on very high seas at 3.30 pm.'

The wind increased to 40 knots as the *Oceanos* ploughed through the huge waves, rolling and pitching. In the main lounge a grand piano fell off the stage and skidded across the dance floor. Passengers in the dining room risked injury as their cutlery slid about and a cupboard door opened, sending piles of plates crashing to the floor.

Mrs Audrey Allister, 83, and her daughter, Anne Amezdraz, laughed at the spectacle as plates and glasses slid off tables. They were admonished by a waiter, who said, 'Don't laugh, it is a very serious matter.'

Merlyn Wright recalled the meal, 'Dinner that evening was a crazy affair as the ship lurched and rolled and swayed and glass, crockery and cutlery slid from one side of the table to the other – breakages galore! We ended up putting the spare wine glasses into the bread basket as it meant less to control.

'We went to our cabin after dinner as Fred, a man nearly 85 years old, was tired so I helped him to bed. Just by the way, he had broken his thumb whilst on board before East London when the door swung and his thumb was jammed. Consequently I helped to undress him, which later proved to our advantage.

'Well after tucking him in I went up to have my last go on the one-armed bandits and to collect the photo taken on the Thursday night. We were all gathered in the lounge for the evening show when the ship's engines stopped, lights went out, flashed a few times and thank goodness the emergency lights came into play. This happened at about 9.40 pm.'

Suddenly there was a muffled thud and the lights went out. The emergency generator then started and dull lights flickered on. The engine stopped and the *Oceanos* wallowed sideways against the wind and waves.

Huge swells, in excess of 15 metres, coupled with hurricane-force winds exceeding 100 kilometres per hour, had damaged the *Oceanos* and caused it to take in water through the plating.

Captain Avranas ordered both forward anchors dropped so that they would hold the bow into the wind. The chief engineer then burst onto the bridge to report that the starboard hull plates had fractured and that the generator room was flooding. Closing the watertight doors wouldn't help as there was a hole in the bulkhead between the generator room and the sewerage tank, as the ventilation pipes had been removed for repairs.

The *Oceanos* would inevitably sink, for water would rise through the toilet pipes throughout the ship. No warning was given to passengers, but the ship's officers and crew rushed to pack their bags. Avranas went to tell his wife and 11-year-old daughter to pack.

Two of the TFC staff were due on the stage that night. Moss and Tracey Hills were guitarists whose daughter would be meeting them in Durban. When Tracey went to her cabin she saw that the sea was boiling against the porthole and was spurting through the seal. Moss saw some of the ship's officers running in the corridor and was ignored when he asked what was going on.

Lorraine Betts was the only TFC member trained to deal with emergencies, so made her way to the bridge. When she arrived there the staff captain was shouting 'Mayday . . . Mayday . . .' into the radio transmitter. She then hurried to the main lounge where she tried to reassure the passengers and told them to remain there.

She then returned to the bridge and demanded to know from Avranas what was happening. He admitted that there was water in

Capt Yiannis Avranas.

Robin Boltman (*You Magazine*).

the engine-room and suggested that the passengers get their life-jackets. Betts relayed the information to her staff then told one of them, Robin Boltman, to alert the passengers in the lounge that there would be lifeboat drill.

While on his way Boltman noted incredulously that the crew were panic-stricken and had commandeered the most serviceable lifeboat, No 1. He reported to Betts, who wasn't surprised after having experienced the officers' fear on the bridge. She then went to her cabin to change into warm clothes and get walkie-talkies.

Boltman proceeded to the main lounge, where hundreds of passengers sat in the gloom, waiting for the show to start. He took a loudspeaker on the stage and joked that they had forgotten to pay the electricity bill. He requested the passengers to put on their life-jackets, then he and other entertainers circulated among them and cracked jokes to avoid alarming them.

Merlyn Wright was among the passengers in the lounge, 'The magician/compere assured us that it would be all right to remain where we were. The cruise leader said that as a precaution we were all to don a lifejacket, but so as not to cause confusion the staff would collect them from the cabins. Some passenger joked, "Jolly good that Dolly Parton doesn't have to put on a life jacket". The reply was, "Never mind, she wouldn't need one." The entertainers then began singing again.

'My main concern was, of course, that my husband was in the cabin but I was assured they would bring him up as they did the

The *Oceanos* sinking (*Gary Horlor, Daily Dispatch*).

rounds of the cabins. Well after a while a call went up "Is Merlyn there, we have your husband". What a relief that we were together at last; Fred in a pyjama jacket, shoes and trousers hurriedly put on by one of the TFC members. Fortunately his wallet was in the pocket. I had on an evening top and skirt. Then Fred mentioned having put his glasses down on the table. When we went on deck there was no sign of them.'

Two TFC men then went below to assess the damage. Julian Russell, a magician, and Moss Hills, 35, a guitarist, descended into the bowels of the ship. They reached the propellor shaft and heard a roaring, like a river in flood, otherside the bulkhead. They wisely decided not to open the watertight doors to take a look, but rather reported their findings to Lorraine Betts.

She decided to start loading the women and children into the life-boats. Her staff were to go and fetch the elderly, and the mothers and children, and bring them to the boats without making a fuss or making any public announcement.

Piet Niemand recalled, 'I really felt very sorry for them. It was horrible to see the fear on people's faces.'

Merlyn Wright was among those who moved, 'At about 10.30 pm all the older folk were taken up on the covered deck and told to remain there. As it was freezing cold and the wind cut us to the bone the young folk, TFC cruise officials, dancers and singers gathered whatever blankets they could from the cabins and we were able to have a little protection'.

Lorraine Betts, Moss Hills and Julian Russell organised the women and children at the second lifeboat, calming them and in-sisting that they climb into the wildly swinging boat. Captain Avranas brought his wife and daughter, then tried to board with them. He was roughly pulled back by some of the crew and a tour staffer.

Mercia Schultz, her husband Leon and their 10-month-old baby struggled among brawling, shouting seamen to get aboard the second lifeboat. When there were about 50 people aboard the lifeboat, Betts had it lowered into the stormy sea. Her grandmother was among those in the wildly bobbing boat.

Ms Liezel Louw, one of the TFC hostesses, checked cabins and found people sleeping in the cabins as late as 11 pm, almost two hours after the crew had their first warnings. 'I tried to wake some guys up but they did not believe me when I told them what had happened.'

According to Mercia Schultz, 'The first lifeboat, a motorised one, had already gone into the sea full of passengers and many crew members. Ours had no engine and was packed with 33 passengers and 12 crew members. The crewmen fought amongst themselves and pushed passengers aside to get aboard.

'It was farcical. We managed to swing out from the side of the *Oceanos* at 11 pm on Saturday, but we never managed to touch the water until midnight because the lifeboat stuck half way down the side of the ship. The crew members efforts to free the dangling lifeboat were pathetic. They had no idea what to do. At one stage a block and tackle swung loose and struck an 85-year-old passenger, grandmother of a TFC member, cutting open her head.

'Every time passengers asked crew members what was going on and whether the lifeboat would be freed, they just shook their heads and did nothing. It wasn't just that they couldn't speak English. That was obvious, but so was our situation and they should have known what to do.'

The lifeboat was eventually launched, only to find that there were no oars and the automatic rowing mechanism didn't work. 'There were only two flares in the lifeboat and these were used in the first hour. One of them did not ignite properly.

Back in the *Oceanos's* lounge, gloom had descended on the passengers as they realised that the ship could sink at any time. Some of the young men sang rugby songs while Robin Boltman tried to cheer up others. Moss Hills and his wife, Tracey, picked up their guitars and in no time had a sing song going.

A third lifeboat was launched and again Captain Avranas tried to board it, but was prevented by the cruise staff. Robin Boltman had, nevertheless, managed to obtain place at 2 am on one of the lifeboats for the captain's dog, for which he was later commended by Earth-life Africa. The dog had thanked Boltman by biting his finger.

SOS signals were sent out by Lorraine Betts. It was picked up by the South African Navy in the Cape Peninsula, almost 1 000 kilometres away.

The Naval Maritime Intelligence Base at Silvermine, near Simon's Town, gathered from radio transmissions that the *Oceanos* was sinking. Accordingly, the assistance of the SADF was called in around midnight. A naval contingent of divers from the SAS *Simonsberg* and SAS *Scorpion* were rushed to the area, together with elements of the following SAAF squadrons: 15, 19, 28, 30 and 35. Brigadier Theo de Munnink of the SAAF co-ordinated the rescue, sending 15 Puma helicopters from Durban, Pretoria and Bloemfontein.

Captain Chaz Goatley, 36, was woken at Durban. He was a former Rhodesian helicopter pilot of 17 years flying experience and knew that his squadron of Pumas was the closest to the scene of the disaster. Shortly afterwards he was briefing his four crews.

The *Oceanos* was foundering in rough seas off Coffee Bay, on the Transkei coast, two hours' flying time away. It would be pointless and unnecessarily dangerous to try any rescue at night. With gale force winds and a heaving deck they would need daylight to be of any use. The superstructure, masts and cables would have to be avoided while passengers were hoisted to safety. They would leave at first light.

During the long night the TFC officials kept up the spirits of the passengers, who huddled together on the open deck. By then it was apparent that the *Oceanos* had developed a severe leak and was sinking, yet no effort was made to call in other ships to help pump the sea water out. In the mountainous seas it would have been impossible in any event.

Merlyn Wright decided that as Fred would not be able to climb up rope ladders from lifeboats into ships, they would remain on the upper deck: 'Then the women and children were lowered in lifeboats – it was much colder out there so we handed out our blankets. More came to hand but as the next boat went, so did our blankets. The trouble was that at that time we had no idea of the full extent of the problem, but realised it must be serious for the lifeboats to have been launched.

'One reassurance was the appearance of the lights of ships that came around us. A Japanese trawler, a Norwegian ship, a Polish ship etc. Those lights were indeed a wonderful sight. Where they came from goodness only knows as on our cruise we only once spotted another ship. But once the message went out they all converged around the *Oceanos*.

'About this time a passenger brought along specs that one of the crew had picked up and, low and behold, they were Freds – a real stroke of luck. The specs then joined the photograph and my purse down the front of my blouse.'

The passengers were filled with trepidation as it seemed that the ship could capsize and sink at any moment. Merlyn Wright recalled, 'As we watched the mountainous waves and felt them battering the ship and saw the impact of that gale-force wind, we realised the great strength of the elements – so strong and cruel they are and what little hope we humans have when they are in full force.

'Then came midnight and then Sunday 4 August. Happy Birthday was sung to the young photographer who was to have a really memorable birthday. I then realised "Sign on Sunday" was here and my prayer to the heavens was – "Dear Lord I have tendered my excuse to my parish, do you now want me to sign on to St Peter?" In my heart of hearts I felt I still had a good bit of living to do but if that was God's will, well so be it.

'Fortunately in my purse I had my finger rosary so I was able to pass that through my fingers as I said my rosary. We held hands and prayed together, told one another how much we loved each other, and so time passed. I think it was about 2.30 am when we

A grey dawn and mountainous seas (*Personality*).

were told that the Transkei government had been contacted and with full co-operation with the South African authorities a pad was being prepared for the use of helicopters, who at first light would be able to start a lift-off of passengers.

'No matter what one thought, prayer was uppermost. Material things had faded into the background; luggage, clothes, etc, all meant nothing. We all just prayed that there would be some way in which all of us could get safely off the ship.'

The second lifeboat approached the Panamanian registered tanker *Great Nancy*, which had come about to provide a windbreak. A large wave smashed the lifeboat against the ship's hull, opening seams and terrifying its occupants. A ladder was thrown down and one of the Greek sailors grabbed hold of it. He swung clear of the lifeboat and in the howling wind managed to climb up to the deck. He told the captain that the boat contained women and children and that a safer way would have to be found to uplift them.

A large rubber bucket was then thrown down at the end of a line and instructions were shouted that children were to be sent up one at a time. Gail Adamson placed her daughter, Kari, 2, in the bucket which was hauled up. Other children followed, then her second daughter, Samantha, 8, who had to crouch below the rim as the bucket bounced against the hull on its precarious trip. Her baby, John, 17 days, was then packed in tightly with a blanket and sent skywards.

The mothers then were hoisted up in a harness. Gail Adamson

broke three fingers before being hauled aboard, but her hands were so numb with cold that she felt no pain. She found her daughters safely tucked away in bed and baby John crying angrily. Adamson then went to thank the Greek sailor for his heroism in climbing the ladder in the gale and thereby saving them.

Two hours later Number 1 lifeboat pulled alongside. The crewmen, all carrying their luggage, sheepishly came aboard and walked past the passengers. Not a word was spoken to them and they could feel the contempt everyone felt. There was not one passenger on their boat.

The third lifeboat to pull alongside included Gail Adamson's husband, John, 35, who had been sent to row the boat. He and his fellow survivors were wet and half-frozen. She threw her arms around him and told him that their children were safe, then led him away to dry off.

On the *Oceanos*, Lorraine Betts took stock after Lifeboat No 5 was launched. There were still 260 people on board of the original 571. The three remaining boats had faulty gear or had got stuck. She told Boltman that when the ship went down they were to line the rails and jump into the sea.

At 3 am two frogmen, Paul Whiley and Gary Scoular, boarded Puma helicopters at Louis Botha Airport, Durban, and left for the Transkei coast. In his book on shipwrecks, José Burman recalled the wrecking of the SA *Seafarer* on 1 July, 1966, Alouette helicopters from 17 Squadron at Ysterplaat, Cape Town, assisted in the rescue. Captain Branch was the last man to be airlifted off the wrecked ship. Burman pointed out that the lesson learned was that 'the true rescue craft of the future is no longer the lifeboat, but the helicopter.' This was proved true in the case of the *Oceanos*.

Meanwhile, the *Nedlloyd Mauritius*, a Dutch container ship, radioed that they were launching a lifeboat to assist with the rescue. Moss Hills told them that they had possibly two hours left. He had seen furniture floating in the dining-room and knew that only two decks separated the remaining passengers from the rising water. Betts ordered that they be moved from the lounge to the open deck in case the ship capsized.

Piet Niemand, 42, his fiancée, Angela Stavrou, and son, Peter, were among those who moved. She asked him whether there were sharks in the sea and he said not, although he knew that the water was infested with man-eaters.

Merlyn and Fred Wright spent an uncomfortable night huddled together on the upper deck. 'Dawn broke after what seemed an endless night. Planes circled around the ship and as the sun rose we could see land and the form of the ships and not just lights. Then

Piet Niemand (*Sunday Times*).

came the helicopters. It almost seemed as if they were queueing up, as they came and went so quickly.

'Then we heard that the ship would go down in four hours. If your heart had not already sunk into your boots it certainly did then. Prayers, prayers and more prayers. We all felt and knew that despite the wonderful help there was still the Dear Lord who would know whether that sign was up to be with St Peter.

'An African gentleman went by and he was very scared. I tried to reassure him that with the lifejacket on he would float and be saved in due course. His great fear I then realised is "Lady, I can't swim". Well to one who has always loved the sea and the last breaker a must when bathing – those mountainous waves were something else, so to a non-swimmer more than terrifying. They were about eight metre waves fanned by a gale.'

Lifeboat No 5 was rudderless and tossed and turned wildly in the mountainous seas. Derek Grove, his wife Jenny, and about 40 others stood knee deep in water which sloshed about in the bottom of the boat. He kept watch in the bow, to warn of breaking waves. Behind him the wretched passengers were terribly seasick. Then he heard the sound of aircraft and moments later spotted the lights of a circling C-160 transport, which acted as a search aircraft and directed aerial rescue.

After being adrift for five hours they were approached by a Norwegian trawler, the *Anik*. The propeller narrowly missed the boat, which was slammed against the trawler's hull the next minute. Grove saw one of the seamen on the lifeboat grab at a rope, then was jerked out of the boat and after banging against the hull was hauled aboard the *Anik*.

Another sailor jumped for a rope and fell into the sea. A lifebelt was thrown to him and after grabbing hold of it he, too, was pulled onto the trawler. The lifeboat was then dragged toward the propeller. The captain of the *Anik* hearing the screams and shouts, stopped the engines, just in time to save them from being smashed into oblivion. He then sailed away as it was too dangerous to try and transfer the women and children.

Joanne Daley (*North Eastern Tribune*).

Joanne Daley, 19, from Lombardy East, Johannesburg, was a junior travel agent who had boarded at East London. She and a colleague had been told by a chef at the hotel there that the seas were rough and that the ship shouldn't leave. After dinner aboard they had been told by the TFC officials not to worry, so they didn't.

They believed it was routine procedure when lifebelts were handed out and the mothers and children left in lifeboats. 'We spent the night talking and laughing,' she said, 'and trying to get some sleep. The entertainers helped us through the night. I was slightly hurt by a falling couch while I was lying down.

Passengers on the steeply-leaning deck (*P Niemand*).

'At 4 am we heard helicopters outside and that was when we realised there was something wrong. Some people started to panic. We were sent onto the pool deck and told to line up. A colleague and I were first in line and it was awful because the ship was at an angle and we kept on sliding down.

'We were afraid the whole mass of people lined up behind us would fall on top of us and crush us. My hands were full of splinters and blisters from trying to keep myself up.'

In an article 'Hero of the *Oceanos*' *YOU* magazine quoted Robin Boltman, 'By 5 am everybody was outside on the pool deck. It was still pitch dark, but not long afterwards the day began to break. We could see more clearly now and I noticed that the captain was on deck with us.

'As our surroundings were slowly illuminated by the rays of the sun an incredible sight greeted us: seven ships circling, waiting to pick us up. Suddenly there was no more doubt – we knew we would be safe. People talked to one another and huddled close for comfort. I remember Terry Lester was sitting beside the swimming pool on a bench. I sat nearby with a group of passengers on the heaving deck.

'Suddenly Terry said: "Look at the dolphins!" I couldn't believe my eyes. In our hour of need, with the shadow of death hanging over us, a group of dolphins swam and frolicked in front of a lifeboat on its way to the ship.

'Somebody had earlier spoken about the likelihood of sharks, but now I knew the waters around us were safe. The dolphins were visible for a few minutes and then they were gone. Perhaps they were the bringers of glad tidings . . .

'From the pool deck I went up to the bridge. It was just after 5 am and there was nobody up there. Moss, Julian and Lorraine had taken their turns at manning the bridge since 3 am. Now it was my turn . . .'

'When day broke that Sunday morning I was standing on the bridge. I greeted the world with the words that Moss recorded on his video: "Good morning, South Africa, the latest news from the *Oceanos* . . . we're all deep in the sh . . ."

'I couldn't help it, I had to lighten things up with a bit of humour, even though we were staring death in the face. At least it made Moss laugh. And so until I was picked up I played at being a captain on the bridge, communicating with the rescue teams on the coast, in the helicopters and on the other ships.'

Linda Bezuidenhout.

Linda Bezuidenhout, a former deputy mayoress of East London, had a lucky escape. 'Yes, this *Oceanos* was certainly a night to remember for ever. I don't believe it will ever leave my mind. It is ironic that I wasn't scared during the night, but once we were sent outside to sit on the deck for hours – I only then realised that maybe we wouldn't make it in time.

'The appearance of the dolphins calmed me for a while, but soon after my foot slipped and I slipped down to the door, with waves hitting into the ship. Luckily a friend helped me up with a blanket, which was thrown down to me as no one could reach me. It was then that I "cracked".

'One couldn't really relate what was going on in our minds as to why this was happening to us. But, believe me, God knew . . .'

At 6.45 am the first diver was lowered by hoist from a Puma helicopter. Able Seaman Paul Whiley, 23, swung wildly at the end of the hoist rope as the ship was pitching and rolling unpredictably in the mountainous seas.

Born at Lyttelton in 1967, Whiley had attended Kearsney College, Durban, then the Pietermaritzburg University where he graduated BA. He did his national service in the Navy and trained at the Diving School at Simon's Town. As a crew member of SAS *Scorpion* he had volunteered for the rescue mission when he heard that the *Oceanos* was sinking.

After 20 minutes of hovering, during which Whiley swung against the ship's railings several times, he finally reached the deck at the confined quarterdeck area. He immediately took charge of the evacuation there.

Able Seaman Paul Whiley (*SADF*).

According to Joanne Daley, Whiley secured her friend's harness first, 'My colleague, who became hysterical, was the first in the helicopter. The captain pushed in front of me and went on next.' Whiley was surprised by Captain Avranas's attitude. He could tell by the insignia on the man's uniform that he was either the captain or the second-in-command.

When first approached by Avranas, Whiley thought that it was to discuss the rescue operations, but when he indicated that he wished to be lifted off Whiley explained that they were dealing with the women and elderly people first.

At first he ignored the captain's insistent requests and began helping other people into the harnesses lowered two at a time by the helicopters. After securing a woman into one harness he turned and found that the captain had helped himself into the second harness. The helicopter lifted the two people off.

'He was very pugnacious about it,' Whiley said, 'I thought then that perhaps he wasn't the captain as he had left the ship.' Then the ship's radio officer demanded to be next, followed by the purser and a deckhand. Whiley didn't argue – his job was to get people off the ship.

Joanne Daley was next, 'Being hoisted in the helicopter was terrifying. Just before they pulled us into the helicopter it felt as though they were dropping us. I fainted from fright and only came to when they were unharnessing me.'

Whiley accompanied the next woman being lifted. When the first helicopter left it contained Whiley, the four crewmen and three women. The helicopter landed at Coffee Bay at 7.30 am. They were then flown south to the Haven, where Avranas was the seventh person to check in. Meanwhile, Whiley returned to the *Oceanos*.

It was more difficult to return to the deck. After 10 minutes of hovering and being beaten against the railings, he was flung out of the hoisting strop and fell to a lower deck. The crew of the Puma thought that he had been killed or critically injured, then saw him stagger to his feet and continue assisting the passengers and crew.

At about 7.45 am the crew of the Polish trawler *Kaszuby II* rescued the occupants of a lifeboat which had been adrift for nearly eight and a half hours. Mercia Schultz recalled the dreadful night adrift as the boat was exposed to the high winds, waves and spray: 'We later found a cover for the boat in an orange box, but couldn't put it up because three of the four supporting struts had broken off.'

The boat was approached by a Norwegian trawler. 'The trawler could not get near enough. The seas were horrendous and the trawler's captain kept warning us to be careful. He tried but it was no use and too dangerous, even when he managed to get close enough. Once, when he did get close, one of the *Oceanos*'s crew pushed us all aside and leapt aboard the trawler just before it moved away.'

One of the passengers had brought bottles of bourbon and whisky aboard to keep the passengers warm, but found instead that the crew fought over them. 'Two of them flattened two bottles in no time and just passed out. But they were as much use as their colleagues.'

Mercia Schultz and her family said their goodbyes, as they had given up. After being rescued by the *Kaszuby II*, she said, 'But the Polish seamen were wonderful. They gave up their cabins for us and even looked after my daughter and another baby by finding enough cottonwool to make nappies.'

L/Seaman Gary Scoular (*Natal Mercury*).

Meanwhile, another frogman had dropped to the deck. Leading Seaman Gary Scoular, also of the SAS *Scorpion*, manned the second pick-up point at the forward sundeck. Originally from Rhodesia, he had immigrated to South Africa with his family and lived at Johannesburg. Scoular was required to assist passengers and crew members into the hoisting strops, but his task was considerably complicated by the pitch and slope of the deck.

Scoular found that he had to cling to the ship's railings with one hand, while assisting the survivors into the strop and signalling by hand to the helicopter crew. From the Puma it was obvious that whenever he left his post to assist survivors elsewhere on the deck, the evacuation process slowed down noticeably and the passengers became panicky.

Despite the existing hazards on the deck, Scoular had to clear a cable carrying lights in the area, which made the task of the helicopter crews easier and safer. As the evacuation area on the forecastle was partially hidden behind the superstructure, few people were aware of what transpired there. Compared to Whiley at the quarterdeck, Scoular's task was extremely hazardous and he performed superhuman feats in evacuating the survivors in an orderly and safe manner.

Angela Stavrou was lifted by the second helicopter. Piet Niemand and his son, Peter, then tried to assist other passengers. He linked arms with Whiley and calmed the passengers, then instructed them how to don the harness. He was very impressed by a couple, Tony and Jenny Rooney, who refused to be hoisted before their sons, Michael, 29, and Mark, 24, had been lifted.

The passengers were hoisted two at a time, jerking into the air as the ship rose and fell, then reeled upwards to where the helicopter crew waited anxiously to assist them to safety. They were then flown the 3.2 kilometres to the nearest land at Coffee Bay.

Robin Boltman, the ship's comedian, then played the role of his life. He manned the radio on the bridge and helped to co-ordinate the rescue of the passengers still on board. Boltman guided rescue vessels over an emergency frequency. The last time he had used a two-way radio was as a serviceman at Katima Mlilo, in the Caprivi.

He believed the mountainous waves to be as high as eight metres and the wind 40 knots. 'We took over the bridge because the captain and his officers disappeared. At one stage I had to climb to the top of the funnel to cut down a string of lights that was in the way of the helicopters. The view from up there was terrifying.'

Meanwhile, the National Sea Rescue Institute had set up a rescue headquarters in a nearby inn at the mouth of the Bashee River, appropriately named 'The Haven'. Their workers were assisted by army medics who met all incoming helicopters with stretchers. The survivors were then taken to the inn and given tea and coffee. A TFC staff member kept records of all the rescued, which they matched to the crew and passenger lists. No telephone calls could be made, though, as the lines had been blown down by the storm.

At about 8.30 am the *Nedlloyd Mauritius* approached Lifeboat No 5. A scramble net was thrown over the side of the ship and as the lifeboat smashed against it one of the passengers threw his wife into it. The damaged lifeboat then slid away and drifted to a Polish cargo carrier, *Kaszuby II.*

Fenders were lowered to save the lifeboat from too much damage against the hull, ropes secured the boat and Polish seamen came down in a cargo net to organise the rescue. Three or four passengers at a time were loaded into the net and hoisted up until all were safely aboard. The *Kaszuby II* had already picked up 45 passengers and 20 crew from another lifeboat.

An unlikely heroine was an 80-year-old woman with a broken hip. Dulcie Hutton-Brown and her husband, Charles, were in the process of moving from Hout Bay to St Winifred in Natal when she had to have a major hip operation. Her doctor recommended that the couple take a sea cruise.

When they left Cape Town on the *Oceanos* she had to learn to cope with the ship's motion while on crutches. Charles Hutton-Brown was a former South African Navy man, who soon realised that the ship was unsuitable for rough seas.

'It was designed for Mediterranean cruises, and just couldn't cope with the rough Cape seas. I quietly told my wife we were in trouble but she didn't panic – she is a fatalist.'

They sat with the passengers on the windswept deck alongside the railing. According to Dulcie Hutton-Brown, 'As people came sliding towards me on the deck, I stuck out my crutches for them to grab on to, and clung to the railing with my other hand.'

She received a battering in the process and later had hospital treatment for two broken ribs and extensive grazes. The skin on both her forearms was rubbed off. As she said later, 'I feel very sore, but at the time I didn't feel any pain.'

Scoular saw that some passengers who had jumped overboard were in danger of being sucked under the vessel in the mountainous seas. He worked his way to the starboard side, which was awash and found three rubber boats. When he attempted to launch the first it was smashed against the superstructure.

He boarded the second and asked a Greek seaman to hold the painter until he had started the engine. The man must have misunderstood, as he released it and the wind swept the dinghy astern. As the *Oceanos's* stern rose, water rushed under it and dragged the rubber duck along.

In the darkness beneath the ship's hull Scoular made a desperate decision. As the ship's stern came down on top of him he lunged for the propeller, wrapped his legs around a blade, and hung on tightly. He held his breath while he rode the propeller down into the depths. Blood pounded in his temples, then, when he felt the stern rise he let go and popped to the surface like a cork.

While gathering his wits in the stormy seas Scoular found that his wetsuit had been ripped down the front. He swam back to the starboard rail where he was further knocked about and buried by breaking waves. When trying to launch the third boat he found that his strength had dissipated.

A Filipino crewman saw Scoular struggling so he helped him launch the dinghy. He started the motor then signalled to Betts that passengers should jump overboard and he would pick them up. Julian Russell jumped overboard with a non-swimmer and assisted him to the dinghy, then sat in the bow to stabilize it. They made six trips to the *Nedlloyd Mauritius* lifeboat, taking 40 people to safety.

Scoular called to Lorraine Betts to jump. She checked that Moss Hills had control, then at 10.20 am jumped into the sea. Robin Boltman was on the bridge where he remained in radio contact with The Haven and kept tally of the passengers being airlifted. Meanwhile, Scoular and Russell continued patrolling in the dinghy, looking for swimmers.

While Whiley was supervising the hoisting at the quarterdeck George Walton, 55, from Boksburg, was inadvertently lifted before his harness was secured. His wife, Gerda, was in the accompanying harness and clung to him. Walton realised that if he was hoisted too high and fell he could be killed, so he let go and dropped about 60 metres into the sea.

On impact with the water Walton's lifejacket hit him under the chin and he was knocked unconscious. He revived in time to see his

George Walton and
A/Seaman Paul Whiley
(*C Uys*).

wife being helped into the helicopter, then, finding the water warm in relation to the wind, splashed to draw attention to his location.

Disregarding his own safety, Whiley dived approximately 40 metres into the debris-strewn, gale-whipped sea. He swam towards Walton, guided by shouts and whistles from the deck. When he reached him Walton was semi-conscious and floating face down.

While being assisted, Walton began splashing again and Whiley warned him not to do so as it would attract sharks. They were picked up by the *Nedlloyd* lifeboat, which took Whiley close to the looming port hull, where he dived overboard to return to his post.

The helicopter crews had, in the interim, found that due to Whiley's absence the hoisting operation was a lot slower and lacked direction. Whiley swam strongly through the stormy sea and reached the stricken ship, only to have great difficulty in boarding it. While climbing a rope ladder, which was draped over the ship's side, he was repeatedly beaten against the hull, but persevered until he reached the deck.

Robin Boltman had unexpected calls from Avranas: 'The captain phoned me on the bridge a few times. I don't know where from. I didn't ask. He said things such as: "How is it going there?" and "Hang in there" and "It's OK, you've still got time".

'It seems he knew how much time the ship had left before it would sink. But he didn't pass this information on to me. Just: "Hang in there, things are going to be fine." '

Fred and Merlyn Wright remained on the upper deck. 'As Fred had the handicap of a broken thumb, arthritic knees and old age, we were asked to stay put, rather than end up with broken legs or something and then be far more of a burden. We kept being re-assured that they would come for us.

'Perhaps the spot where we were was rather important, as at some

152

time the hatch had been opened to try and get the rope ladder. When closing it the catch had broken and, being on the port side, should the door handle have been opened they would have crashed onto the side of the ship and ended up injured and possibly killed. So Fred and I became "the keeper of the door", which made it a bit more difficult to get along the deck but we felt that lives were saved.

'As time went on we knew the list was worse as we could no longer see the sea or the ships and were lying back in the chairs. To get to the rails one needed at least one more person to form a human chain. All the time the ship was pitching and rolling, up and down and side to side. The waves were mountainous.

'The helicopters came in a never-ending stream. Fortunately I had on lace-up shoes, as many people lost their shoes when being winched up to the helicopters. When one is uncertain as to whether we would all be rescued it is amazing how unimportant material things are and how valuable life is.

'Able Seaman Whiley, who was wearing a frogman outfit, passed us several times. On one occasion he had a can of cooldrink. We were terribly thirsty but didn't ask for any as we considered his need more important.

'Time goes very slowly when one is just waiting. Eventually a super little crew member, Costas, came to fetch us and took us to the front of the ship. It was too dangerous to be hoisted there so we returned. The trip along the deck was quite a feat, hanging onto the railing. I held onto Fred's jacket belt to make sure that if he lost his hold at least there was an extra anchor. Costas coped with us wonderfully and took complete charge of Fred when another youngster came to assist me.

'When we came to the end of the upper deck we virtually slid down the steps on our backsides. They wouldn't hoist two elderly people together, so I made sure Fred went first. He went up with a young man, then those two loops were suddenly there for myself and a young Afrikaner. We clung tightly to each other as we were whisked up.

'The whole process is very quick and heights are the least of one's worries. I looked up into the concerned eyes of Staff-Sgt Scott who operated the winch. We were brought into the helicopter and quickly unleashed, so that the next lot could be fetched. We had to move in as far as possible to make room for new arrivals.

'When we landed a blanket was put around our shoulders and we were transferred to another helicopter to take us to The Haven, a nearby holiday resort. When we arrived I was helped out while Fred was put onto a stretcher. The lounge of The Haven became an emergency hospital and the treatment from the young men of the medical corps and the staff of the resort was tops.'

Piet Niemand had been helping passengers into the harness while Peter Niemand had assisted them up the steeply canted deck to the lifting point. Peter had refused to leave the ship without his father, but when asked to take a frightened, elderly lady up with him he complied.

Whiley and Niemand then checked the ship for any more passengers, but found none. As they passed the bridge Robin Boltman said that he calculated that there were still 14 on board. He then sent his last message to the NSRI, 'Oceanos is about to go down. I'm leaving the bridge.' He then released a canary from a nearby cage.

They noted that the helicopters had all left and Whiley surmised correctly that they had all gone for refuelling at Umtata. Boltman saluted Scoular and Russell, who were still patrolling the seas, and was rewarded with a wave. As tension mounted the Filipino crewman, who had assisted Scoular, read Psalm 23 aloud: 'Yea, though I walk through the valley of the shadow of death, I will fear no evil: for thou art with me . . .'

Tracey Hills was the only woman still aboard. She and her husband, Moss, waited side by side for rescue, or for whatever fate had in store. Then with a sigh of relief they saw the specks of returning helicopters. The 14 passengers went first, then Moss and Tracey Hills, Boltman and the Filipino.

After they had landed many of the passengers rushed over to thank Boltman and Hills. Moss Hills collapsed from the cumulative strain and was rushed away on a stretcher by medics.

Boltman modestly replied, 'Don't thank me, we did it together.' Then military personnel descended on him. 'Defence Force officers, doctors, chaps in brown uniforms all clustered around, asking: "Who's Robin?"

'They were all curious to see who they had been chatting to for the past six hours. "I am," I replied, quickly adding as we had learned in the army: "I didn't do it! I didn't do it!"'

Whiley and Niemand did a final check that no one was left aboard. In the main lounge they helped themselves to cokes 'on the house'. According to Niemand, 'It was a shambles and quite eerie. We stopped in the bar for a cooldrink. It had been really thirsty work. Back on the pool deck Paul turned to me and said, "Piet, let's get the hell out of here."'

They signalled to the helicopter and were lifted from the deck. The helicopters winched Scoular and Russell from their dinghy as well.

When they arrived at The Haven it was apparent how the survivors felt about Whiley. They showered him with appreciation and thanks in a moving display of hugging and affection. He had clearly won the hearts of those he had assisted and rescued.

A survivor and
L/Seaman Gary Scoular
after alighting from a
Puma (*Natal Mercury*).

Once the last of the passengers were lifted off the ship the Rescue Control Centre found that 21 passengers were unaccounted for. As they could have been trapped inside the sinking ship, volunteers were called for to search for them. Four men from the SAS *Simonsberg* stepped forward: Lieutenant-Commander Andrè Geldenhuys, Chief Petty Officer Frans Mostert, Leading Seaman Darren Brown and Leading Seaman Luke Dicks.

They were taken by Puma to the fast-sinking *Oceanos* to conduct an organised search for trapped or disabled survivors. According to Geldenhuys, 'We did some surface swimming around the ship and went on board, which was quite dangerous as it was tossing about quite a bit.'

Under extremely dangerous sea conditions, the foc'sle awash and waves breaking over the ship, they clambered along the slippery deck, which had a 75 degree list. They miraculously escaped injury. Then they undertook one of the most dangerous tasks of the rescue operation.

The frogmen had to descend dark passages, slithering down the walls to the sound of creaking bulkheads and the thunder of waves against the ship's side. Oily sea water full of debris rose menacingly, threatening to cut them off in the cabins they feverishly searched.

They clawed their way through the dangerously listing ship, without regard to their own safety and in a dramatic last-minute search for passengers. From the movement of the ship it was clear that it could sink at any minute but, disregarding their own safety, they

Lt-Comdr Andrè
Geldenhuys (*C Uys*).

155

A Simon's Town function: Major L van Wyk, L/Seaman Luke Dicks, Brig T de Munnink, Mrs N Holderness, CPO Frans 'Mossie' Mostert, Commander J de Vos, L/Seaman Darren Brown and Lt-Cmdr Andrè Geldenhuys (*SADF*).

kept on searching. Should the ship have sunk during this time their chances of survival would have been negligible.

Having completed the search and having ascertained that there were no passengers left behind in the ship Geldenhuys, Mostert, Brown and Dicks were lifted off the deck.

The *Oceanos* was gradually dragged down by the tons of water rising within her. Her bow struck the continental shelf 90 metres down while her stern was still visible above the sea. Then she slowly toppled over and sank at 1.46 pm.

That afternoon at 2 pm the pilot of a DC-3 Dakota spotted a man in the water about six kilometres south of the *Oceanos's* grave. It was Avgerinos Tsikis, 46, who'd been in the water for 10 hours. He said that as he was getting into one of the lifeboats, the ship hit a swell and pushed the steps to the lifeboat upwards, causing him to fall into the sea. He tried to swim to the *Nedlloyd's* lifeboat, but had been swept away. After being rescued he was flown directly to hospital at Umtata. Apart from an injury to his chin and pain in the right knee, he was pronounced fit.

By sunset the crisis centre had accounted for all but one man, Tsikis. Merchant ships had picked up 344 people (The *Great Nancy* saved 176, the *Kaszuby II* 106, the *Nedlloyd Mauritius* 51, the *Reefer Duchess* 8 and the *Anik* 3) and the Air Force 226, a total of 570. Then it was found that Tsikis was in the Umtata hospital. Everyone had been miraculously saved.

The Captain's Story

In an interview in his private room at The Haven, Captain Avranas denied abandoning ship. He said that he had wanted to get ships to anchor upwind of the *Oceanos* to facilitate the rescues. He later added that he had wanted to re-establish contact with the lifeboats.

He was interviewed on television and his explanations were

screened around the world. The *Philadelphia Inquirer* of 7 August reported: 'No matter how many passengers actually were on board when Capt Yiannis Avranas took the second rescue helicopter off his ship after his officers had bolted with one of the lifeboats, his remarks afterward on TV pretty much describe his attitude on the unwritten code of the sea about a captain going down with his ship.

'"When I ordered 'abandon the ship' it doesn't matter what time I leave', Avranas told ABC News. "Abandon is for everyone. If some people like to stay, they can stay" . . .'

The librarian at the Philadelphia Maritime Museum couldn't believe that Avranas had left the foundering vessel when he did, and said, 'This doesn't sound like proper protocol. It's not the usual procedure for the captain to abandon ship while passengers are still aboard.'

The *Philadelphia Inquirer* then compared Avranas's action to that of the captain of the *Titanic*. 'Certainly Capt Edward Smith didn't. Smith was the captain of the *Titanic*. He died with 684 other crew members as well as 832 passengers when the *Titanic* sank in less than two hours after hitting an iceberg on its maiden voyage from Southampton, England, to New York in April 1912. The crew managed to launch 703 people in lifeboats before the *Titanic* went under.

'"Of the many stories told by survivors, all seem to agree that both the officers and crew behaved with the utmost gallantry and that they stuck by the ship nobly to the last," reads a section from *The sinking of the Titanic and Other Great Disasters,* edited by Logan Marshall, a book in the museum's library that describes itself as the "only authoritative book" about the disaster based on interviews with survivors. It was published later the same year.

'Smith remained on board until all the lifeboats had been lowered, then he leapt into the icy water "with a little girl in his arms", according to the book. The captain swam a few strokes to a lifeboat and helped put the child into it.

'After two attempts to climb aboard himself, Smith clung to the side of the boat and then "took off his life preserver, tossed the life buoy into the inky waters and slipped into the sea again with the words, 'I will follow the ship'." '

The British tabloids were equally damning. The *Daily Star's* headline was 'Captain Coward', whereas the *Daily Mirror* spat out 'Crew abandoned passengers on sinking liner', then added a sub-headline, 'Brit girls were heroes'. The *Daily Mail* had a British girl tell of her nightmare hours on the sinking liner, under the heading, 'Crew left us all to drown'.

Avranas then went into hiding. In an interview published in the Afrikaans *Beeld* newspaper, Mrs Ingrid Avranas said that her husband was being kept in a safe place because it was feared that angry passengers would attack him.

In *Travel Times* magazine, in an interview before the *Oceanos* sailed, Avranas was quoted as saying that if it went down, 'I'll be on the first boat off the ship.'

The cruise director, Lorraine Betts, came to his defence, saying that he wanted to conduct rescue operations from the shore. She added that some 60 Greek crew members had stayed aboard to assist passengers onto lifeboats and with the airlift.

For his brave and selfless conduct Able Seaman Paul Whiley was awarded *Honoris Crux* Gold decoration, the highest award any South African serviceman had won since the Second World War.

Leading Seaman Gary Scoular was awarded the *Honoris Crux* Silver and Lieut-Cmdr Geldenhuys, Chief Petty Officer Mostert, L/Smn Brown and L/Smn Dicks were awarded the *Honoris Crux* for exceptional bravery in the face of imminent danger to their lives.

The SA Air Force awarded 27 Air Force Crosses to the gallant air-crews, who had miraculously plucked so many people from the sinking ship in the midst of a gale. It had been the largest and most successful sea-rescue ever. On 23 October, 1991, a medal parade was held at the Air Force Gymnasium where the medals were awarded to the following:

Honoris Crux

Cmdt E Elphick and A Hunter
Major P Fenwick, M Louw, A Johnson, A Stroebel and H Steyn
Capt H Meintjes, S Thomas, C Goatley, F Weyers, P Hanes,
         R Coulon, P Jooste, J Hugo, L Pienaar and A Botha.
Lieut M Fairley
WO2 W Riley
F/Sgt F Campher, F Schutte, D Bezuidenhout, D Jacobs,
         C Pedlar, P Scott, W Steyn and N Askew-Hull.

The following were mentioned in dispatches to the State President:

Brig T de Munnink SD and R Lord SD
Col   G Hallowes, B Kriegler and L Weyer
Cmdt D Janse van Rensburg
Major W van Wyk

Lieutenant-General Jan van Loggerenberg, the Chief of the Air Force, said in his address: '. . . I congratulate the recipients on parade. We are very, very proud of you who held the Air Force flag so high under very difficult and even dangerous flying conditions. You did us proud and we all salute you. This salute is also directed

A/Seaman Paul Whiley,
Vice-Admiral Lambert
Woodburne and the
author in March 1992
(*C Uys*).

at all those who participated by getting our aircraft ready and by ensuring that the command and control organisation functioned smoothly and efficiently. We are equally proud of the awards you received today.

'. . . The Air Force Cross, which may only be awarded to aircrews, is merely a recognition of the fact that aircrews very often operate under conditions that are unique to airmen. I believe that no other profession can be as demanding of man's skill and judgement as ours. The failure of an aircraft system in flight can spell instant hazard for the pilot who has lost his concentration only momentarily.

'The influence of the elements, the high winds and heavy seas, the clouds hiding terrifying turbulence behind a façade of innocent beauty; these are the challenges that constantly confront the airman. These are the factors which demand sound judgement and sharp reflexes. It makes the profession of airmen very demanding but also very exciting . . .

'To obervers, who are not familiar with the requirements of flying, the camps in the mountains and the annual helicopter competition may appear to be a waste of taxpayers' money. After the *Oceanos* rescue operation, I am sure that everyone will agree that money invested in those exercises was money very well invested.

'It enabled our aircrew to fly the helicopters with the confidence born out of the knowledge that they have exploited the performance of their helicopters to the limits. They knew that they could do the job . . .'

As one of the passengers who could have perished, Merlyn Wright summed up the feelings of the survivors: 'To the sung and unsung heroes of that day we owe our lives. When one looks back on the whole proceedings and realise what a terrific amount of organisation was behind our rescue we say a big "thank you".

'Please convey to all who were in any way responsible for the rescue and in particular those "wonderful men in their flying machines" our grateful thanks. They will always be remembered in a very special way in our hearts and prayers.

'I must say how proud I am to be a South African. We have had sanctions for many years, but despite that we could show the world that in a short time we were able to put into operation the greatest sea rescue of our time. It had to take a disaster to make us realise what a beautiful, thoughtful, caring and loving place our world can be.

'If the future could be as that day was, with no thought of colour or creed, as we were all just people, what a wonderful world it would be. The calibre of the young folk was of the highest and we are all so proud of them.'

In May 1992 a Greek Maritime Board found that five of the senior Greek officers and Captain Yiannis Avranas were guilty of negligence. Nevertheless, Captain Avranas was to set sail as commander of other vessels. In July 1992 he captained the *Panagia*, a small ferry boat which plied between Greece and Cyprus.

Among the TFC staff commended for their bravery by the Johannesburg Rotary Club were senior cruise hostess Lorraine Betts, Geraldine Massyn, Robin Boltman, Lynn Greig and Julian Russell.

Lifeboat No 5 is on display outside the East London museum. On 4 August, 1993, two years after the sinking, a commemorative plaque was unveiled alongside it while former *Oceanos* passengers clambered into it. The museum director, Nancy Tietz, said that the unveiling highlighted a remarkable sea rescue in which all passengers had been saved.

Paul Whiley left the navy and began a scuba diving school at the Umkomaas River mouth in Natal, north of where the *Oceanos* sank.

The bravery of the passengers and rescuers of the *Oceanos* will long be remembered. What will probably never be forgotten is the haste with which the captain abandoned ship – the first recorded incident of a master leaving his ship before the passengers. Branded by the international press as 'Captain Coward', he proved that one cannot rely on the '*Birkenhead* tradition' on all ships. Had the *Oceanos* sunk further out to sea the loss of life could have been horrendous.

Survey of the wreck

Within a week of the sinking sonar pictures were taken of the wreck by the SAS *Umkomaas*. It indicated that the hull was intact with no visible holes, was lying on it starboard side and had 80 metres of water above it.

During September divers from the Transvaal Deep Water Diving Club and M-Net's Camera 7 News Team shot videos of the sunken ship. Cross-currents tore them backwards and forwards at high speed. One of the divers' masks was whipped off his face by the current.

The spectral footage of the *Oceanos* showed rope ladders and a gangway trailing from the ship. The treacherous seas off the Transkei coast had claimed another victim to add to its long list.

Incongruously, two of the most famous, the *Grosvenor* and the *Oceanos*, were wrecked on 4 August. A painting of the two ships and the significant date was done by Dave Gerber of Durban and a print was presented to Cmdt Hunt, CO of 15 Squadron, which had effected the greatest sea rescue of all time.

CHAPTER 8   Solo-Sailor

Anthony 'Ant' Steward was born in 1962 and raised at Deneysville, on the banks of the Vaaldam, one of South Africa's largest man-made lakes. The son of a boat-builder, he took to sailing like a duck to water. After schooling at Vereeniging he attended Natal University in 1982 to study law. Steward found the lure of ocean sailing to be irresistible.

In 1987 he sailed around Cape Horn with a yacht owner who had never sailed before. 'We really got hammered', he said, 'but after that trip I knew I had what it would take to circumnavigate the world alone in the smallest open boat ever.'

During 1990 he decided to become the first man to do so. Joshua Slocum had been the first to single-handedly circle the globe and Robin Knox-Johnson, from England, the first to do so non-stop. Whereas Sir Francis Chichester had sailed a 54 foot yacht, Ant's mono-hull sailing dinghy was only 19 foot long.

Challenger

He left from Cape Town on 18 February, 1991, aged 29, leaving behind his fiancée, Sue Middleton, from Port Elizabeth. He sailed across the Atlantic via St Helena, Brazil and the Caribbean to the Panama Canal, relying on a sextant for navigation. Steward had logged 70,000 nautical miles of ocean sailing by this time.

Americans came to hear of his venture and sent him a waterproof GPS (Global Positioning System), which proved a boon for the crossing of the Pacific. As he only carried 30 days of food and water he had to stop five times before reaching Australia.

Steward recalled the welcome he received from the Polynesians, 'The people related to me as I was in a small boat. Their attitude differed toward those in large yachts as it was then very much a question of "have's and have not's". I learnt of the *Oceanos* disaster from them. They were very disparaging about the Greek captain and his officers who had abandoned the passengers to their fate.'

Dismasted at Samoa, he sailed under a jury-rig for 2 000 miles to Brisbane, where repairs were effected. He then sailed from Australia for Africa. 'I carried 75 litres of water, tinned food, navigational equipment, books in plastic bags and spares. I was never lonely at sea as there was always something to do and I had contact with birds and even whales out in the deep ocean.'

When he rounded the northern side of Madagascar he hit horrendous weather. 'The pilot charts don't show the gales which sweep around the island, sometimes reaching 50 knots.'

Monday 13 July

Steward opened his radio hatch to send a message to Sue that all was well. His logbook recorded, 'About 4.30 am a massive wall of

Ant Steward in the cockpit (*Fair Lady*)

NCS *Challenger* sails from Brisbane (*AS*).

black cloud appeared and I knew wind was on the way. I tried running with the storm and no sails, but just as I was preparing to speak to Cape Town radio it hit me at about 40 to 50 knots. There was a crash as a wave broke over *NCS* and capsized her.'

The squall had appeared and borne down on him at terrific speed. Ant was thrown into the sea and would have been swept away in the stormy water if he hadn't grabbed hold of the boat. He had hardly ever worn his lifejacket, as it was uncomfortable on a long trip, so clung desperately to the hull.

'Suddenly, I found myself under water. I surfaced next to the boat, which had turned turtle. For a long time she wouldn't right herself. Two opposing swells were keeping her upside down. It was very dark, but I managed to climb onto the keel and slowly but surely she started to right.

'Finally, I was able to climb on board to find she was full of water in the bow among the water-resistant foam we'd packed in to keep her afloat. I was furious with myself. This wouldn't have happened if I'd resealed the compass properly after I'd changed a bulb in it a week before. The sea doesn't suffer fools and I was now to pay the price. I felt like the biggest fool to cross the ocean'.

He had spent almost an hour in the raging sea, standing on the keel and transom to right the boat. She had eventually came up sluggishly and he climbed into the waterlogged interior.

'My main locker was open when I capsized, so I lost a lot, including the radio. It was a seven-day storm and I had to stay awake most of the time as I drifted and hand-steered into the waves. The wind was 30 knots, gusting 40 and I was exhausted. Besides suffering from salt sores I had to drink salt-contaminated water.

'To run with the storm I'd lashed all the sails down. But now one of them, the Genoa, had unfurled at the top. It was jammed solid and flogging violently in the wind. I realised the whole mast was bent and swaying around and making the boat list to port.

'The swells were breaking frequently now. I'd soon capsize again if I didn't do something quickly. She was low in the water so there was a good chance of the yachtsman's worst nightmare – pitchpoling, the whole boat diving nose first and flipping over.

'Until then I'd been too busy to be frightened, but now all these thoughts running through my mind were making me terrified. My brain was becoming my worst enemy – not the sea.

'I decided the only way to stay upright was to cut the rig away. The wind was howling a steady 50 knots and the heavy rain meant there was no visibility. Every time I looked behind, I'd get stinging rain in my eyes, blinding me. Anyway, it was pitch black. The only thing I could really see was the white water of the breaking swells.

'I couldn't find the torch. It must have fallen out of its pocket when the boat was upside down. Nor could I find the spare in the mess in the port locker. I groped in the central locker for bolt cutters to cut the rig, but the catch had broken and the locker was full of water – I seemed to have lost everything from it.

'One swell after another was breaking over *NCS*. Every time I heard the crash, I'd grab for the winch, thinking, "Here we go again", and she'd lean right over. Eventually, I found the only tool left – a hacksaw in the starboard locker. I started cutting the starboard stays very carefully, knowing if the hacksaw blade broke, I wouldn't find another.

'My hands felt very sticky, so I licked them. All I got was the taste of blood mixed with salt. It felt like a long, long time but was probably only about three minutes until the stays finally gave way and the mast fell to port.

'Immediately, the motion felt better, and at least the flogging Genoa wasn't tearing at my nerves. The boat was now more stable, so it was much easier to cut the port stays. I began to feel relieved that I was doing the right thing.

'But the worst was having to go right to the front to cut the forestays. I dived from the cockpit to the "bullhorns" we'd fitted specially to the bow. I knew that I'd be OK hanging onto them, but with my weight there, *NCS* was lying low in the water and the swells were coming right over the bow. I had to hang on very tight most of the time, and sawing under water was really exhausting.

'Suddenly, there was nothing to cut – I was through the forestay. But the next moment I was in the water. I think I was pulled off by a loose halyard as the mast broke free. I shuddered at the thought of being entangled in the rigging and sinking with the mast.

'I ripped off my weather gear because it was weighing me down. Back on board, I really wished I could find my life harness, but that was impossible in the mess of the cockpit. With the mast gone, I could turn the boat to run with the swells. She felt safe and even comfortable.

'I rested for about 10 minutes, but that made me notice the pain of my cut hands and my aching, bruised shins and started me shivering uncontrollably. I couldn't believe how cold it was in these latitudes – it felt more like the southern ocean.

'I started baling out the bow with the dog bowl I ate out of, at the same time steering with my foot to keep *NCS* directly with the swells. They felt frightfully steep, but with the mast gone she had less wind resistance and didn't surf out of control so often.

'I felt really freezing just in jeans and a T-shirt, but managed to find my dry-suit which would seal out the cold. How it stayed in the cockpit, I don't know – but thank goodness it hadn't been washed away or I'd have been in serious trouble. I kept steering, hoping that at dawn the wind would die down.'

Tuesday, 14 July The wind remained strong. 'When dawn finally came, I wasn't too happy because the light meant I could see the state of the sea. You were supposed to find this kind of sea between Durban and East London, not here. What the hell was wrong with the weather?

'The swells were between five and six metres, but occasionally some really dangerous ones at seven metres. I put out a drogue, like an open cone, to create resistance and stop the boat surfing out of control.

'The clouds started clearing, which relieved me because I thought the weather would too. But the wind fell only to 35 knots. There was nothing I could do but keep running with it, still steering by hand because the windvane which could turn the rudder automatically had been ripped off when the boat capsized. The autopilot also wouldn't work.

Next disaster – I took a sip of water from the container I'd bought in Aussie. All I got was a great salty taste and a burning throat. My only fresh water had been fouled.

'I tried to mend the autopilot and at 3.30 pm got it to work by connecting it straight to the battery. But I decided to carry on steering myself for as long as possible and save the battery power for the night, when I knew I'd be really exhausted.

'Wave after wave broke over the boat and I was almost permanently awash. It was making my hands so sore that it was painful even to touch the tiller, never mind try to tie a knot.

'I also noticed that the tiller stock was breaking. If it went, I'd lose steering – not a pleasant thought in those conditions. I steered till about 12.30 that night, I think. I'd lost my watch, so I had only the sun and moon for time. By then I'd been working for 30 hours and was exhausted.

'I put on the autopilot and it steered till 4.30 am, when it stopped working. I did manage four hours' sleep – not too blissful as half the time I was under water. The wind had fallen a bit to 30 knots, but rain squalls crossed almost every hour with winds of up to 50 knots. It all kept the seas big and confused.'

Wednesday, 15 July Steward was exhausted but carried on mechanically. 'Wind and seas still the same. Thank goodness for the dry suit. I was still cold because my underwear was wet, but at least I wasn't shivering. So much for the so-called tropics.

'The cuts on my hands were festering badly and throbbing continually. Whatever I tried, I couldn't manage to keep my hands dry. The waves kept crashing over the stern and my eyes were burning from the salt. To make things worse, the salt sores and rash on my backside were now so painful I couldn't sit for longer than five minutes. I had to kneel to steer – not comfortable, either, but better.

'I discovered that the cockpit floor was permanently awash because the two back compartments were full. Next disaster – the navigation system wouldn't work to give me a position. I knew my average course since Monday night had been 330 degrees, and I estimated that I'd averaged about 60 nautical miles in 24 hours, but I didn't know the strength of the current. So, to tell the honest truth, I had no clue where I was.

Sue Middleton.

'How I stayed awake through Wednesday night I will never know, because I was exhausted. I sang, shouted, screamed and mostly thought of Sue to stay awake. I kept telling myself, "I'll be OK because the boat is unsinkable. I must just stop her capsizing. The weather has to abate sometime."

'I still couldn't believe this sort of weather prevailed so long in these latitudes. But then, this is the Indian Ocean, the worst of all oceans.'

Thursday 16 July One day seemed to merge into the next. 'No change in the weather. I was deteriorating fast so I don't remember much. Sores were festering on my hands, which were puffy and swollen.

'I remember eating a tin of something, but I can't recall what it was. Thank goodness I found my angio-oedema medication – an attack would be fatal in these conditions. I took a double dosage and put the rest in my dry-suit. The steering was getting worse, so I had to steer very carefully to avoid the disaster of losing steerage completely.

'I found the best thing was to think of Sue and plan things we'd do together when this was over. I wished I'd told my folks that I love them, but I've always battled with emotions. I regret that now. For their sakes I mustn't give up.

'Kept dozing off, dreaming of what I'd eat if I got home – hunks of French bread filled with banana and honey, and definitely a big pizza with lots of salami. Then I'd be wakened by white water all around me and find the boat off course.

'I felt like an automaton. I wished I had my harness instead of having to clutch onto something all the time – that was so painful on my hands in the end. I tied a rope around my chest and around the track that the mainsheet sail moves on.'

Friday 17 July

Steward's strength was rapidly draining away. 'As the sun rose, the wind dropped to 25 to 30 knots. I decided to hove to and get some rest because I was losing my will to carry on. It was just too much.

'*NCS* would lie side on to the swell and be thrown about violently, but at least it didn't feel as if she'd capsize. I rested for about two hours, but was too tense to sleep.

'The stern was really low in the water, so I decided to bail out the back compartments. I built a wall of ropes stuffed in sailbags to stop the water coming in, and started bailing. As I worked, something made me look up. In the distance, about three miles away, I could see trees!

'It was when I felt myself starting to go that I saw the palm trees on the horizon. I knew from the chart that it was Cerf Island, the southern point of the Seychelles, and it was surrounded by a reef. The Provident Reef was about 60 km by 15 km, but fortunately very narrow at the point I would cross it. So I rigged a jury mast with the spinnaker pole, put up a jib and tacked south.

'As I got closer I could hear a thunderous roar of the waves smashing on the reef, which was about $2\frac{1}{2}$ kilometres from the beach. I had been given a one-man raft, so inflated it with the intention of climbing in, but saw it deflate at once. It was apparently holed. I then tried to surf over the reef. The waves were about three metres high – it was like surfing the Banzai pipeline in Hawaii – and I hunkered down.'

The rig was thrown with a crash onto the reef and Ant hung on grimly. A second wave rolled the boat head over heels. If he was thrown out he knew that he would be ripped to pieces on the coral. The third wave lifted the boat and the water boiled about it, ripping the boat's keel and rudder off on the jagged reef – then suddenly he found himself on his back floating serenely in the lagoon and staring up at the sky.

'A really huge wave had catapulted *NCS* over the reef onto which we'd been battered and into the calm of the lagoon. As I looked towards the island I knew I was going to live. "Thank you, Lord," I said, "Thank you."

'We drifted towards the beach. I hate beaches and refuse to take Sue to one, but now I was excited about the sand ahead.' He was badly bruised but thankful to find that the boat was drifting towards the island. 'About 700 metres offshore *NCS* smacked into a second line of coral. I jettisoned all the containers that would float and watched them drift to shore. Even in the lagoon it was still choppy and the keel was pounding quite heavily against the coral.

'I hesitated for a long time. I didn't want to leave *NCS*. I'd built her and she'd carried me all the way round the world. Now I was deserting her. My first real success in life, and this was the end.

'I rocked her but she wouldn't come free. I then threw some floatable articles overboard and saw them drift toward the beach. After about an hour I decided to swim ashore.

'Something made me grab a marlin spike, which had been given to me by the Royal Navy, as well as a Teddy Bear which the Cape Town 'Juniors' had given to me, then jumped into the lagoon. As I slowly swam and drifted I noticed that my hand had been cut badly by solar panelling on the boat.

'I was in about three metres of water, was pretty exhausted and thankful for my lifejacket. Something made me stick my head under water. Even though my eyes were stinging, about 20 metres away I could make out two small sharks. Now I was nervous. I looked at my hands. The left one was still bleeding.

'I panicked. I fear sharks more than anything else. I stuck my head under again. Now I saw four shapes. I started frantically to rip off the lifejacket, because it was stopping me from keeping my head under water to watch the sharks.

'They had probably been attracted by the blood and were excited. Three were smallish black-tipped sharks but the larger one, I don't know what kind, was about one and a half metres long and could have taken off my leg. Rather than be attacked from below I decided to try and walk on the bottom, about 10 feet down.

'I knew I must keep my eyes on them. I went under again. There were definitely four – and one was pretty big. The big one was pretty excited, swimming up and down on my left-hand side. It suddenly came straight at me. I lunged with the spike. The shark was too far away, but the movement must have put it off. I had jabbed with the marlin spike like a boxer, but you can't believe how slowly your hand moves under water.

'I went up for air, gasping because I'd been down too long. As I went down again, I realised he was right under me. I must have lunged again, because I struck him and he shot off to the right.

Detail from a painting *Sharks* by Rosemary Clark.

The large shark came at me again and again. I lunged at it with the spike and it veered off.

'I tried to swim towards the beach under water while at the same time turning round and watching. Almost out of breath, I shot up for air. When I submerged I couldn't see the big one, but there were definitely four small ones around me now.

'When I turned full circle, there he was – coming right at me. It was almost on top of me and there was no time to ward it off. I must have screamed in terror and lunged at the same time, because I swallowed a lot of sea water. I was choking, but as I came up for air, I couldn't see him. I must have got him or frightened him off temporarily. Then it came back.

'The water was shallower and I could now stand, but it was quicker

169

and so safer, to swim. The big one was behind me, so I frantically used the spike to push myself along the bottom. When I reached knee height, I stood up. I didn't run. I couldn't run. My legs wouldn't move.

'I just kept my eyes on the big shark. He was swimming about 20 metres away from me, up and down, very fast. I didn't know what type he was, though I could see the others were small and black-tip, so I knew they weren't dangerous.

'I started walking backwards. Twice I must have fallen, but I got up like a shot. He was still there, swimming up and down fast. When I got to ankle-deep water, I turned and ran until I reached the beach. I just lay on the sand shaking uncontrollably.

'It felt as if I was going to faint. My heart was pounding so hard that I couldn't hear anything else. I don't know how long I lay like that, but I felt faint for a long time. My mouth was dry and my throat burning. When I was able to think again, I just felt angry – to go through all this and suffer a shark attack so close to safety. It was just so unfair.

'The water container was about 200 metres from me, lying on the beach. I tried to stand. My legs were so weak that I fell down when I took my first step. So I crawled. I got to the water. It tasted great, even though it was foul. I just lay in the sand, not caring. I was hot, but it started to rain and I cooled off. I must have fallen asleep right there.

'I woke up just as it was getting dark. I could see *NCS*, now lying on the beach about 200 metres away. Her keel and rudder must have finally been ripped off by the pounding surf. I felt happier – at least she was close to me.'

Saturday 18 July

Steward slept like a log. 'I must have slept right through the night. I don't remember waking up at all. I felt so stiff that I could hardly move. My bruised left shoulder was really painful. My hands were throbbing because of the festering sores and I couldn't close them.

'My throat was very dry. My tongue felt swollen. All I wanted was water, but I knew there wasn't likely to be any on this island. I retrieved the big screwdriver and knife from the boat and set about opening a coconut that had fallen from a palm by the beach.

'I had to stop often because I felt so weak. I just didn't seem to have any strength. Each time I hit the shell I would have to rest for a few minutes. After almost two hours of effort, which felt like a very long time, I finally managed to remove the husk. For as long as I live I will never forget that sweet taste – or the complete relief I felt in my body and to feel the inside of my mouth wet again.

'After having a second coconut, I finally felt I had the strength to salvage as much as I could from *NCS*. I didn't feel hungry at all, but I knew that if I didn't eat something I'd become weaker. I love my food and for me the first time I had to force myself to eat. The coconut flesh tasted sweet and took a long time to chew and my jaw ached.

'Sitting down and looking at my boat stranded on the beach, it finally sank in that I was marooned on an island. I felt devastated. The realisation made me anxious to see if by any chance there might be someone else on the island. I was right at one tip and reckoned that if anybody was there, they'd be on the leeward side. I knew it was crazy to try walking all that way in my state, but I was determined to check. Suddenly I needed company.

'It was the worst walk I've ever had to endure. My legs felt like jelly and my clothes were irritating the sores on my backside. Finally, I took my clothes off. It was a great relief because the sores had nothing to rub on. I had to stop often to rest my legs. I reckon I walked about three kilometres, the longest three kilometres I've ever covered. And at the end there was just an abandoned hut among the undergrowth. I felt alone and lost.'

Sunday 19 July

Steward found the nights surprisingly cool for the tropics. 'Last night I slept under a bush close to my boat. I surrounded myself with what I'd retrieved. That was all the company I had, but at least it was something. Coconuts for breakfast. Again I had to force myself to eat, because I still didn't feel hungry – my stomach must have shrunk.

'It seemed the only thing to do was to get to the leeward side as soon as possible and set up camp. I knew I must keep busy. I must have a mission. "Don't think. Just work." I told myself. If I stopped to think, depression would set in.

'There was a lot of bamboo around, washed up from where I don't know. In a couple of hours I managed to make a raft on which to float everything I'd recovered from *NCS* to the leeward side. I couldn't carry things across the length of the island – it would take days and I didn't have the strength.

'I managed to pile everything I'd salvaged onto the raft so I could move it in one go, but pulling it through the lagoon was tiring. I had to be very careful not to stand on the stingrays that dig themselves into the sand in the shallows. I kept worrying whether a shock from one of them could possibly be fatal to me in my weak state, though I didn't know how dangerous they were. What I did know was that they were everywhere.

'With time to think, I was neurotic the whole day about getting to the leeward side, as I believed this was the only place where I stood a chance of being rescued. But who will rescue me? Maybe a passing trawler, as the reef extends far out – but will they see me?

'I hope Sue and Mom and Dad aren't worrying too much. It's now six days since I was supposed to speak to them.

Ant Steward.

171

'I found gold! – pawpaw trees. Dinner was three overripe paw-paws and one drinking coconut – better than the tins I had on the boat. I'll sleep in the abandoned hut. All I have to read is a Bible, because it was in a case that didn't get wet. I started reading the Old Testament and found it too boring, so I went on to the New Testament – much better.'

Monday 20 July

Steward was awake before dawn. 'I woke about 5 am and got up to watch the sunrise – also the best time to check for any trawler lights in the area. At about 6 am I had pawpaw and coconut for breakfast. It rained and I managed to collect about 50 litres of fresh water from the roof of the abandoned hut, which should last easily for about 25 or 30 days. I can't begin to explain the pure relief of tasting fresh water after such a long time.

'I've walked all over the island and established that I'm the only inhabitant besides the birds and lots of pawpaws. Every time I collect pawpaws I have to dash into the sea to wash off the spiders because they get all over me, especially in my hair. I hope none are poisonous – it would be terrible to die of a spider bite after surviving so much.

'I'm very depressed because I couldn't get the Emergency Position Radar Beacon to work. All I wanted to do was get a message through to Sue and my folks that I'm alive. They must be worrying because I should have been in the Comores by now. I'll try to fix the EPRB tomorrow. I wish I'd told mom and dad that I love them, but I've always battled.

'Dinner was one pawpaw and crushed coconut. The New Testament is quite interesting. I'm starting to feel lonely.'

Tuesday 21 July

I couldn't sleep, mainly because of rain leaking through the hut's rusty roof. But I'm terribly restless, my mind turning over ways to be rescued. I'm also considering salvaging *NCS's* hull to build a trimaran to sail to the next island. I'm still not quite sure where I am – probably Cerf Island – but it's so isolated by this massive reef that the chances of a fishing trawler finding me are very slim.

'Worked on the EPRB all day – the batteries and some parts are completely corroded, but luckily *NCS's* satellite navigation uses similar parts. I've rebuilt it, but I'm scared to see if it works because it's my last hope of rescue. I will try tomorrow.

'Tried my luck at fishing, but it looks as if I'll have to build a platform in the lagoon because I've got only a spear made of bamboo and a nail. I wish I had some hooks.

'I have discovered one source of amusement – the small black-tip sharks come right up on the shore at high tide. It's great fun chasing them – revenge! I even managed to kick one. Now I know what loneliness is. I love you, Sue.'

Wednesday 22 July   Boredom was getting on Steward's nerves. 'Nothing to do at night as I have no light or fire. So restless, I spend half the night staring out to sea.

'The EPRB works! I'm really happy – never in my life could I imagine that I'd be capable of fixing such a complicated device. At least now there's hope. I just pray that an aeroplane passes close overhead to pick up the signal.

'It's funny how a little device has cheered me up – I must have a mission to keep my mind off depressing thoughts. To make myself visible I put up a seven metre flagpole using bamboo and a piece of red canvas as a flag.

'I spent the afternoon exploring the island. The undergrowth is very dense in some places, impossible to get through. I wish I had a machete. The spiders are my biggest worry. So far I've identified 11 types and I don't know whether any are poisonous – worrying as they are everywhere. At least they're keeping the mosquitoes at bay.

'Gathered some eggs from fairy-tern nests, but raw eggs are definitely an acquired taste, which I'll have to get used to. They were so rich that I could only eat one every two days. My salt sores and cuts are healing quickly. It must be that the fresh food I'm eating is a lot healthier than what I had on the boat.

'I read the Bible just before the sun goes down. I must say it's very interesting, maybe because there are no distractions. It's nice to watch the sun set. I can't read by moonlight, so I'm terribly lonely after dark because there's nothing to do.

'I can't stop thinking of Sue and how they must all be worrying by now because I should be in the Comores. It makes me hate what I'm doing. It's so selfish and unfair on my family. I noticed that I've stopped talking to myself. On the boat I used to have long conversations, but now I prefer the silence.'

Thursday 23 July   Nothing seemed to go right. 'Feeling very despondent. The EPRB signal is starting to fade and I don't have any more batteries. I hope an aircraft has picked it up. Started constructing a fishing platform in the lagoon, using bricks from the hut. It makes me realise how weak I still am – this ordeal has really sapped me.

'I've seen a lot of whiting in the shallows at high tide, but it's much harder to spear a fish than I thought. All those stupid Hollywood movies make it look so easy.

'Tried rubbing sticks together as the Bushmen do to make fire. No luck. I must definitely go and live with them if and when I get back. Surviving on the sea is no problem for me but I'm rather lost on land.

'Yippee! I found a rusty machete hidden in the roof of the hut. Opening coconuts is now great fun. Dinner was two pawpaws and a tin of mushrooms I salvaged off the boat.

'Have named the hut "Shackleton's Place" in honour of Sir Ernest Shackleton, the bravest of the brave. I wish I felt as brave as he was.

'I hate night-time because it's too dark to do anything and I can't keep my mind off my parents and Sue. I screamed at the top of my voice that I'm still alive. Maybe telepathically they'll know.'

Friday 24 July

He finally realised that he might never be rescued. 'The EPRB isn't working as the batteries are flat. I'm very depressed. If they'd picked up the signal, a plane would have been despatched from Diego Garcia.

'I'm all alone and only I can save myself, so I've decided to salvage *NCS* from the windward side. It will be easy to build a trimaran, because I've found two large floats that the Japanese trawlers use, and there's a lot of cedar planking on the beach that a ship must have lost overboard. I'm feeling a lot better now that I have a plan.'

Saturday 25 July

Steward then set to work. 'Managed to salvage *NCS* from the windward side. It took about five hours – thank goodness she's so small. I dug a trench in the sand and at high tide she floated free.

'I nearly stood on a stingray while bringing her round – they're almost impossible to see. This lagoon is a dangerous place. I must be more careful.

'I can't believe the change that's come over me now that *NCS* is at the camp. It's so good to have her nearby. I really missed her.

NCS *Challenger* on Cerf Island (*AS*)

174

Besides Suzie, she's all I've got and she's been so good to me. If I'm rescued I hope some day I can salvage her from this lovely place.'

'He felt more confident now that he had decided to try and build a trimaran in which to head for Africa. In the boat he found that his Nikon underwater camera and video camera were undamaged, so amused himself by taking photographs and filming.

Although the island had been inhabited 10 years before, Steward counted five chickens scratching around. Steward salvaged some waterproof paper and began writing, catching up on his diary and to leave a record of what had happened to him in case of mishap.

First he would have to build up his strength, 'I'm starting to get tired of this diet of pawpaws and coconuts and I still don't like the taste of raw eggs. The sooner I complete the fishing platform the better.

Sunday 26 July

A miracle then occurred. 'This morning when I woke up I could just see what looked like a ship further down the reef, but it was only a speck on the horizon. I watched all day, too scared to move off the beach in case it disappeared.'

He found that he was growing weaker as he had insufficient nourishing food. The boat was about two kilometres away along the beach and if he tried to run there it might leave before he could attract their attention. Steward then grabbed his last rocket flare and fired it.

The 25-year-old skipper, Frank Bibi, had decided to work the island's outer reef, then, owing to storm damage, came inside the reef to repair his fishing boat. He saw the trail of smoke which arced skywards, so had some of his men row him in a dinghy along the beach.

'At about 4 pm the boat started to come closer and I fired off a flare. After what seemed a hell of a long time, I thought I could see a dinghy heading towards the shore. Seconds felt like minutes. I grabbed the red flag and started waving furiously. I was so emotional that I didn't realise I'd be rescued until they spoke to me.'

Steward stumbled into the lagoon as they arrived. 'I almost broke down, and Frank said "We're here, man". I couldn't speak properly. I had looked at death so often I couldn't believe it was all over. I was really well looked after. But I can tell you this: it's all still too big to grasp mentally. I am still too scared to think about what's happened. All that I know is that I have been given a second lease of life, and I will never waste it.'

'I'm now on a Seychelles fishing trawler, the *Verseau*, heading for Farquhar Island. The skipper, Frank Bibi, tells me there's an airstrip on the island and they'll fly me to Mahè.

'Frank organised a call through to Suzie on the radio. After speak-

NCS *Challenger* at Mahè (*Fair Lady*).

Anthony and Sue
Steward (*Fair Lady*).

ing to her I couldn't stop crying. I can't believe she still wants to
marry me after all this.

'I feel sad because I've left my boat behind. I really miss *NCS* –
we were so long together. Thank goodness I still have Suzie. I really
can't believe she still wants to marry me. She's all I've got now.'

He was taken to Farquhar Island, then flown to Mahè for medical
treatment. The radio call to Cape Town was passed on to Sue, who
had last heard from Ant three weeks before. He returned to South
Africa in time to marry her on 28 August, a date which he had
almost not kept.

Frank Bibi's fishing boat returned to Cerf Island to salvage the
NCS Challenger. He placed the hull in a fishing net and towed it
back to Farquhar Island, then it was sent to Mahè for repair. The
boat required a new keel, rudder, mast and rigging.

Four months later Steward returned to the Seychelles and resumed
his voyage. It took him four months to complete the remaining
1,670 nautical miles to Cape Town, 'Those last miles were the
toughest,' he said, 'As I'd lost faith in my boat.' Yet he never lost
faith in himself.

After 25 months and 25,000 nautical miles, he became the first
person to circumnavigate the globe in an open dinghy – one of the
last frontiers for the solo yachtsman. His achievement was only possible because of his success as a survivor.

Appendix: **Man-eating Sharks**

Deep sea sharks, also known as pelagic sharks, generally feed near the surface. They have been known to bump and deliberately try to capsize boats, rafts or rubber dinghies. The Oceanic White-Tip shark (*Carcharhinus longimanus*) is responsible for attacks on survivors of sinkings far out at sea. It has been maligned with the attacks on the survivors of the *Nova Scotia*.

The White Tip shark is generally greyish, which fades to a dirty white below, and the tips of the fins are white. Their usual length is two metres, while specimens over three metres long are exceptional. The sharks are found in all oceans between 20 degrees north and south and are among the most abundant large species of animals on earth.

They usually feed on squid but are known as man-eaters. Generally brazen, the shark can become aggressive and difficult to deter. Even after receiving blows from an oar it will repeatedly return. Such was the experience of the *Nova Scotia* survivors.

Jacques Cousteau regards it as an especially dangerous species as it is aggressive and abundant in the open sea. They are quick to gather at the scene of any mid-ocean shipwreck.

One of the most appalling attacks by sharks took place in 1945 when a United States cruiser, the *Indianapolis,* was torpedoed. The men floated in the Pacific for five days and grouped together to fight off the sharks. Eventually, of the 1,196 casualties, 880 were dead. Captain McVay was court-martialled for not having taken evasive action against submarines. He took his own life in November 1968.

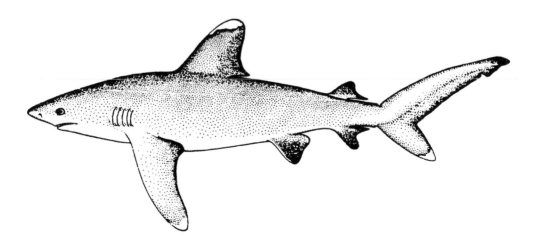

Oceanic White-Tip (Steel).

Coastal sharks have some anomalies. While the Zambezi or Bull shark (Carcharhinidae leucas) is a known killer in South African waters, it is merely regarded as aggressive elsewhere. On the other hand the Tiger shark (*Galeocerdo cuvier*) is the number one coastal killer in Australia, but has no confirmed victims on the South African coast.

The Blue Pointer, or Great White shark (*Carcharodon carcharias*) has its breeding ground off the south-west Cape coast and was probably responsible for some attacks on the *Birkenhead* survivors. Kerr states that the Black-Tip sharks, 'nowadays gone from this coast', were responsible for the attacks on the men and horses from the *Birkenhead.*

Malcolm Turner, in writing of the *Birkenhead,* states, 'Death by drowning came quickly to most of them, but some of the men – and the horses – were taken by Great White sharks (Blue Pointers) and even today the locals in Gansbaai call this shark the "Tommie-haai" (Tommy Shark), after the Tommys who died . . .'

Theo Ferreira spent many years hunting Great Whites and was credited with having killed 28. Then, in January 1980, he came up against a 7,6 metre, three ton Great White, which he nicknamed the 'Submarine'. He fought the Sub on three occasions and finally nearly lost his life and his boat when the Sub turned on him. The hunter has subsequently turned conservationist.

Great White (detail from a painting *Sharks* by Rosemary Clark).

Bibliography

Addison, A Christopher, *The Story of the Birkenhead* (1902) Simkin, Marshall, Hamilton, Kent & Co Ltd.

Bevan, David, *Drums of the Birkenhead* (1972) Purnell & Sons (SA) (Pty) Ltd, Cape Town.

Bond, Cornet, *Notable Shipwrecks,* being tales of disaster and heroism at sea, as retold by Uncle Hardy. London Liquor Tea Company, Postern House, Tower Hill.

Burman, Jose, *Great Shipwrecks off the Coast of Southern Africa* (1967) C Struik, Cape Town.

Busch, Harald, *U-boats at War* (1955) Ballantine Books, New York.

Clarke, James, *Man is the Prey* (1971) Panther.

Clothier, Norman, *Black Valour* (1987) University of Natal Press, Pietermaritzburg.

Cruise Shipping Report (1989) Sea Trade Organisation, United Kingdom.

Duffus, Louis, *Beyond the Laager,* Hurst & Blackett Ltd, London.

Dunn, Laurence, *Ships of the United Castle Line* (1954) Adlard Coles Ltd.

Edwards, Bernard, *The Grey Window-Maker* (1990) Futura.

Harris, C J, *War at Sea* (1991) Ashanti Publishing (Pty) Ltd, Rivonia.

Harris, John, *Without Trace* (1981) Methuen.

Home Front, the Moth magazine, March and October 1988, November 1992.

Hough, Richard, *The Longest Battle, The War at Sea 1939–45,* (1986) Weidenfeld and Nicolson, London.

Jeffries's papers, Miss; See SA Archives, Cape Town.

Jenkins, Geoffrey, *Scend of the Sea* (1971).

Johnson, R H, *Sharks of tropical and temperate seas,* H S Editions du Pacifique.

Kayle, Allan, *Salvage of the Birkenhead* (1990) Southern Book Publishers.

Kerr, J Lennox, *The Unfortunate Ship,* The Story of HM Troopship *Birkenhead* (1960) George G Harrap & Co Ltd, London.

Kirby, Percival R, *The True Story of the Grosvenor East Indiaman* (1960) Oxford University Press, London.

Lenton, H T, *Navies of the Second World War,* German Submarines 1 (1965) MacDonald.

Muggeridge, Sir Malcolm, *Chronicle of Wasted Time,* the Infernal Grove.

Murray, Marischal, *Ships and South Africa* (1933) Oxford University Press, London.

Nesbitt family records

Personality, 19.6.1989, 28.8.1992, 4.9.1992.

Potgieter, Coenraad, *Skipbreuke ann ons Kus* (1969) Tafelberg Uitgewers.

Rand Daily Mail

Reader's Digest New Pocket Companion: 'They Remembered the Birkenhead' by Keith Monroe. The *Reader's Digest:* Article 'Death off Durban' by J D Ratcliff; The *Reader's Digest* Illustrated Story of World War II (1980) *Reader's Digest,* November 1992, *Miracle of the Oceanos* by Frank Bate.

Rosenthal, Eric, *Cutlass and Yardarm,* Howard Timmins, Cape Town.

SA Archives, Cape Town: Miss Jeffries's papers.

SADF Documentation Centre, Pretoria.

Standard Encyclopaedia of South Africa (1975) Nasou Ltd, Johannesburg.

Steel, Rodney, *Sharks of the World* Blandford Press, London.

Stern, Robert C, *U-boats in action* (1977) Squadron/Signal Publications, Inc. Texas.

Sunday Star, 25 June, 1989. Article 'Three men and a boat' by Gary Brennan.

Sunday Times – various editions.

Sunday Tribune, 2 August, 1992.

Time-Life Books, *Wolf Packs* (1989) Joseph J Ward.

Turner, L C F, Gordon-Cumming, OBE RN, Cmdr H R, and Betzer, J E, *War in the Southern Oceans* (1961) Oxford University Press, London.

Turner, Malcolm, *Shipwrecks & Salvage in South Africa – 1505 to the present* (1988) C Struik, Cape Town.

Uys, Ian S, *For Valour,* the History of Southern Africa's Victoria Cross Heroes (1973) Uys Publishers.

Uys, Ian, *Cross of Honour* (1992) Uys Publishers, Germiston.

Uys, Ian, *South African Military Who's Who* 1452–1992 (1992) Fortress Publishers, Germiston.

Willcox, A R, *Shipwreck and Survival on the South-East Coast of Africa* (1984) Drakensberg Publications, Winterton, Natal.

Birkenhead: Addison; Bateman; Bevan; Burman; Bond; Edwards; Kayle; Kerr; Nesbitt; Potgieter; *Reader's Digest* 1; Turner, M; Uys, *For Valour,* Uys, *Who's Who.*

Challenger: Fair Lady, 11 August, 1993, article 'Overcoming Obstacles' by Mike Behr; Interview with Ant Steward; *Personality,* 28 August, 1992, and 4 September, 1992; *Sunday Tribune,* 2 August, 1992, article 'Never say Die' by Graham Spence.

Galway Castle: Home Front; Murray; SADF.

Grosvenor: Burman; Edwards; Kirby; Potgieter; *Saturday Star* 1 December, 1990; Willcox.

Ligonier: Rosenthal; SA Archives.

Laconia: Duffus, Stern.

Llandaff Castle: Burman; Dunn; *Home Front,* the *Moth* magazine, November 1992; Interviews with Harry Brotton, Vic Harms and Lady Taylor; Potgieter; Rand *Daily Mail,* Account by 'A survivor'.

Mendi: Clothier; *Standard Encyclopaedia; The Star* 24.2.1951.

Nova Scotia: Clarke; Interviews with Lady Alda Taylor, George Kennaugh amd Nat Herman; Lenton; Muggeridge; *Observer* 23.3.1969; Reminiscences of George Kennaugh and Nat Herman; *Sunday Times:* 13, 20 and 27 April 1969 and 22 November, 1992; The *Reader's Digest:* Article 'Death off Durban' by J D Ratcliff; The *Reader's Digest Illustrated* Story of World War II (1980); Turner; Typescript by Sir Robert and Lady Taylor.

Oceanos: Cruise Shipping; Interviews with Paul Whiley, Ian Scoular and Merlyn Wright; *Reader's Digest,* November 1992, *Miracle of the Oceanos* by Frank Bate; Uys, *Cross of Honour.*

São João, São Benedictus and *Santo Alberti:* Burman; Potgieter; Turner, M; Willcox

Sharks: Clarke; Interview at the Natal Shark's Board; Steel; *Sunday Times magazine* 13.9.1992.

Waratah: Harris J; Jenkins; *Personality* 19.6.89; Standard *Encyclopaedia;* Sunday Star 25.6.89

Index